THE COMPLETE BOOK OF
WOODCARVING

THE COMPLETE BOOK OF
WOODCARVING

Everett Ellenwood

FOX CHAPEL
PUBLISHING

© 2008 by Everett Ellenwood and Fox Chapel Publishing Company, Inc., East Petersburg, PA.

ISBN 978-1-56523-292-1

Interior Photography by Jeff Ellenwood and Greg Heisey.

Publisher's Cataloging-in-Publication Data

Ellenwood, Everett.

      The complete book of woodcarving / Everett Ellenwood. -- East
Petersburg, PA : Fox Chapel Publishing, c2008.

         p. ; cm.
         ISBN: 978-1-56523-292-1

         1. Wood-carving--Handbooks, manuals, etc. 2. Wood-carving--
Technique. 3. Wood-carving--Patterns. I. Title.

TT199.7 .E45 2008
736/.4--dc22   0804

To learn more about the other great books from Fox Chapel Publishing, or to find a retailer
near you, call toll-free 800-457-9112 or visit us at *www.FoxChapelPublishing.com*.

Note to Authors: We are always looking for talented authors to write new books.
Please send a brief letter describing your idea to Acquisition Editor,
1970 Broad Street, East Petersburg, PA 17520.

Printed in China
Seventh printing

ACKNOWLEDGMENTS

Trent Busch
Ron Bymers
Kent Duff
Walter Grittner
Wayne Hendrickson
Randy Kinnick
Garry Kolb
Slim Maroushek (owner of Slim's
   Woodshed and Carving Museum)
Ron Morrow
Bob Nowicki
Myron and Laverne Schettl (Shady Haven Tree Farm)
Kathy Ward

For allowing me to photograph their carvings and providing
me with various items which enhance my book

A SPECIAL THANK-YOU TO:

John Krantz—retired Department of Natural Resources
forester in Forest Products Utilization—for his assistance
with and input on Chapter 3, "Wood for Carving"

W. F. (Bill) Judt—for allowing me to reference his
"Four-Quadrant Carving"

Dale Knoblock—the developer of Pentacryl and owner
of Preservation Solutions—for his contribution on
curing woods for carving

Bob Montagno—plant manager at Norton Abrasives,
Littleton, New Hampshire—for his review of and input to
the information on sharpening stones

Stan Watson—technical director for DMT (Diamond
Machining Technology), Marlborough, Massachusetts—
for his assistance with and contribution to the sharpening
stones information

Robert B. Hanna—professor and director at SUNY,
College of Environmental Science and Forestry, Syracuse,
New York—for sharing his knowledge and providing me
with micrographs of wood

Greg Heisey for his photographic expertise and fellowship
while shooting the bird, flower, and snowman projects

Peg Couch, book acquisition editor for Fox Chapel
Publishing, for her patience and assistance in making
this book a reality

Gretchen Bacon, editor for Fox Chapel Publishing, for
correcting my spelling and grammar errors, plus creating
magic by condensing the 400 pages and hundreds of
photographs I sent her into a book of 288 pages

Troy Thorne, creative director for Fox Chapel
Publishing, for his creative layout to make my
book aesthetically interesting

AND A MAJOR THANK-YOU TO:

My son, Jeff, for the many hours he spent doing photography
for the body of this book. It would have been next to
impossible to have completed this book without his
assistance. He's more of a perfectionist than I am.

My wife, Deloris, for her patience and understanding.
Many "Honey Do's" were left undone during the two
years I lived inside this book.

And to all my family, friends, and students who gave
me support and encouragement as I made my dreams
of writing this book a reality.

CONTENTS

INTRODUCTION

If you're searching for a hobby that will be with you for a lifetime—not just some fad that's here today and gone tomorrow—woodcarving puts you on the right track. It's not a stagnant hobby but one that is stimulating, yet relaxing. Woodcarving is done in many styles, from simple repetitive patterns to intricate sculptures, so it's a hobby in which you will never run out of ideas for what you can create. It can become a very satisfying and fulfilling part of your life.

In this age of mass production, it's gratifying to take a piece of wood and create your own piece of art, and because wood comes from a once-living tree, no two pieces will ever be the same. It grows and changes, even after it's harvested. Each piece will have a beauty and character of its very own. This beauty of wood makes woodcarving a special art.

During the 30-plus years I have been carving, I've held classes, written articles and books, and produced videos and DVDs—all to help woodcarvers at different stages of their carving careers. Woodcarving can't be learned through books alone, but books are a great way to start your journey into woodcarving and a great resource to turn to when you need help on a specific topic.

With that in mind, I've included material in this book to help you develop an understanding of woodcarving basics so you have a solid foundation on which to build.

Experienced woodcarvers can expand their knowledge of this beautiful art form as well. I recommend you read this book in its entirety, and then refer back to specific chapters if you have questions on a particular topic. This book will take you through

- a history of woodcarving
- the various types of carving
- the anatomy of wood and how its characteristics affect how you carve it
- why some types of wood are better to carve than others
- what to look for when buying wood for carving
- why wood may crack or split and how to minimize it
- what to look for when buying carving tools
- the different types of sharpening stones and their characteristics
- how to sharpen your carving tools
- how to use your carving tools safely
- how to develop an idea into a finished carving
- techniques to finish a carving

I've also included seven projects, each one specially selected to help you become proficient with your carving tools and expand your knowledge of how to carve wood.

Working with wood as a medium, and carving in particular, requires only a few tools to get started, and you can create an unlimited number of things within this art form. I find it totally relaxing and gratifying to see a piece of wood come alive with each chip I remove. Carving is a very satisfying and fulfilling part of my life; I hope it can be a part of yours.

—*Everett Ellenwood*

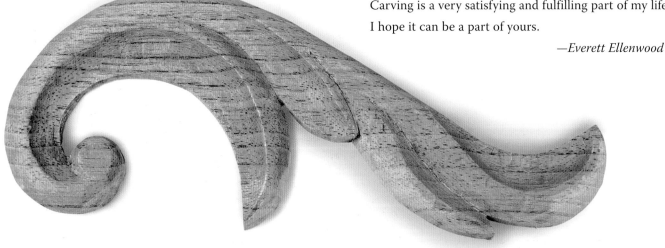

THE WOODCARVER

by Everett Ellenwood

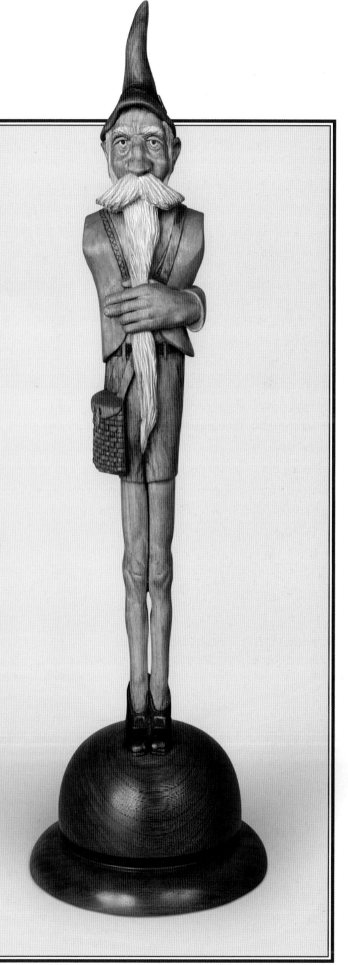

I saw this piece of wood one day
When I picked it up it seemed to say

There's something hiding inside of me
Remove some chips and you will see

I looked to see what I might find
And soon an image came to mind

My task was now to set it free
What's hidden in this piece of tree?

With loving care each cut was made
Wood peeled off with a sharp-edged blade

And as each chip fell to the floor
I could see the object more and more

By one final cut it was set free
My work of art for all to see

This piece of wood which would just lay
And see its body soon decay

Was now transformed and given life
With careful cuts of gouge and knife

By carving something from this tree
It lives again because of me

Chapter One

 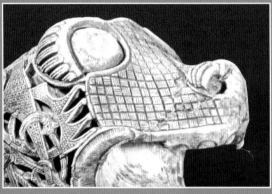 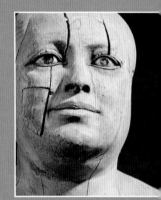

A History of
Woodcarving

1

Woodcarving is one of the oldest developed skills known.

Studying the past can do more than inspire and show you some of the different possibilities; it can also add value to your work by providing a context for it. Whether you eventually fit into the community of caricature carvers or create techniques and works that parallel or advance those of furniture carvers, knowing the history of carving can bring self-satisfaction and a sense of worth, especially if you ever decide to sell your work.

As you will see here, woodcarving is a common thread that has flowed through every nation and culture since the beginning of mankind. No country in the world is without a history of carving in one form or another; it is one of the oldest developed skills. Carving also has a presence in every era. In tough times, men decorated practical objects; during wealthy times, they created more luxurious carved items. The availability and workability of wood—for practical and indulgent purposes—helped woodcarving gain its place in history.

WOODCARVING'S BEGINNINGS

Some of the earliest examples of woodcarving include everyday items found in China that were crafted with simple stone tools, fine wooden hunting spears found in Germany, and a wooden club and digging sticks found in Africa. All of these wooden articles trace carving back to the New Stone Age (about 9000 BCE to 7000 BCE). Even though writings indicate woodcarving's presence prior to the New Stone Age, any actual examples do not exist because of wood's susceptibility to the elements.

Although woodcarving was practiced in all parts of the ancient world, ancient Egyptian works provide us with some of the best examples and have survived because of Egypt's arid climate. Of particular interest is the focus on figure, furniture, and relief carving. Numerous tombs have been excavated, yielding many examples of human and animal mummy cases with likenesses and figures carved on them and their lids. Detailed intaglio wooden molds, used to impress patterns into dough, have also been found. Additionally, expeditions have unearthed wooden furniture with folding seats, similar to modern campstools, and chairs with legs terminating in the carved heads or feet of animals. One

of the oldest toys, a little carved boat, was found in a child's tomb there, and excavations have uncovered seafaring wooden vessels with carved human and animal figureheads dating back before 3000 BCE.

An amazing example of Egyptian woodcarving that withstood the test of time is a three-foot-by-seven-inch lifelike statue, most of which was carved from a solid block of sycamore around 2500 BCE. Wood was not plentiful in Egypt, and sycamore, so scarce that it was considered sacred, was the only tree suitable for carving. The statue immortalized Ka-Aper, a priest who recited prayers for deceased kings (see photo on page 4).

In 1860 CE, the tomb of Hesy-ra, the royal physician of ancient Egypt, was opened to reveal yet another tribute to woodcarving's past. Eleven wooden relief-carved panels, each measuring two feet high, were discovered. These exquisite low relief panels may have been carved around 2500 BCE.

While the Bronze Age (3000 BCE to 1300 BCE) saw the creation of functional carved items, such as coffins found in Germany and Denmark, carvers also worked in figure, incised, and relief carving. In Germany, fine wooden animal statues in bas-relief were found. In southwest China, archaeologists uncovered a painted woodcarving of a head, which measures 31½ inches long.

In Norway, the Oseberg ship, dating back to 800 BCE, is one of the prime examples of Iron Age (1300 BCE to 300 BCE) woodcarving. The Oseberg is one of only two Viking ships found from this era and is believed by some to be the burial ship of the Viking queen Åsa. Built of oak, the ship measures 70 feet long by 16 feet wide by 5 feet deep and was filled with items for the buried woman to use in the afterlife, such as a wooden cart, bedposts, and rudimentary farming implements.

Carved relief depicting a knight and two figures from a wagon found at Oseberg, Norway. The ninth-century woodcarving is on display at the Viking Ship Museum in Oslo, Norway.

WOODCARVING IN THE COMMON ERA

Few examples exist of very early Common Era carvings, but it's clear that woodcarving served many of the same purposes it does today. Dating back to the fifth century, panels found in a Roman basilica and adorned with figures and designs provide an excellent example of the religious carving of the time. In northern Canada, a Dorset culture mask from 500 CE to 1000 CE was excavated from the permanently frozen Arctic soil. This painted, life-size mask was carved from driftwood. Culturists think the mask was probably worn in rituals for curing the sick, controlling the weather, or influencing the hunt.

Religious devotion and extensive carved detail marked the art of the Gothic period (1200 CE to 1450 CE). Many of the religious woodcarvings of Europe, including panels, choir stalls, and crucifixes, were executed with proportions and detail that have never been paralleled. Some scholars speculate that the heightened religious devotion of the time spawned the extreme attention to detail. Craftsmen carved not just for carving's sake; they carved to glorify God and religious ideals. During this time, multitudes of apprentice carvers throughout Europe, Scandinavia, and the Far East worked under the watchful eyes of master carvers.

Because the transition from the Gothic period to the Renaissance (the fourteenth to the seventeenth century) happened gradually and because their spans overlap, it is useful to look at the characteristics of both periods together. Foliage designs were prevalent in both periods, although Gothic artists did not use the scroll design and avoided the repetition of details, which Renaissance artists used to maintain balance and symmetry. As the Renaissance neared, foliage became more

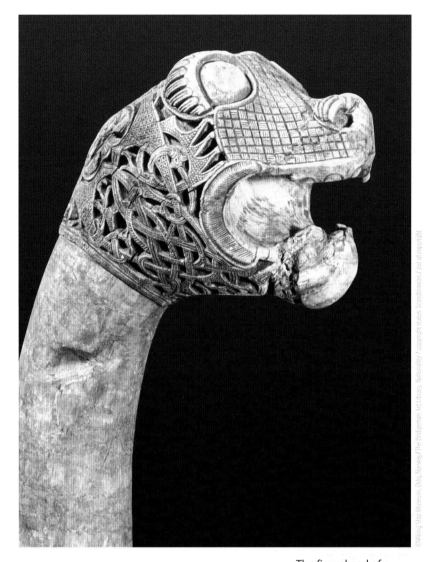

The figurehead of a Viking longship found at Oseberg Norway. From the ninth century, the figurehead is on display at the Viking Ship Museum in Oslo, Norway.

realistic, and carvers favored the vine over traditional foliage.

Renaissance and Gothic artists both ornamented many features of the church. Relief-carved foliage and figures appeared in many places, including coves, bosses, ribs, and other architectural elements; roofs; pulpits; rood screens, which separated the clergy from the laity; misericords; and seats. More than just carved with decorative foliage, seats in particular included "green men"—faces in, or often spewing, foliage. Piercing and undercutting techniques were employed to create shadows and realism. Carving in the round also had its place. Baptismal font tops or bench ends were shaped into doves,

A carved wooden statue of Ka-Aper, known as Sheikh el-Beled, a headman of his village, from his mastaba tomb in North Saqqara, Old Kingdom. The eyes in the statue were made from rock crystal rimmed with copper. The sycamore carving, which was lifesize, comes from the Egyptian Fifth Dynasty. The piece is on display at the Egyptian National Museum in Cairo, Egypt.

scrollwork, pilasters with capitals, coats of arms, and figures. Chests and staircases both often displayed coats of arms or other heraldic images. Solid-backed chairs received low relief carvings, and table legs were sometimes decorated with acanthus designs. During the Renaissance, house fronts provided a large canvas for the carver, and animals and acanthus leaves were often used.

During this same time, Arabic craftsmen carved many of the same motifs. Architectural elements and screens of complicated joinery were decorated with geometric designs, scrollwork, intricate interlacing patterns, foliage, and sometimes animals and figures in low relief. In places such as Persia, spoons, boxes, and other small items were embellished with low relief patterns or designs that resembled chip carving patterns.

The Reformation dealt a damaging blow to European woodcarving in 1548 CE. During the reign of Edward VI, the council ordered all rood screens and images of saints removed from churches and destroyed. Almost all of the beautifully carved roods in medieval England were removed or defaced. The only religious carving during this era was done by monks in the secure confines of monasteries. After stabilization of Puritan rule, this edict was reversed. By 1556, almost all churches had altars, images, and rood screens once again, but many exhibited defacement suffered during the Reformation.

Woodcarving continued to gain momentum in the seventeenth century. Deep relief carvings became popular, with vines as a key element. Chip carving and acanthus designs were commonly used for decorating buildings, furniture, and household items. Figurework was also widespread.

In England, Grinling Gibbons, one of the most famous decorative woodcarvers of all

representing the Holy Spirit, or angels, and life-size carved figures of the Virgin Mary or the Lord also appeared in many churches. Doors and windows were adorned with rosettes or other geometric patterns that resemble some of today's chip carving. Many carvings of all varieties were beautifully colored through painting.

Not reserved for churches alone, foliage and geometric designs were also common in the home on mantelpieces and cabinets. Because the fireplace mantel was the focus of a room, it was exceptionally ornate and could include time, carved for some of England's kings and brought decorative carving to new heights. His work still decorates several English churches, most notably Saint Paul's Cathedral, and aristocratic mansions, including Windsor Castle. Best known for his technical skills, Gibbons' specialties included foliage, fruit, flowers, birds, and an almost endless array of objects intertwined with drapery, all carved in lime wood up to a foot thick. Flower petals, leaves, and feathers were undercut and stood off the surface in unbelievable detail. The delicacy of his carving has arguably never been surpassed since. Gibbons' work had an enormous influence on the interior design and décor of this period, along with having a profound influence on furniture craftsmen, such as Thomas Chippendale. Although Chippendale did not carve the variety of motifs that Gibbons did, scrolls, shells, ribbons, and claw and ball feet, all done in very fine relief, are abundant in Chippendale's work.

WOODCARVING IN NORTH AMERICA

The early 1600s saw the beginning of emigration from Europe to North America, which continued for more than three centuries. Early settlers carved primarily utilitarian items, such as spoons, wooden bowls, and yokes. Parts of wagons, such as spokes for wheels, were also carved. These early settlers were more concerned with survival than making decorative items.

As migration grew from a few hundred to millions of immigrants in the eighteenth century, some of the best carvers from Europe and Scandinavian countries moved to North America. This influx of talent had a tremendous influence on the newly discovered American continent, where immigrants decorated their homes and churches with carvings and architectural moldings.

As more and more businesses developed, carvers were in great demand to create

The coat of arms of the sixth Duke of Somerset was carved in lime wood by Grinling Gibbons (1648–1721). The carving was part of the ornamentation at Petworth House in Sussex, United Kingdom.

A high relief carving from the fifteenth or sixteenth century, *Altarpiece of the Passion* was carved by Veit Stoss (1445–1533).

wooden signs to advertise shops. Because so many immigrants couldn't read English, signs displayed carved objects instead of words to bridge the language barrier. Pubs were often named after eclectically grouped but easily illustrated elements. The Bell-in-Hand Tavern, established in Boston in 1795 by James Wilson, featured a town crier on its sign. Other popular examples of illustrating a product rather than carving out letters were cigar store Indians in front of tobacconist shops. (Native American Indians were equated with tobacco because they introduced the early explorers to it.) Yet more examples of symbolic carving include the carved barber pole, a key for the locksmith, scissors for the tailor, a shoe for the cobbler, a hat for the haberdasher, and so on. Some signs were so well designed and crafted that they are highly collectible if still around today.

Furniture makers were also in great demand. Records dating from before the American Revolution show at least 150 cabinetmakers in Boston and an equal number in Philadelphia. Craftsmen in some southern states also made fine furniture, especially from cherry and mahogany. Many of these cabinetmakers employed several skilled carvers to produce Chippendale-style furniture with highly decorated hand-carved cabriole legs, backs of chairs, drawer fronts, and bonnets across the tops of chests and highboy furniture.

The use of decorative hand carving declined in the nineteenth century, except in works

Before the American Revolutionary War, many furniture makers employed skilled carvers to produce Chippendale-style furniture with interlaced splat backs and square chamfered legs. The chair is owned by Mallet & Son Antiques Ltd., London, United Kingdom.

made for churches and mosques. However, fun and relaxing projects known as whimsies emerged. Duplicating machines, capable of making large quantities of one item, began to replace carvers. Additionally, the price of labor increased, so only the wealthy could afford to beautify their homes with the carvings of skilled craftsmen.

The Depression era (1930s to mid-1940s) significantly impacted all skills, including carving. In 1935, President Franklin D. Roosevelt spearheaded a program called the Federal Arts Project (FAP), meant to establish community art centers to educate children and adults in the arts, to provide artwork for nonfederal buildings, and to create jobs for unemployed artists on relief rolls. Through this program, woodworking and whittling classes for men and boys were operated in settlement houses, YMCAs, schools, museums, and recreation halls. The FAP was the largest employer of artists during the Depression, giving jobs to more than 5,000 artists. Today, many of the artists' works are displayed in post offices and public buildings throughout the United States. In addition to providing jobs, the program also created a new awareness of American art and exposed thousands of would-be carvers to woodworking.

The Second World War gave way to modern, straight-lined architecture in buildings and furniture; very few decorative accents were used. Because of this trend, and because people were focused on the war effort, carving faced another decline.

When the war ended and the world economy began to grow, people could devote more free time to hobbies. Carving witnessed another revival. Today, thousands of people throughout the world enjoy this beautiful art form. With the retirement of the baby boomers, who will be looking for hobbies to fill their free time, woodcarving in the United States may continue to grow in popularity. And with all of the different types of woodcarving, artists and hobbyists alike will have plenty of options to explore.

A shop sign for a shoemaker in France depicting St. Crispin at his workbench. The sixteenth-century French school carving is displayed at Musee de la Ville de Paris, Musee Carnavalet, in Paris, France.

This painted totem pole was carved by a Native American tribe from the Pacific Northwest. The pole is on display at the Horniman Museum in London, United Kingdom.

Chapter Two

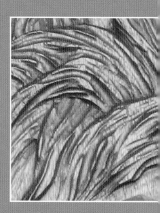

Types of Carvings

Once you begin carving, only your imagination will limit what you can create.

If you've read Chapter 1, "A History of Woodcarving," you probably noticed terms such as relief carving, chip carving, and architectural carving that describe some varieties of carving throughout history. Just as most arts and crafts have different styles— impressionism and cubism, for example, are styles of painting—carving also has different types. Within each specialty, you will find an unlimited number of things to carve. For instance, realistic carvings could encompass everything from birds to fish to human busts, all in exquisite, true-to-life detail.

How do you decide what to carve? If you feel overwhelmed and aren't sure where to begin, start with what inspires you. Do you want to create something usable for your home? Try a utilitarian carving project. A simple spoon is ideal. Do you want to capture the human figure in wood? Make a bust your first carving. Do you want to memorialize a friend's favorite pet? Create a realistic carving of a dog or a cat.

In the following section, I'll show you examples of each style so you can recognize the types and their characteristics. If you're a new carver, try as many varieties as possible. After carving for a period of time, you'll probably find that you prefer certain types to others, but don't be afraid to experiment with the different styles at first.

Two-Dimensional Carving

Two-dimensional carving refers to carving done only on the surface of a flat piece of wood. Don't be fooled, though. Two-dimensional carving can range from relatively simple, like incised carving, to more difficult, like chip carving and relief carving.

A dolphin exquisitely done in incised carving.

Incised Carving

In incised carving, only the outline of an object is carved into the wood; the rest of the wood is normally left untouched. Cuts are made with V-tools, veiners, or knives of varying sizes, and deeper or wider cuts create highlights. Incised carving is used on furniture, for wood block printing, and for carving lettering into wood.

Tools: Tools capable of outlining cuts

Uses: Furniture decorating, carvings for wood block printing, letter carving

Incised Carving. The piece of basswood board was first painted black and then carved using a V-tool, making the outlines easy to see.

Chip Carving

One of the oldest forms of decorative woodcarving, chip carving has been used throughout the world to decorate homes, household items, and vessels. Chip carvers remove selected chips of wood to create patterns. The patterns are often repetitive and can have free-form chips, such as curves, or geometric chips, such as triangles.

Tools: Chip carving knives
Uses: Decorating items of all types

Chip Carving. Notice the characteristic geometric patterns in the borders and main designs of this chip carved box. A key to its beauty is the neat and even removal of chips.

Small Basswood Giftbox, with the pattern and carving by Todd Moor, measures three inches by five inches. The chip carving features a flower motif on the sides and is mirror-imaged on the top.

Basswood Bowl, a carving by Wayne Boniface of Kitchener, Ontario, is an excellent example of chip carving.

INTAGLIO

In intaglio (pronounced in-TALL-yo), a recess is carved, and the subject is carved into the recess. The surrounding surface is normally left untouched. This style of carving is effectively negative relief carving. Typically, intaglio is used to make designs in butter molds, candy molds, chair backs, and other furniture. Albrecht Dürer, who created the famous *Hands of the Apostle*, is one of the most renowned intaglio artists.

Tools: Various carving tools, especially long bent and short bent

Uses: Molds, furniture decorating, printmaking

Intaglio. An excellent example of negative relief carving, this candy mold from the Philippines shows the depth of the main image and the untouched surrounding wood.

Another carving by Gene Wilson—his largest cookie mold—of King William III. Carved from beech, the mold measures 5½ inches wide by 12 inches long.

Butter molds carved by Gene Wilson of Belleville, Illinois. The molds were used to identify who had made the butter.

RELIEF CARVING

In relief carving, wood is carved away around an object to make it look as if the object is standing off the surface of the wood. This variety of carving uses techniques such as undercutting (cutting under an element to hide the line where the element meets the background) to create shadows and depth. Relief carving can be further divided into three categories:

■ In **low relief**, or bas-relief, only a small amount of wood is relieved from around the object, which extends off the background. These carvings normally have no undercuts but can be very detailed.

■ **High relief** is basically the same as low relief, except more wood is removed around the object and undercuts are made to create more shadows. Normally, at least half the object's circumference projects off the wood. These differences make high relief more dramatic than low relief.

■ In **pierced relief**, areas of the carving are completely removed so you can see through those areas.

Usually, finished pieces of all three types are viewed only from the front. As you probably remember from Chapter 1, "A History of Woodcarving," relief carving traces back to ancient Egypt and has been used throughout time to decorate homes, furniture, jewelry boxes, and household items.

....

Tools: Knives and other carving tools, especially gouges, V-tools, and veiners

Uses: Decorating items of all types

....

Low Relief Carving. Notice how little wood I removed from the surface of this low relief carving. The iris flower is raised no more than ⅛ inch at any place on the carving.

High Relief Carving. This highly detailed high relief carving is an antique from Europe and more than 100 years old. Carved in linden wood, the panel measures 11½ inches wide by 20 inches long. Notice how the deeper cuts of high relief create very dark shadows.

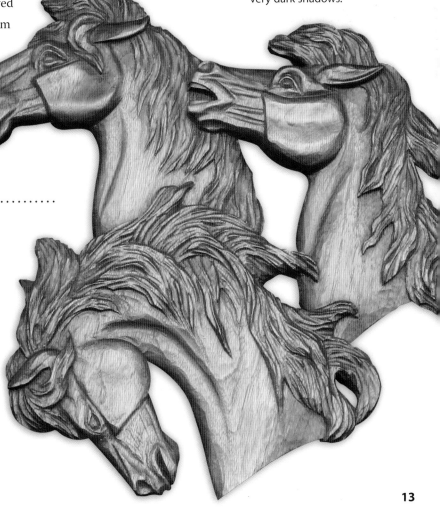

Pierced Relief Carving. The open spaces between the horses, where I removed the wood completely, make this a pierced relief carving.

ARCHITECTURAL CARVING

In this style of carving, designs are carved in, or attached to, items such as furniture or architectural elements.

Acanthus carving is one of the most popular specialties of architectural carving and can also fall under the category of relief carving. The ornate acanthus style incorporates concave and convex cuts to make flowing, stylized designs based on the acanthus plant. The Greeks and Romans used the acanthus in Gothic art and architecture; it carried into the Renaissance, and it also became very popular in the Scandinavian countries. It is still recognized as a Scandinavian style of carving today. Acanthus carving is used on furniture, on picture frames, and architecturally as a decorative accent.

Tools: Gouges, veiners, and V-tools of various sizes
Uses: Furniture and architectural decoration

Architectural Carving. This 32-inch-long-by-4½-inch-wide cherry piece adorns the front of a fireplace mantel. The scroll-like form is typical in architectural carving.

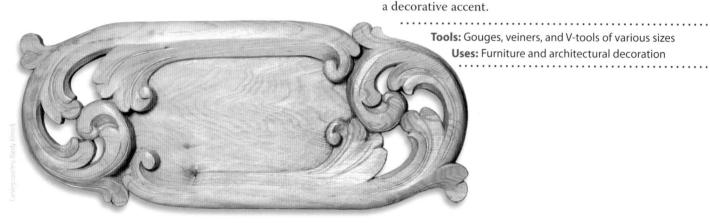

Carving courtesy Randy Kinnick

Acanthus Carving. In this acanthus carving done in butternut, you can see how the leaves flow in convex and concave shapes.

An excellent example of rustic architectural carving by Greg Young of Germantown, Wisconsin.

From *Fireplaces and Mantel Ideas*, Second Edition, by John Lewman, 2004. Fox Chapel Publishing, Inc.

BARK CARVING

Bark for carving, such as cottonwood bark, is thick and dense. Every piece of bark has a unique size and shape, so each carving conforms to an individual piece. Bark carvings are typically carved and viewed from only one side; however, they can sometimes be partially hollowed out. Though its medium is the first thing that sets it apart, bark carving also has some distinct techniques because it carves differently than solid wood. Fantasy buildings and wood spirits are two popular items carved in bark.

Tools: Knives and other carving tools
Uses: Fantasy decorative items

Bark Carving. *Silent Sentinel*, a 3½ inch thick, 6 inch wide, 22 inch long carving from plains cottonwood bark. The finished piece is treated with lacquer and wax finish.

Untitled Wood Spirit, 4 inches thick, 6 inches wide, 23 inches long. Carved from plains cottonwood bark with lacquer and wax finish.

Images on this page from: *The Illustrated Guide to Carving Tree Bark*, by Rick Jensen and Jack A. Williams, 2004, Fox Chapel Publishing, Inc.

CARVING IN THE ROUND

Any three-dimensional carving where wood is removed all around the subject, giving the work height, width, and depth, is called carving in the round. Carvings in this category can be viewed from any angle and have a subject that is visible from any side.

REALISTIC CARVING

Realistic carvings present a subject as true to life as possible. Carvers of this style rely heavily on photographs and direct observation of their subjects. Every scale, feather barb, or wrinkle is recreated in wood. Painting is equally detailed.

- Amazingly detailed, **bird carvings** range in size from the smallest hummingbird to the largest goose.
- Rarely done as life-size carvings, **animal carvings** are often miniature versions of the real creatures. No details, from the way the fur lies to the highlights in the eye, are overlooked.
- **Fish carvings** vary in size—smaller fish, such as freshwater trout, are carved life size; larger game fish, sharks, and dolphins are often carved in miniature. Special tools exist for getting each and every scale correct.
- **Human figure carvings** include life-size sculptures, busts, and miniature figures. Carvers who specialize in this subcategory work hard to capture facial expressions and body language.

Tools: Knives, gouges, veiners, V-tools, micro tools, and sometimes power tools

Uses: Sculptures or decorative items

Realistic Carving. This bust of a male figure in basswood shows the human figure variety of realistic carving. I used a ⅜-inch veiner and a V-tool to detail the beard and cap. I sanded only the face to create the smooth appearance of skin.

Cedar Waxwing, by Lori Corbett, is a fine example of realistic carving.

From *Carving Award-Winning Songbirds,* by Lori Corbett, 2005, Fox Chapel Publishing, Inc.

STYLIZED CARVING

Stylized carvings emphasize form over detail; these carvings represent a subject without recreating it exactly. Normally, stylized carvings are sanded to give smooth, flowing lines, and many works are left unpainted so the natural wood grain shows in the finished piece.

. . . .

Tools: Knives and other carving tools
Uses: Sculptures or decorative items

. . . .

Stylized Carving. The smooth lines and natural finish of this 12-inch-high stylized cat are characteristic of most stylized carvings. You'll also notice that the majority of the details have been left out.

An outstanding example of realistic carving: *The Sentinel* by Ralph Mueller. The great blue heron is carved in cedar.

Caricature Carving. Like most caricature carvings, this golfer has exaggerated features, such as his hands and nose, but he still has elements of realism. I carved the golfer in a class given by one of the premier caricature carvers, Marv Kaisersat.

CARICATURE CARVING

A very popular type of carving, caricature deliberately exaggerates a familiar subject's distinctive features or peculiarities. Emil Janel (1897–1981), one of the masters of caricature carving, referred to it as "exaggerated realism." Artists in European countries carved in caricature to some degree, but Sweden had the most profound and lasting effect on this style of carving. Most caricature carvings are done in basswood.

Tools: Knives and other carving tools
Uses: Decorative figures, sometimes bottle stoppers

Pair of Pirate's Parrots, by artist Joe You, is an excellent example of caricature carving.

FLAT-PLANE CARVING

Flat-plane carving, native to the Scandinavian countries, has become popular in recent years. It features simple, controlled knife cuts, which leave flat surfaces on the finished carving. Typical subjects are people and animals. Flat-plane carving was almost extinct but was revived primarily because of one person: Harley Refsal. Refsal spent an extensive period of time in Scandinavia, interviewing elderly carvers and studying this dying art form. He wrote books documenting the style and has traveled around the world demonstrating and teaching.

....

Tools: Knives
Uses: Decorative figures

....

Carvings courtesy Wayne Hendrickson

Flat-Plane Carving. Flat-plane carvings are easily recognized by the flat knife cuts left on the surface of the finished carving. The bright coloring is also characteristic of this style.

From: *The Art and Technique of Scandinavian Style Woodcarving*, by Harley Refsal, 2004, Fox Chapel Publishing, Inc.

Scandinavian Kick Sled by Harley Refsal. From the collection of Walter and Marcia Sanders, Jamestown, North Dakota.

Oscar, by Harley Refsal, is an example of flat-plane carving.

From *The Art and Technique of Scandinavian Style Woodcarving* by Harley Refsal, 2004, Fox Chapel Publishing, Inc.

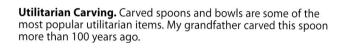

Utilitarian Carving. Carved spoons and bowls are some of the most popular utilitarian items. My grandfather carved this spoon more than 100 years ago.

UTILITARIAN CARVING

Items intended to be useful and practical, such as spoons, bowls, and drawer pulls, are part of utilitarian carving. These carvings can include other styles; items can be created as stylized carvings, with natural finishes and few details, or carved in the realistic style, with highly detailed, decorative markings and beautiful painted colors.

Tools: Knives and other carving tools
Uses: Functional items that also can be decorative

Utilitarian carvings can be both beautiful and functional. I carved these drawer pulls from cherry wood.

This oak leaf candy dish carved from walnut is a good example of a utilitarian carving that can also be used as a decorative item. It is 5½ inches wide by 6½ inches long.

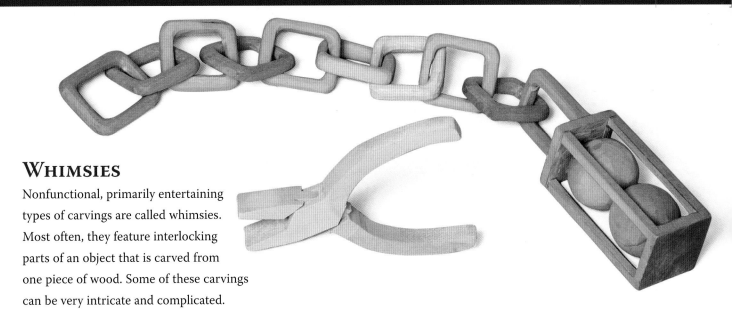

WHIMSIES

Nonfunctional, primarily entertaining types of carvings are called whimsies. Most often, they feature interlocking parts of an object that is carved from one piece of wood. Some of these carvings can be very intricate and complicated.

. . . .

Tools: Primarily carving knives
Uses: Toys

. . . .

Whimsies. Items such as this wooden chain with a ball in a birdcage and these jointed pliers are whimsies that can be toys, puzzles, or games.

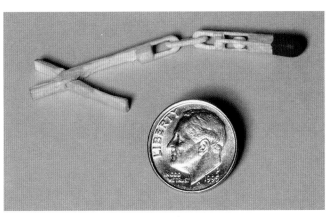

Whimsies can be any size, such as this incredible chain carved from a matchstick.

With its trapped ball, this carving is another excellent example of a whimsy.

Chapter Three

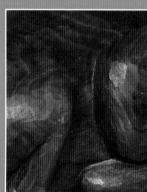

WOOD FOR CARVING

The more you know about wood, the more effectively you can use it.

Now that you've gotten a good look at the different types of carving and hopefully found one that sparks your imagination, let's take a look at the medium you'll be working in: wood. You'll want to learn as much as you can about wood before you actually start because the more you know about wood, the more effectively you'll be able to use it.

Selecting the right wood involves much more than just thinking about the finished product. To get the most out of the medium, you'll also want to understand the makeup of wood and why it reacts to the environment and to carving tools the way it does. In this chapter, we'll take a look at the various characteristics that determine how carvers use a tree for carving.

Anatomy of a Tree

A tree consists of three primary components: the trunk, the roots, and the crown. Each part can provide different types of carving wood. The way a tree grows and the health of that growth affect the quality of the carving wood.

Trunk

Also called the bole, the trunk connects the roots to the crown and transports food to the roots and food and water throughout the trunk. The trunk is usually considered the portion of the tree without limbs. Because it has the least tendency to crack or split, wood from the trunk is generally the most stable wood for carving.

The bark of a tree's trunk acts as a protective skin, keeping moisture and gases contained in the tree and resisting life-threatening attacks by insects, microorganisms, and weather. Bark consists of living and dead cells. The tree adds new bark cells each year to replace the outside bark, or dead cells, which will crack. If no new bark cells are made, the cracked area will expose the wood to the elements. Bark can be carved by itself if it has considerable thickness, or it can be carved through to expose the wood beneath.

Roots

The roots grow into the ground and anchor the tree, keeping it erect. They also absorb water and minerals from the ground, which are transported through strawlike vessels up through the trunk, limbs, branches, and twigs, and finally out to the leaves. While many carvers enjoy working with roots, these parts of the tree aren't a good medium for beginning carvers. Roots are embedded with dirt, which dulls carving tools quickly. Also, many roots have a twisted grain, which is very difficult to carve.

Crown

The limbs, branches, twigs, and leaves form the crown of the tree. Leafy branches offer habitat for many animals, shade from the sun, protection from the elements, and beauty to the landscape in all four seasons. Food, called sap, is produced in the leaves through the process of photosynthesis. Limbs, branches, and twigs can all provide good carving wood. Even small twigs can make great material for carving, especially whittling projects.

INTERNAL GROWTH

The trunk, roots, and crown are the tree's primary visible components, but studying its internal characteristics gives us an even better understanding of the tree's structure. Looking into the cross section of a tree is the best way to see its internal characteristics; understanding what you're seeing helps you avoid costly and time-consuming carving errors.

PITH

At the tree's center is the pith, the oldest part of the tree. The pith, together with the tree's first few annual rings, is what's called juvenile wood. Juvenile wood also forms where the initial growth of branches begins. As the tree grows, the pith usually dries out, becomes softer, and turns darker than the rest of the wood. The pith area also has a tendency to crack.

Because of these characteristics, avoid carving pieces of wood that include the pith. If you do carve wood with the pith intact, design the piece so the pith doesn't show from the viewing angle.

The pith isn't usually included when wood is cut into blanks, but if it is, orient the wood so the pith is less noticeable on your finished carving. On this piece, the pith is located toward the back of the carving.

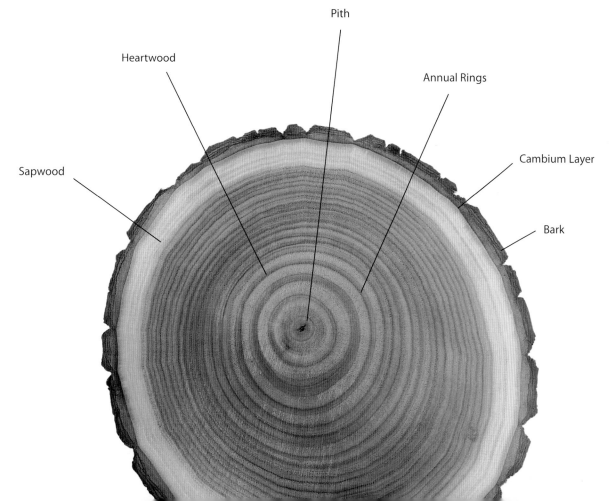

Pith

Heartwood

Annual Rings

Cambium Layer

Sapwood

Bark

Early Wood

Late Wood

ANNUAL RINGS

Radiating out from the pith are the annual rings. Each ring has two components: early wood (also called spring wood) and late wood (also called summer wood). Early wood grows at the beginning of the tree's growing season, the tree's period of active growth. This wood is made of large cells with thin walls. As the season progresses, the growth activity slows down, and the cells become smaller with thicker walls; this is the late wood. Late wood is normally darker than early wood because it has a higher concentration of cellulose. You will normally see one annual ring for each year of the tree's growth. The rings can vary in width because of weather and other conditions during the growing season.

In a tree's limbs and branches, the annual rings can reflect stressful or irregular growth. Because limbs and branches hang parallel to the ground for their entire life, some develop reaction wood, which grows unevenly to help support the branch. Blocks or pieces with reaction wood have a significantly higher chance of cracking or splitting, no matter what precautions you take. To check if the wood you want to carve has reaction wood, look for a pith that's off-center. This phenomenon also will occur in trees that are leaning.

Studying the annual rings also helps us see how the rings appear as grain lines when wood is cut from a tree. Here are some common terms:

- **Plainsawn** (sometimes called flatsawn) wood has arches on the face (the long surface), and curved parts of the annual rings are visible on the end.
- **Quartersawn** boards have straight grain lines on the face and ends.
- **Riftsawn** wood has slightly wavy grain on the face and slightly bent lines on the end.

Reaction Wood. A pith and annual rings that are off-center can indicate reaction wood, like the type found in this tree limb, most likely formed as the limb was drooping toward the ground. This cross section also shows the remnants of a knot and an encased internal flaw.

CAMBIUM LAYER

The annual rings progress out to the cambium layer, located between the bark and the wood. Cell division takes place here, and when the cells divide, they become either wood cells or bark cells. Normally, about 15 wood cells develop for every bark cell. The wood cells are primarily responsible for the tree's increase in diameter.

Knowing when the cambium layer is active helps you choose wood that has been cut at the best times. If you cut a tree in the spring or summer, the cambium layer feels slippery and slimy because cell division is taking place. During this period, the bark and wood are loosely bonded together, so when the wood is dried, the bark may fall off. During the fall and winter, when almost no cell division takes place, the bark and wood are tightly bonded together. It's imperative that a tree is cut in the fall or winter if you want the bark to remain intact.

HEARTWOOD AND SAPWOOD

As you read earlier in this chapter, the trunk transports food to the roots and food and water throughout the trunk. Once a tree grows large enough, only a portion of the trunk is required to supply food and water. This active portion consists of the outer annual rings and is called the sapwood.

The vessels of the center rings, no longer needed to supply food and water, fill with extractives, minerals, and tannins. This section becomes the heartwood. Instead of conducting food and water throughout the tree, the heartwood gives strength, essentially becoming the tree's vertebrae.

With the addition of new sapwood each year, the tree grows in diameter. The heartwood also expands because each tree requires only a certain number of sapwood rings. This number varies from one tree species to another.

In some species, you will see a distinct color contrast between the heartwood and sapwood. Other species, like basswood, show almost no difference between the two parts. Both heartwood and sapwood are ideal for woodcarving, but to maintain the same basic color, most carvings are done using the heartwood of the tree.

Harvesting a tree during the fall or winter, when the bark and the wood beneath are tightly bonded, allows you to incorporate bark into the finished design.

The sapwood, which delivers nutrients to the canopy, is usually lighter than the heartwood, which no longer carries food. Most carvings are done in heartwood, but some carvers prefer to include the varying colors of heartwood and sapwood.

There is little difference between the colors of the heartwood and the sapwood in basswood.

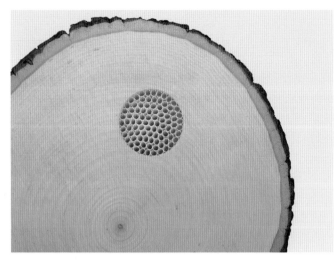

I cut out an area and inserted straws to simulate how it would look if this area were magnified.

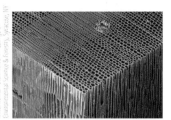

Under a high-powered microscope, the vessels that run up and down a tree's trunk are even more visible.

When a carving tool travels between vessels instead of across them, the tool tends to slip between the vessels, causing the vessels to split apart from one another; this is called "splitting with the grain." Always cut across the vessels, even if you have to change the position of the wood or the grip on your tool, so you never give the tool an opportunity to go between the vessels.

VESSELS

Under a microscope, the cross section of any tree looks like the end of a large bundle of straws. These straws are the vessels that carry water and minerals from the roots to the crown. (In softwoods, or coniferous trees, these are called fibers. In hardwoods, or deciduous trees, fibers make up the walls of the vessels.)

Most transfer of water and nutrients occurs up and down in a tree. However, some transfer of nutrients occurs across the tree from the phloem, the inner bark, to the pith through vessels called medullary rays. The rays transport food (sap) horizontally across the tree and also act as food storage areas.

Understanding the microscopic vessels along with the annual rings is important for working with grain and figure. Though many people use the terms interchangeably, grain and figure are actually different. Grain is a broader term that refers to the arrangement of vessels in wood. Straight grain, spiral grain, coarse grain, and fine grain all refer to what we see when we look at a piece of wood. Earlier, we touched on grain when describing how boards are cut from a tree (see Annual Rings on page 26).

CATEGORIZING TREES

Trees are divided into two classes: hardwoods, which are deciduous (broadleaf) trees, and

softwoods, which are coniferous (evergreen) trees. Hardwoods are angiosperms: trees with a branching and rebranching trunk and leaves that normally drop in the fall. Softwoods are gymnosperms, or conifers: trees, usually evergreens, with needles or scalelike foliage that have a single central trunk with side branches. The terms "hardwood" and "softwood" are not directly associated with the hardness or softness of the

wood; they describe the scientific classification of the trees. For example, basswood, a hardwood, is softer than Douglas fir, which is a softwood.

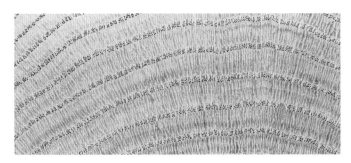

Medullary rays carry nutrients horizontally across the trunk of a tree. The rays can only be seen by magnification in most trees, but they are visible without magnification in a cross section of an oak tree's trunk.

For carvers, grain is most significant in describing how you work with wood. It affects every cut you make. For example, if a knife is allowed to go between these vessels, the fibers that make up the vessel walls will tear apart, and the wood will split. This is called "splitting with the grain" and can cause you to lose control of the cut and easily ruin a carving in progress. Make sure every cut you make with your knife or gouge is cutting across the vessels of the wood, not between them. The following terms are common ways carvers refer to methods of working with grain:

- **Across the grain**—Cutting perpendicular to the wood vessels.
- **With the grain**—Cutting parallel to the wood vessels.
- **Against the grain**—Cutting at an angle to the vessels.
- **Into the grain**—Cutting between the vessels.
- **Splitting with the grain**—Tearing of the wood, which normally occurs when you cut between the vessels.

Figure describes patterns of grain or color in wood. Curly and fiddleback figures, for example, are specific patterns of wavy grain. Figure most often comes into play when looking at the characteristics of the final piece. If you have trouble remembering the difference between grain and figure, just remember that grain *causes* figure.

HEALTH HAZARDS OF WOOD

Estimates are that about two percent of people have some type of wood allergy. Woods from the rain forests (mahogany, for example) pose the greatest threat because of their oily nature. These woods can cause skin rashes, and if sanded, the fine sawdust can create respiratory problems.

Woods from the United States and Canada that create the greatest dangers are western cedar and walnut. Dust from these woods may cause respiratory problems and eye inflammation.

Studies have found that softwoods are less allergenic than hardwoods, but no matter what kind of wood you use, it is best to take precautions. Remember, preventing problems before they occur is better than requiring ongoing treatment after. Here are some general guidelines:

- Wear a good-quality dust mask. Get one that is NIOSH (National Institute for Occupational Safety and Health) approved and fits snugly on your face, especially over your nose.

- If you do much sanding or power carving, make sure you have a good vacuum and ventilation system in addition to your dust mask. (If you install a vacuum system, it should be well grounded. Fine, dry sawdust is highly flammable, and a static spark can ignite it.)

- When handling wood that can cause skin irritation, wear gloves.

- If you have any type of symptoms when using a certain species of wood, avoid using that wood.

- If symptoms persist, have them checked by a physician.

GOOD WOODS TO CARVE

The anatomy and all of the growth characteristics in the first part of this chapter come into play to create well-nurtured wood, but even if it's perfectly grown, you won't want to pick up just any piece of wood and start carving. Of the 50,000-plus species of wood in the world, some are more carver-friendly than others.

Whether it is hardwood or softwood (see Categorizing Trees on page 28), a wood's weight is directly proportional to its relative hardness. The heavier the weight, the harder the wood, and the tougher it is to carve. The best woods for carving weigh between 25 and 50 pounds per cubic foot when dried to about 10 percent moisture content (MC). Woods lighter than 25 pounds per cubic foot are too soft; they dent easily and won't hold good detail. Woods heavier than 50 pounds per cubic foot are very hard and more difficult to carve.

Beginning on page 31, you'll find examples of popular carving woods. Each sample is 5 inches wide and 2¾ inches high. The left diagonal side is the natural wood color; the right diagonal side has a coat of satin-finish polyurethane varnish. The left half of each end piece is the natural wood color; the right half has a coat of polyurethane.

If you're just beginning your carving journey, start with basswood or butternut; then, as you develop your skills, try different species. A common mistake is to start with wood that is difficult to carve, a frustrating experience that causes many people to abandon woodcarving.

CHARACTERISTICS OF POPULAR CARVING WOODS

Wood	Weight[1]	Heartwood color	Sapwood color	Workability
Basswood[2]	26	Creamy to beige	Creamy white	Easy
Butternut[2]	27	Golden brown	Cream	Easy
Catalpa	29	Grayish brown	Grayish yellow	Easy
Tupelo	35	Cream to light tan	Light gray to whitish	Medium
Cherry	35	Light reddish brown	White-yellow brown	Medium
Mahogany	35	Dark reddish brown	Straw	Medium
Walnut	36 to 38	Chocolate	Light cream	Hard
Birch	38 to 45	Golden brown	Creamy white	Hard
Maple	42 to 45	Blond to tan	Cream	Hard

[1]Based on 1 cubic foot at 10% moisture content
[2]Basswood and butternut are the most popular woods for carving because of their density.

Basswood

One of the most popular woods for carving, basswood carves easily and is similar to European linden and lime wood. Because most basswood has a subtle grain pattern, paint is the best finish. Clear finishes tend to make carvings look bland.

Region: Great Lakes region of the United States and Canada; the best carving basswood (whitest and softest) comes from northern Minnesota, Wisconsin, and Michigan

Qualities: Fine, even texture; very little grain figure; holds detail well

Color: Creamy with little difference between heartwood and sapwood

Suggested finish: Paint

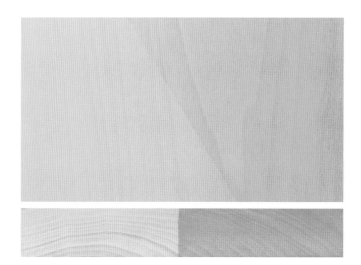

Butternut

A highly favored wood, butternut, like basswood, is easy to carve but has a beautiful grain that carvers rarely cover with paint. Finding good butternut is becoming more difficult because of a blight, called "butternut canker," that is killing the trees. Wood is now primarily gathered from dead but still standing trees. Researchers are working to develop a canker-resistant species or to find and propagate trees with natural resistance.

Region: Central and eastern North America; northeast Canada

Qualities: Beautiful grain pattern; easy to carve; similar to basswood in texture

Color: Warm golden brown

Suggested finish: Varnish or one of the oils

Catalpa

Most catalpa wood has much the same texture as butternut, but its more distinct grain makes it look more aggressive. There can be some variation in density from one catalpa tree to another, so some wood is easier to carve than others.

Region: Central Mississippi river basin and eastern United States

Qualities: Distinct difference between early wood and late wood; wide annual rings; density varies; cures without splitting or cracking

Color: Grayish brown

Suggested finish: Varnish, oil, or lacquer

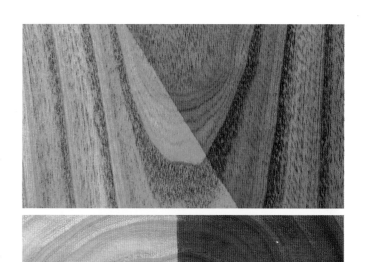

Tupelo

Tupelo is popular with power carvers who specialize in birds and fish because it holds carved and woodburned details well. It is less popular for hand carving because it tends to tear if your tools aren't razor sharp. When selecting tupelo, use only the sapwood from the bell portion (the area of the tree partially underwater and about two to three feet above). Other parts have an uneven texture and stringy grain.

Region: Swampy areas of southern United States

Qualities: Fine, uniform texture with interlocking grain; available in large blocks; avoid wood with grayish green streaks; does not fuzz during power carving and doesn't char when woodburned; tears easily with hand tools

Color: Light cream to grayish yellow

Suggested finish: Painted detail

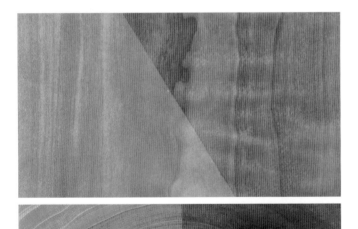

Cherry

Cherry is another wood that is normally finished naturally to display its beautiful color and grain pattern. Though beautiful to work, cherry is very susceptible to burn marks from any power tools, whether it's a power carver for carving or a band saw for roughing out an initial shape.

Region: Midwestern and eastern United States

Qualities: Straight, tight grain; fairly uniform texture; carves nicely with sharp tools; may have brown, pithlike flecks and small gum pockets; susceptible to burn marks from power tools

Color: Distinct variation between darker heartwood and lighter sapwood

Suggested finish: Natural; develops a patina from ultraviolet rays over time

Mahogany

Mahogany is a straight-grained, fine- to medium-textured wood with excellent working and finishing characteristics. It is popular for deep relief carving.

Region: Central and South America (best), Philippines, and Africa

Qualities: Straight, tight grain (Honduras mahogany); works easily with hand tools or power tools

Color: Develops deep red or brown color as it ages

Suggested finish: Varnish, oil, lacquer, or stain

WALNUT

Walnut is one of the harder woods to carve and also one of the most beautiful. Because of its natural beauty, carvers rarely paint walnut. Sharp tools are a must because walnut tends to tear as you cut across the grain.

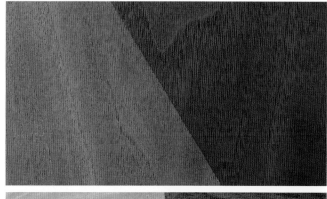

Region: Ohio, Indiana, and Missouri

Qualities: Straight grain with uniform texture; high density; tears unless tools are very sharp

Color: Distinct difference between lighter sapwood and darker heartwood

Suggested finish: Natural

BIRCH

Yellow or white birch (shown here) is the birch species most commonly used for carving. Birch is a light-colored, fairly hard wood with a subtle grain pattern and an even texture. It holds excellent detail. When cured, it is resistant to warping.

Region: North America; the best hard birch comes from the Adirondacks, Vermont, New Hampshire, Wisconsin, and Michigan

Qualities: Carves easily; tight-grained, uniform texture; leaves a polished cut from sharp tools; cracks and splits if not dried properly

Color: Yellow birch has white sapwood and light reddish brown heartwood; white birch has light-colored sapwood and brownish-colored heartwood

Suggested finish: Any

MAPLE

Maple is another beautiful but hard-to-carve wood. It is a close-grained, even-textured wood that takes excellent detail. Because of its density, you must have sharp tools, and a mallet is useful when carving maple.

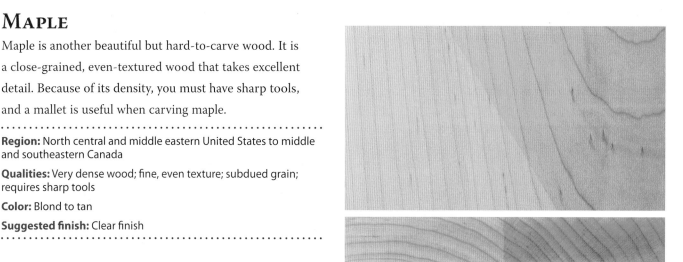

Region: North central and middle eastern United States to middle and southeastern Canada

Qualities: Very dense wood; fine, even texture; subdued grain; requires sharp tools

Color: Blond to tan

Suggested finish: Clear finish

Found Wood

In addition to the various woods mentioned, many people carve found wood. Found wood is any wood in its natural, unaltered state. It can be bark from dead or dying cottonwood trees, cypress knees, knots, weathered wood, or driftwood. Because it is more difficult to carve than boards or other pieces sawn from a tree, I don't recommend found wood for your first project. However, once you have gained some experience, found wood can be an inspiring medium.

Cottonwood trees grow **bark** thick and dense enough to carve—often up to four or five inches. Black cottonwood and plains cottonwood are the two most common species for carving; however, eastern, swamp, Palmer, and Fremont cottonwoods can also produce thick bark in the right growing conditions. Wood spirits or whimsical buildings are ideal subjects for bark carvings.

Cypress knees grow from the roots of the bald cypress trees in the swamps and bayous of the southern United States. Each cypress knee has its own unique shape and size. Cypress knees are soft and require very sharp tools to make clean cuts.

This found wood is part of a root from a walnut tree. Sometimes, the shape of the wood determines what it will become. I plan to use the piece to carve a bear coming out of the piece, with the root area behind the bear left intact.

Bark is the medium of choice for carver Marshal Artime of Addieville, Illinois.

Alabama carver Carole Jean Boyd favors cypress knees as her choice of found wood.

Another cypress knee carving by Carole Jean Boyd of Alabama.

Knots—some of the best and largest—come from dead ponderosa pines. When the pine tree dies, the softer wood body (bole) decomposes, leaving the dense knots behind. Knots can be found in various shapes and sizes and are quite hard, so sharp tools are a necessity. Wood spirits are the most popular subject carved in knots.

Weathered wood and **driftwood** can come from almost any species, but the wood must be hard enough to withstand the elements without decaying. Many carvers like cedar and juniper because of their beautiful colors and grain patterns. Both weathered wood and driftwood can be found in any shape and size imaginable, allowing you to let your mind run with whatever you see hidden in the piece of wood.

Artist Jim Wright of Tennessee finds inspirations for his carvings in driftwood and says the shape of the wood often suggests what the carving will become.

Living in the Gulf Coast region of Florida, carver David Neener finds many opportunities to convert driftwood into beautiful pieces of art.

Selecting Wood

Now that you've learned about wood's anatomy and some of the common species for carving, you're armed with the information you need to select an appropriate piece of wood for your project. Whatever species you choose, keep an eye out for the items that follow.

Grain.
❑ Examine the grain carefully.
❑ Is it straight or twisted?
    Opt for straight-grained wood; it is much easier to carve.

Deformities.
❑ Has the wood been split or cut vertically through the pith? ❑ Yes ❑ No
❑ If so, look closely for signs of deformities that may extend into the piece of wood.
    Signs of a once-existing branch may indicate internal deformities.

Checks or cracks.
❑ Are there any checks or cracks? ❑ Yes ❑ No
    Do not use wood with checks or cracks.

Heartwood or sapwood.
❑ Is there enough heartwood for your project once the sapwood is removed?
    ❑ Yes ❑ No
    Note: The only wood where you use just the sapwood is tupelo.
❑ Is there little differentiation in color between the heartwood and sapwood so
    that both can be carved? ❑ Yes ❑ No
❑ If they are different colors, will the colors add another dimension to the carving?
    ❑ Yes ❑ No

Blemishes.
❑ Are there any blemishes? ❑ Yes ❑ No
    These may indicate a deformity inside the piece.
❑ Are there external flaws with openings through their centers? ❑ Yes ❑ No
    Deformities may be hiding inside.

Wormholes.
❑ Does the wood have wormholes? ❑ Yes ❑ No
❑ Will the wormholes complement your intended carving? ❑ Yes ❑ No

Knots.
❑ Does the wood have knots? ❑ Yes ❑ No
    Knots and the surrounding wood are extremely difficult to carve.
❑ If the knots are small and tight, can they be worked around? ❑ Yes ❑ No
❑ Would the knots end up right in the middle of the viewing area of the carving?
    ❑ Yes ❑ No
❑ If the knots are loose, would they fall out? ❑ Yes ❑ No
❑ Could any voids be plugged? ❑ Yes ❑ No

Many problems with wood are superficial and can be spotted easily, but no matter how closely you evaluate a tree's external characteristics, you may still get some surprises when you cut into a piece. Trees often grow new wood around a damaged area, completely separating the infected area from the healthy wood. Soft spots or dark spots sometimes appear where a wound has been "treated." You may also find internal knots or twisted grain. If you find an internal flaw, you can

1. continue carving if the deformity is not too bad or if it is in an area that will not detract from the finished carving,
2. change your design to incorporate the deformity or avoid it,
3. cut out the bad section and use the good wood for another project, or
4. use the piece in your fireplace to warm your house.

Though this piece of wood showed no deformities on the outside, a small deformity was exposed by cutting the blank. When cut in half, you can see what was inside the piece.

Curing Wood for Carving

As you've learned, many species and types of wood make good carving wood. Although you can carve wood freshly harvested from a tree, many projects require cured wood.

Curing wood is defined as stabilizing the wood for carving or as drying or seasoning the wood. Basically, all of those phrases boil down to one thing: Most of the internal water needs to be removed from wood before it is carved.

Let's take a look at how much water is in a tree and what happens to that water when a tree is cut, and then review the processes of air-drying, kiln-drying, and chemical-drying.

You can see how much this piece of wood has shrunk from its wet state to its dry state. The piece was originally cut straight across, but it shrank this much as it dried.

Reaching Equilibrium

A tree requires a large quantity of water, and its structure is designed around the transportation of water. A mature tree, for example, can give off up to 100 gallons of water vapor in a 24-hour period. Further evidence of just how much water trees store is the fact that most freshly cut trees weigh at least two times their dry weight.

When a tree is cut and removed from its water supply, it immediately begins to release the water contained within the wood in an attempt to reach equilibrium with the atmospheric humidity around it. Wood that has not reached equilibrium is called wet or green wood. Wood that has reached equilibrium is called cured, dried, or seasoned wood.

Free Water and Bound Water

As you learned earlier in this chapter, all hardwood trees consist of strawlike vessels that carry water from the roots to the leaves. Because the vessels are open at the ends, they contain two types of water that need to be reduced through evaporation: free water and bound water. Free water fills the insides of the vessels. Bound water saturates the walls of the vessels, and when the vessel walls are fully saturated, they are at their fiber saturation point (FSP).

Eliminating free water is relatively easy and causes very little change to the tree's characteristics, except to decrease its weight. When bound water leaves the vessel walls through evaporation, it profoundly affects the tree's characteristics because each vessel can shrink up to three percent in diameter.

Understanding how and why wood loses water shows the importance of properly drying wood to keep your carvings from cracking. However, if you need to carve wet wood, you can take the following precautions to reduce—but not eliminate—the chances of it cracking as it dries:

- If possible, **split the piece of wood in half through the pith** and split off the juvenile wood (the pith and the first few annual rings).

- If you don't split the wood, **drill a large hole through the middle of the piece of wood** to relieve the internal stresses as the wood dries. This is another method of removing the pith and some of the juvenile wood.

- At the end of each carving session, **wrap the piece of wood in plastic** to stop the evaporation process. Don't leave it wrapped too long, or it will develop mold spores. If several days pass between carving sessions, unwrap the wood from time to time to allow air circulation, or punch holes in the plastic so some of the moisture can escape, reducing the chance of mold developing.

- **Hollow out the back of the carving** to relieve some of the stresses and facilitate drying. This process is a time-proven remedy: Carvings with hollowed backs have been found dating back to the thirteenth century.

- When you complete your carving, **put a finish, such as polyurethane varnish, on it immediately** to seal the wood and slow down the migration of water out of the end vessels.

- **Know the state of dryness before you start carving.** If you aren't sure your wood is dry, take precautions to lessen the chances of it splitting through the surface area of your carving.

Split the wood through the pith and eliminate juvenile wood.

Hollow out the wood to relieve stresses.

Always check the moisture content of your wood. A vendor assured me that this sassafras wood was completely dry, so I didn't take precautions to minimize splitting. Soon after I started carving, a small crack appeared through the face. If the crack had been larger, it would have destroyed the carving.

The Two Phases in the Drying Process

Wood dries from the outside in, and there are two phases in the drying process. During the first phase, free water in the cell cavities closest to the bark area evaporates until the cavities reach the humidity of the surrounding environment. The evaporation from the cavities starts immediately after

> " *When a tree is cut and removed from its water supply, it immediately begins to release the water contained within the wood in an attempt to reach equilibrium with the atmospheric humidity around it.* "

the tree is cut. As this process takes place, moisture content in the cavities becomes lower than the FSP of the cell walls, and phase two occurs. During phase two, moisture (bound water) migrates from the area of higher moisture, the cell walls, to the area of lower moisture, the cell cavities. This is called differential drying, and it will continue until the entire tree has reached the relative humidity of its surrounding environment. It can take several years, depending on a number of parameters that we will discuss later.

What Happens When Wood Dries

As wood dries, several things occur. When wood reaches 25 to 30 percent moisture content, shrinkage begins. Normal wood shrinks negligibly in its length (along the grain) but substantially in its width and thickness, and it will always shrink toward the bark side. Species differ in the amount of shrinkage that occurs. Dense woods shrink more than less-dense woods.

Wood shrinks toward the bark side because each vessel in a tree is basically the same diameter, so as the circumference of the tree increases from the pith to the bark, the number of vessels also increases. If each vessel shrinks up to three percent, far more shrinkage happens at the bark side than at the pith because there are more vessels to shrink.

A check forms when vessels split apart from one another and is evident in the end grain of the wood.

For example, if a log has a circumference of 25 inches and each vessel shrinks just two percent, the log will shrink a half-inch more near the bark than at the pith area. If the shrinkage isn't controlled, the wood will form a crack or a check a half-inch wide. This half-inch could be at one place or in multiple places that add up to a half-inch. Cracks are separations in wood that create visible gaps, usually running lengthwise through the piece of wood. Checks occur when the vessels split apart and are evident in the end grain of the wood. If cracks or checks develop through the surface of a carving, it may ruin the carving.

How Juvenile Wood Affects Cracking and Checking

Wood has a much greater potential of cracking if the juvenile wood (pith and first few annual rings) remains in the piece. Juvenile wood shrinks up to six percent along the grain direction. If the juvenile wood is not removed from the log, this dramatic change in shrinkage between the juvenile wood and the rest of the wood puts tons of differential pressure in the log as it dries. In some places, the pressure will be relieved and create cracks.

How a piece of wood is cut from a tree has a major impact on whether it will dry without splitting or cracking. You can virtually eliminate splitting if the wood is sawn properly. When the juvenile wood is removed, the remaining wood will shrink only about 0.1 percent along the grain direction (the length of the piece of wood) as it dries.

Cracks are separations in wood that create visible gaps, usually running lengthwise through the piece of wood. Cracks can easily spread to ruin a carving.

AIR-DRYING WOOD

If you air-dry wood, it's important to do it right or not at all. Sure, you can throw a piece of wood from a freshly felled tree in a corner and hope for the best, but you'll have a better chance of the wood not splitting if you use a controlled process to air-dry the wood. Two of the biggest mistakes carvers make when air-drying wood are that they try to dry too much at one time and that they don't follow through.

"A few months before you start carving, bring the wood you're going to carve into an environment similar to the one in which the finished carving will reside."

If you have the space and time, try this method in a corner of your garage. You can use it for all wood, except basswood (see Special Treatment for Premium Basswood on page 46). Before you begin, go through the following steps to prepare the wood:

- Seal the ends of the wood as soon as possible after the log is sawn. Use polyurethane varnish, aluminum paint, or commercial sealants. If the wood is very wet, first apply a coat of water-based acrylic paint and then apply polyurethane varnish or aluminum paint. Commercial sealants won't need the extra coat.

- Split the piece in half lengthwise, through the pith, to help relieve the internal stresses. It's even better if you can remove the juvenile wood as well.

- Cut the pieces in lengths longer than needed for your carving. This way, if the wood checks on the ends while drying, you can cut off the ends and still have an intact piece to carve.

- If the bark is loose, remove it. Loose bark is a breeding ground for fungal spores that will ruin the wood.

- If the bark is tight, leave it on to slow down the evaporation rate through the vessel walls.

- If the piece needs to be glued, either for size or for strength, glue it after it dries.

Once all of the prep work is done, start by making a base about four inches off the floor to allow good airflow under the wood. Lay the wood you're drying on the base so the pieces are not touching one another. Place wooden spacers (called stickers) between each row of wood you stack to

Leave tight bark on to slow evaporation.

Remove loose bark to avoid the formation of mold or fungus.

allow airflow around each piece. You can air-dry more than one species of wood at a time, but make sure a large-diameter sample of each species is accessible to serve as a control piece. Accurately weigh at least one control piece for each species. Write the weight and date on a piece of paper and attach it to your control piece.

Every six months, accurately weigh each control piece and record the weight and date. When there is no change in weight for at least six months, under normal conditions, the wood is at its equilibrium moisture content (EMC), about 13 to 15 percent moisture content.

It's impossible to overdry wood by air-drying, so you can allow the wood to cure as long as it's protected from the elements, such as rain and snow. When the total piece of wood has achieved equilibrium, the only variation in moisture content will occur when the environmental humidity changes.

A few months before you start carving, bring the wood you're going to carve into an environment similar to the one in which the finished carving will reside. To minimize the chance of it ever splitting, the wood should be down to about 10 percent moisture content before carving (see Measuring Moisture Content at right).

Not all the wood you attempt to air-dry will be usable. Even if you take precautions, some wood will still split or crack during the drying process and not be salvageable; however, it's better to have it crack before you start carving rather than afterward.

When air-drying wood, use spacers, or stickers, to allow air to flow freely among the pieces.

MEASURING MOISTURE CONTENT

When the weight of your control piece has been stable for at least six months, confirm the moisture content (MC) with a moisture meter. There are two basic types of moisture meters: resistance and capacitance.

Resistance moisture meters rely on the conductivity of electricity through the wood. Moisture is an excellent conductor, and this characteristic helps measure moisture content. Two or four pins are driven into the wood, and the resistance of the wood between the electrodes is measured. The meter then converts this resistance to percentage MC.

The capacitance moisture meter generates a radio frequency field, which penetrates into the wood via electrodes laid on the wood. Depending on the type of capacitance meter, it measures either power loss determined by the MC or the capacitance of the wood. The data is then calculated by the meter into percentage MC.

If you don't have access to a moisture meter, cut a one-inch-thick cross section slab, from the middle of one piece. Then, cut three or four one-inch-square pieces from the middle of the slab, and weigh them to a fraction of an ounce. Put the pieces in an oven heated to 220 degrees Fahrenheit for about 24 hours to completely remove all water from the wood. This is called oven-drying, and it will result in an oven-dry weight. After removing the pieces from the oven, immediately weigh them again, and use the following equation to calculate the MC of the wood before it was oven-dried.

% MC = weight of wood before drying – oven-dry weight ÷ oven-dry weight x 100

If you don't have access to a scale that weighs to a fraction of an ounce, your local post office will have one. If you need to drive to a scale, put the pieces in a sealed plastic bag immediately after removing them from the oven, so they don't start absorbing water from the surrounding environment. If the dried pieces absorb water, the percentage MC will not be accurate.

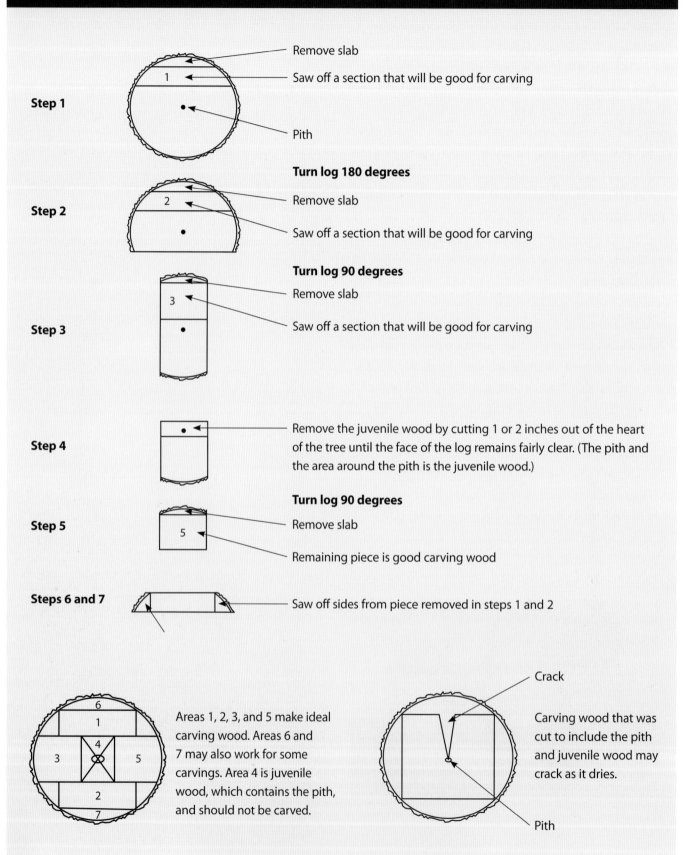

Step 1

Remove slab

1 — Saw off a section that will be good for carving

Pith

Turn log 180 degrees

Step 2

2 — Remove slab

Saw off a section that will be good for carving

Turn log 90 degrees

Remove slab

Step 3

3 — Saw off a section that will be good for carving

Step 4

Remove the juvenile wood by cutting 1 or 2 inches out of the heart of the tree until the face of the log remains fairly clear. (The pith and the area around the pith is the juvenile wood.)

Turn log 90 degrees

Step 5

Remove slab

5 — Remaining piece is good carving wood

Steps 6 and 7

Saw off sides from piece removed in steps 1 and 2

Areas 1, 2, 3, and 5 make ideal carving wood. Areas 6 and 7 may also work for some carvings. Area 4 is juvenile wood, which contains the pith, and should not be carved.

Crack

Carving wood that was cut to include the pith and juvenile wood may crack as it dries.

Pith

KILN-DRYING WOOD

Kiln-drying wood is the most efficient way to remove water from wood. This process uses a kiln, a well-insulated chamber in which airflow, humidity, and temperature can be accurately controlled. The wood is stacked in the kiln with spacers (stickers) between each row of wood to allow airflow around each of the pieces.

The kiln-drying process starts with a high-humidity, low-temperature environment and air being driven around the stacked wood. Sample boards are monitored for moisture content using a moisture meter, and the kiln is set to a humidity slightly lower than the monitored moisture level. The kiln remains at this setting until the moisture drops to a predetermined level. When the moisture level is reached, the temperature is increased and the humidity is decreased. This sequence continues at a kiln schedule for the specific species and thickness of the wood, until the wood reaches 6 to 8 percent MC. When it is removed from the kiln, the wood will normally recover a small amount of moisture.

> **"** *Kiln-drying wood is the most efficient way to remove water from wood.* **"**

You'll want to note the following information about the kiln-drying process:

■ The thicker the pieces of wood being dried, the longer it takes to dry them.

■ Most kiln operators prefer to dry wood less than four inches thick. Kiln-drying heftier wood becomes cost prohibitive for the average carver.

■ When you purchase kiln-dried wood, protect it from the elements. If the wood gets wet, you defeat the purpose of buying kiln-dried wood.

■ A few months before beginning your carving, bring the kiln-dried wood into the environment in which it will reside to make sure it's stable.

■ Buy wood from reputable suppliers who are well versed on how to kiln-dry wood. If wood is kiln-dried at temperatures that are too high, it will dry too fast, have a tendency to case harden, and may then splinter when carved.

DRYING TIME RULES OF THUMB

Though you'll hear many rules of thumb to determine drying times, none of those rules is accurate, because the drying environment (thickness of the pieces, local humidity, number of hot days, amount of air circulation, and manner of stacking) and the differences in densities between various species of wood have a major impact on how fast wood will dry. It is not unusual for a 4-inch-thick piece of basswood to dry in six months, whereas a 4-inch-thick piece of walnut can take years.

SPECIAL TREATMENT FOR PREMIUM BASSWOOD

If you want premium basswood for carving, you'll need to take extra care, but the results are well worth the effort. Pay special attention when the wood is harvested and cured. Here are the things you need to know:

- Basswood should be harvested during the dormant season (fall/winter) and sawn by the end of May. The best drying times are April, May, and June.

- Never leave basswood in the log during hot weather. The sugars in basswood react to high temperatures, causing the wood to stain rapidly.

- After sawing a basswood log into blocks, stack the blocks in an open area where wind can blow through the pile. Build a base at least four inches off the ground, and leave space between each piece so air can flow around it.

- If you stack more than one row of wood, place stickers (spacers) between each row. Basswood must have a large amount of airflow when first sawn because it demands rapid evaporation of the free water to prevent stains from developing internally. It turns a dark color if the initial moisture does not evaporate rapidly.

- Cover the pile with a stiff material slightly larger than the pile to prevent discoloration from spring and summer rains. By midsummer, the moisture should be reduced enough so that the basswood can be moved into a building. Add new stickers, and allow the wood to dry to about 12 percent moisture content.

- If basswood is kiln-dried, it should be dried at about 120 to 125 degrees Fahrenheit. If it is kiln-dried at too high of a temperature, a reaction with the sugars can cause it to yellow slightly.

- While many species take years to dry, basswood dries rapidly. A piece four-inches thick by four-inches thick will air-dry to about 10 to 14 percent MC in 130 to 180 days, solar-dry to about 6 to 8 percent MC in 30 to 60 days, and kiln-dry to about 6 to 8 percent MC in 15 to 25 days.

DRYING WOOD WITH CHEMICALS

Chemicals can be an efficient way to dry wood if you have the time and money to do it correctly. Talk with other carvers who have used the products on their carving wood. As I've found, the results may not always be to your liking.

PEG 1000

Using polyethylene glycol 1000 (best known as PEG 1000 because its average molecular weight is 1000) is one way to stabilize wood. This white, waxlike material is not used much because of the time and cost required and its instability with high humidity. PEG replaces the water molecules in wet wood with the waxlike glycol molecule and bulks the wood at its wet diameter, stabilizing the wood and preventing it from shrinking and cracking.

Because it is reactive with humidity, PEG will never feel completely dry to the touch. If the humidity at the surface of a carving is higher than the humidity on the inside of the carving, PEG will try to migrate to the higher humidity area, and the surface of the carving will feel tacky.

Pentacryl

Preliminary testing shows that Pentacryl, a liquid composite of siliconized polymers, may treat wet wood in a timely, cost-effective manner. (Because I have not had time to test Pentacryl in order to give historical data, I can only relate here what my preliminary testing shows.) The polymers penetrate the wet wood and prevent it from checking or cracking as it dries. Pentacryl also acts as a lubricant, which makes the wood easier to carve.

Whereas PEG-1000 diffuses into the wood, replacing water molecules inside the vessels with PEG molecules to bulk the wood, Pentacryl coats the walls of the vessels to keep them from shrinking. Pentacryl is less costly than PEG and penetrates and stabilizes wood much faster. (Stabilizing a piece of wood using PEG takes weeks or months of soaking; Pentacryl penetrates the same piece of wood in hours.)

Originally developed to treat and stabilize waterlogged wooden Native American artifacts, Pentacryl will not discolor wood, is nontoxic, and will not migrate when exposed to high humidity. You can also carve wood when it's still wet with Pentacryl. Additionally, wood treated with Pentacryl can be finished with any type of finish and glued with any type of glue, once the wood has dried to at least 15 percent MC. Applying finish before the wood is dry can trap water inside the wood and cause mold to form under the finish.

Pentacryl-treated wood air-dries about 20 to 70 percent faster than untreated wood. Dry the wood slowly; fast drying times will crack the wood. The ultimate curing environment is a cool area with approximately 60 percent humidity. Stack the wood so there is good air movement around each piece, and cover the pieces with a large cardboard box. Drying takes about three months per inch of wood, but drying times vary depending on the type of wood, thickness, original moisture, and environmental humidity and temperature.

The wood for this cat was stabilized with PEG and carved at least 15 years ago from freshly cut walnut. Even now, when the humidity gets high, the surface becomes tacky.

Pentacryl is used in its undiluted form. Brush it on until the wood is saturated, or soak the wood in the solution; there is no need to treat the cut ends with a sealer.

To cure a large piece of wood, pour some Pentacryl in a nonmetallic pan, put a couple of nonmetallic spacers in the pan, and after each carving session, set an exposed end of the carving on the spacers. Wrap plastic around the carving and pan, and let the Pentacryl wick up through the wood.

Another trick is to leave excess wood at the top of your carving, hollow out a bowl-like recess in the excess wood, and fill the hollow with Pentacryl. By setting your carving in a pan of Pentacryl and filling the top cavity with the chemical, the piece is treated from both ends at the same time, and the Pentacryl wicks to the middle. When you pour Pentacryl in the recessed area and it no longer wicks into the wood, the wood has been sufficiently "bulked" with Pentacryl.

" Originally developed to treat and stabilize waterlogged wooden Native American artifacts, Pentacryl will not discolor wood, is nontoxic, and will not migrate when exposed to high humidity. "

To save time on finishing the piece after carving, consider adding oil-based or water-based dyes and stains to the Pentacryl in which the wood is being treated for a preliminary coat. How much dye or stain to add will depend upon the desired effect.

Chapter Four

  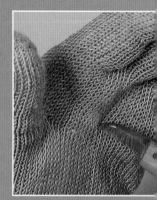

CARVING TOOLS

Carving tools come in an almost infinite variety of shapes and sizes.

Now that you have some basic information about the different styles of carving and the various woods, it's time to select your carving tools. Carving tools come in an almost infinite variety of shapes and sizes, and your choices will depend on what style of carving you'd like to do. Let's take a look at the carving tools available and what makes them comfortable, efficient, and long lasting.

Basic Carving Knives

A carving knife is one of the first tools most carvers purchase. Knives come in a variety of shapes and sizes. With all the types of carving knives on the market today, understanding their differences and similarities will help you make a smart choice.

Blade shape. Standard carving knives have either straight or curved blades. I personally find a straight blade easier to sharpen and more versatile than a curved blade. A straight blade also allows you to easily visualize where the tip of the blade is in the wood as you make cuts. Whichever type you choose, a presharpened blade saves time and effort.

Blade size. Carving knives are available with long or short blades. If you're a beginning carver, I recommend a knife blade no longer than 1½ inches because it reduces your chances of cutting yourself. A shorter-blade knife does not stick out as far, so it is less likely to cut you.

Blade handle. When you buy your first carving knife, do it in person so you can hold the knife in your hand. The handle should be sized and shaped so it feels comfortable in your hand. Some carvers will make their own handles or wrap an existing knife handle with tape or cord to form a shape that's the most ergonomic.

The standard carving knife comes with either a straight blade (top) or a curved blade (bottom).

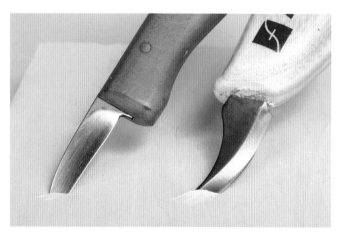

When you insert a knife into wood, it is easier to visualize where the tip of a straight blade is in the wood than it is to picture where the tip of a curved blade is.

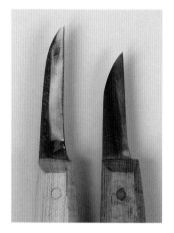

Long and short blades are available, but beginners should start with a blade no longer than 1½ inches (right).

More people cut themselves using long-blade knives because, as you're carving, the primary focus is usually on the area you're cutting and not on the area where the blade is protruding.

DETAIL KNIVES

The detail knife is a specialty carving knife that you won't need when you first start carving. Its blade comes to a sharper point at the end than that of a standard carving knife. It is used to get into tight areas where a normal-size blade won't fit. Wait to buy one of these knives until you start doing fine, detailed work.

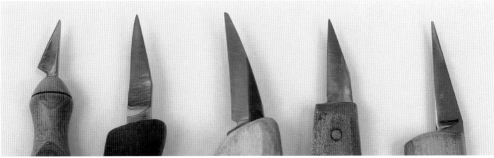

Detail knives have sharper tips and are not necessary for beginning carvers.

CHIP CARVING KNIVES

If you're interested in chip carving, you'll find knives specifically made for it. The two most popular are the standard chip carving knife with a 20-degree angled blade to remove chips and the stab knife to make a decorative stabbing cut.

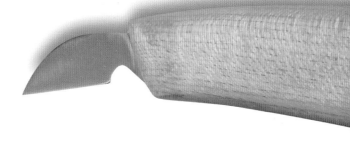

Chip carving knives are specially shaped to remove chips in a geometrical pattern from the surface of a carving.

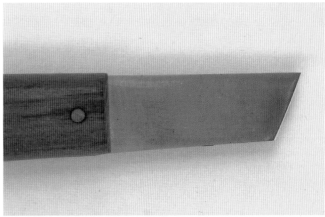

Stab knives are used to make decorative stabbing cuts.

Once you decide upon and invest in carving tools, it goes without saying that you'll want to protect that investment. Of particular importance is preserving the tools' cutting edges. All it takes is one bump against another tool—or some other metal object—and you'll put a nick in that precious cutting edge.

When you're carving, try one of these tips to protect your tools:

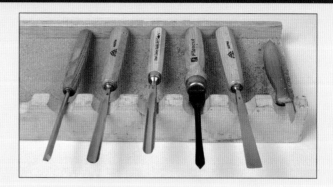

- **Make a tool holder.** Place your tools in the holder with the cutting edge facing forward. The tools never touch one another, and as you're carving, you can see each tool's contour for quick selection.

- **Place your tools on nonskid material** or a terry cloth towel so they don't roll around.

When you're not carving, protect the cutting edges by doing any of the following:

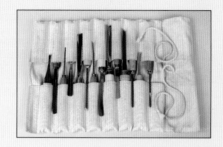

- **Keep your tools in a tool roll.** These are available in any carving catalog, or you can make your own from canvas or heavy cotton material (polyester will dull your tools). The seams are staggered so the tool blades lie between the handles. When you roll up the tools, the blades are protected because the tool pockets are staggered. Cases are available to fit any tools, from regular to micro.

- **Use a fishing tackle box** with multiple drawers and compartments, or make a box for your tools.

- **Place clear plastic tubing or dense foam insulation material over the cutting edge.** Tubing is available at any hardware store, comes in multiple diameters, and can be bought in any length. Scraps of dense insulation foam are available from homebuilder stores or lumberyards—sometimes for free. Cork also works, but avoid cork from a wine bottle. Some wines contain chemicals, which, if they have absorbed into the cork, may rust or pit your knife. **Note:** Never attempt to pull the blade guard straight off the knife; you could easily cut yourself. Instead, place your thumb behind the guard and push it off.

TOOL PARTS

All carving tools, whether they are chisels, gouges, veiners, or V-tools, consist of the following parts:

Handle. Normally made of hardwoods like ash, oak, and maple, handles can be round, hexagon, or oblong and come in various lengths. Handles are classified as long handled or palm handled.

Ferrule. A metal ring, or metal insert, that strengthens the handle, the ferrule prevents the handle from splitting when a mallet drives the tool through wood. The ferrule can be either around the outside of the handle, next to the shoulder, or embedded in the bottom of the handle where it butts up to the shoulder of the tool.

Tang. Driven through a hole in the handle, the tang connects the tool to the handle.

Shoulder. The shoulder is the flared section of the blade at the bottom of the tang. Also called the bolster, the shoulder prevents the blade from being forced into the handle when the tool is driven through wood.

Blade. The blade is simply the body of the tool.

Outside bevel. The outside bevel is the angle ground on the front of the tool that forms part of the cutting edge. It is also known as the face of the cutting area and is located between the toe and the heel.

Toe. The front of the cutting surface is called the toe.

Heel. The back portion of the cutting surface is the heel.

Inside bevel. A small secondary angle on the inside of the cutting edge, the inside bevel adds strength to the cutting edge. It is also called a micro bevel.

Wings. The outside edges of the blade are called wings. Tool width is measured from wing to wing.

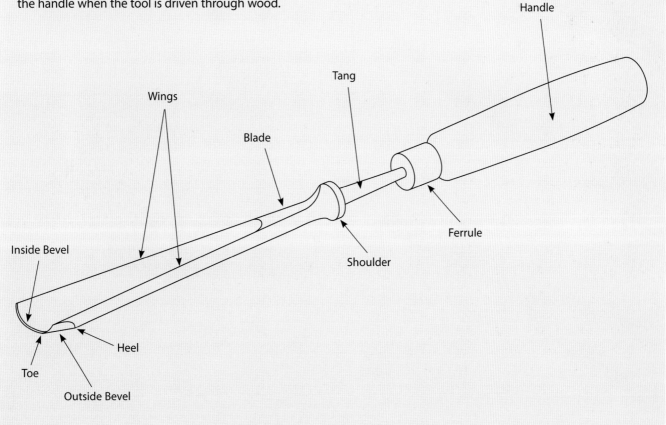

CHISELS, GOUGES, VEINERS, AND V-TOOLS

Chisels, gouges, veiners, and V-tools describe the shapes of specific groups of tools. But with so many different types, shapes, and sizes of chisels, gouges, veiners, and V-tools, it can become confusing as to what kind—and how many—you will need.

As with choosing a knife, consider what type of carving you'll be doing. Many chisels and gouges can make the same cuts as a knife, but others are designed for special purposes and can save you a lot of time.

Also make sure that you understand the universal numbering system, which correlates to carving tool shapes and sizes and makes it easier to tell which tool does what job. Though there are some slight variations between manufacturers, the chart on page 57 will provide the general information you need.

Across the top of the chart is the width of a tool (measured from wing to wing) in both inches and millimeters. This chart goes up to ⅞ inch (22 mm) wide, but tools can go well beyond this width, with some up to 2¾ inches (70 mm) wide.

Along the left side are the universal numbers that correspond to the sweep, or curvature, of the tool. The smaller the number, the less curvature there is along the cutting edge.

Tool width is measured from wing to wing. Wide tools are capable of removing large areas of wood.

CHISELS

A #1 chisel is a flat chisel. Flat chisels, as the name implies, do not have any sweep. They come in a variety of widths and are great for flat or straight cuts. Most carpenter chisels are also flat across the cutting edge, but woodcarving chisels normally have thinner blades than carpenter chisels.

A #2 chisel is a flat skew chisel. Like a flat chisel, the skew chisel is also flat, but it is angled across the cutting edge. Skew chisels can be either left or right and are useful for getting into tight areas, primarily in relief carvings. Some skew chisels are sharpened with a bevel on both sides of

> **"As with choosing a knife, consider what type of carving you'll be doing."**

the blade so they can be used as left or right skews simply by turning them over. A #2 can also be a flat skew fishtail chisel. The name "fishtail" refers to its shape, which is more versatile and allows the chisel to get into even tighter areas than a straight skew can.

Flat chisels have no curvature and come in a variety of widths. Chisels can be helpful when removing wood from larger areas.

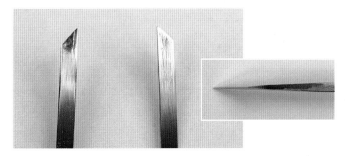

Left and right skews are primarily helpful when working tight areas of relief. Some skews are beveled on both sides to increase their usability.

The angled shape of the fishtail chisel allows it to work in tight corners.

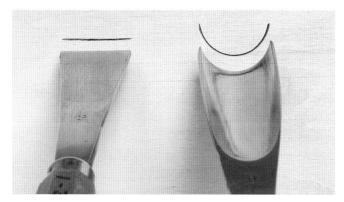

Compare the cutting edges of a #3 (very little curve) and #9 (much more curve) sweep.

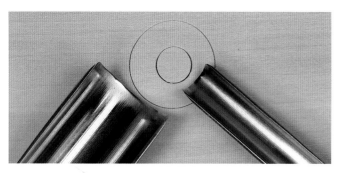

Every gouge will cut a perfect circle.

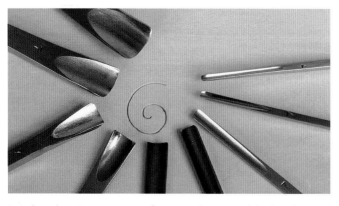

Spiral made using #7 gouges from ⅛ inch to ¾ inch laid end to end following the contour made by the previous tool. Number 5 tools placed end to end will make a looser spiral. Number 9 tools laid end to end will make a tighter spiral.

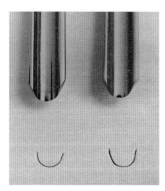

Veiners, also called U-tools. Both of these veiners are ⅜" from wing to wing. The only difference is the one on the left is a #10 and the one on the right is a #11. As you can see, the #11 has higher wings, which will allow it to cut deeper than the #10.

GOUGES

Tools labeled #3 through #9 are called gouges. A gouge is a tool that has curvature on the cutting edge of the blade. As tool numbers increase in numeric value, the sweep becomes more pronounced. The more pronounced the sweep, the more wood you can remove without the wings of the tool going under the surface of the wood. For a controlled cut, the tool wings should never go under the wood's surface.

Both knives and gouges are very versatile and can perform many of the same cuts. However, there are three basic cuts you make with a gouge: concave cuts, where you cut a channel in the wood; convex cuts, where the tool is turned over and you make cuts for a bead or button; and plunge cuts, where you drive the tool into the wood as you do with a stop cut.

Because every gouge blade is a small segment of a circle, any individual gouge will cut a perfect circle. The sweep and width of the tool determine the radius of the circle a tool will create.

Another characteristic of gouges is that any specific tool number series does not have the same radius as it increases in width across the cutting edge. As the cutting edge width increases from wing to wing, the radius of the tool becomes slightly less. For example, a ⅜ inch (10 mm) #9 gouge cuts a tighter-radius circle than a ¾ inch (19 mm) #9 gouge.

This system will become more apparent if you make a stab cut with the narrowest tool of a specific series and continue making stab cuts with the next-width tool of that series, following the previous cut's contour. Laid end to end, any series of the same number will make a spiral pattern.

Gouges are available in numerical sequence from #3 through #9; however, some manufacturers make only #3, #5, #7, and #9 sweep gouges. The odd-number sweeps are the most popular with carvers.

VEINERS

Tools labeled #10 and #11 are called veiners. You may also hear them referred to as U-tools because they make a U-shaped cut. (You cannot cut a circle with a veiner.) The only difference between a #10 and a #11 is that a #11 has higher wings so it can make a deeper cut. Veiners are useful for soft-looking cuts, such as hair details.

V-TOOLS

Also called parting tools, V-tools do not have a universal numbering system. Instead, V-tools are listed by degrees of the cutting angle. They are available with angles of 30, 35, 45, 55, 60, 75, 90, 100, or 120 degrees. A 60-degree cutting angle is the most popular. V-tools are also available as winged and soft V-parting tools.

A winged parting tool is simply a V-tool with curved wings. The curvature of the wings softens the work by rounding the top of the cut.

Because the bottom of a soft V-parting tool is shaped like a gouge, it will leave a soft contour at the bottom of the cut.

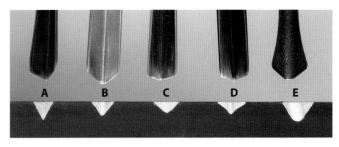

V-tools hold various contours. A is 35 degrees, B is 60 degrees, C is 90 degrees, D is winged, and E is a soft V.

TOOL SHAPES AND SIZES

	1/8" 3mm	3/16" 5mm	1/4" 6mm	5/16" 8mm	3/8" 10mm	7/16" 11mm	1/2" 13mm	5/8" 16mm	3/4" 19mm	7/8" 22mm
1										
2										
3										
4										
5										
6										
7										
8										
9										
10										
11										
75°										
60°										

Long-bent and short-bent tools.

Short-bent gouge.

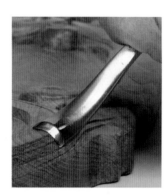

Back-bent gouge.

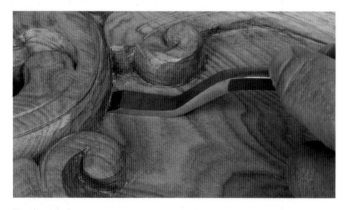

Dogleg tool.

Macaroni (left) and fluteroni (right).

Micro tools.

SPECIALTY TOOLS

Chisels, gouges, veiners, and V-tools are also available in long-bent, short-bent, back-bent, and spoon styles, which have more specialized applications. You may never need many of these tools, but I will show you what they look like and describe their functions so you can see what they are, know what they do, and choose any that may help you in the future.

■ **Long-bent and short-bent tools** allow you to cut into recessed areas without the handle interfering with the surface wood, an application particularly helpful for relief carving. Short-bent gouges are also called spoon gouges because of their shape. Short-bent tools have sharply curved blades and cut deeper recesses than long-bent tools, which normally have gently curved blades.

■ **Back-bent**, or reverse-bent, tools are useful for making cuts on the outsides of curved areas, such as those found in decorative or acanthus carving. Normally, only gouges are back bent.

■ A **dogleg** is used primarily for leveling the background in a relief carving and is useful for cleaning out undercut areas.

■ The **macaroni** is a multipurpose tool with three working edges: a flat chisel on the bottom and a V-tool on each side. These features are useful for architectural carving, moldings, and leveling the background areas in relief carvings.

■ Similar to a macaroni tool, the **fluteroni** has a flat chisel area and two sides that curve to meet the flat area. This shape gives the tool a flat chisel and a small gouge on each side. Because its sides are rounded, the fluteroni leaves a smoother cut on a flat surface than the macaroni.

■ **Micro tools** are very small tools used for fine detail work. They are available as flat chisels, skews, gouges, and V-tools and can be as small as 1½ mm wide from wing to wing.

Buying Carving Tools

Unfortunately, you can't tell how good a tool is just by looking at it. In this section, we'll take a look at some strategies for evaluating and purchasing carving tools.

The Importance of Steel

Selecting tools made of high-quality carbon steel just about guarantees you've purchased long-lasting carving tools because high-quality carbon steel has the ideal composition and hardness for carving. Let's take a look at the blade-making process to help you better evaluate tools.

The first thing that determines a blade's quality is its composition. During the process of making tool steel, trace elements—carbon being a very important one—are added to give the steel certain characteristics. The alloy content, or percentage of these elements, determines the steel's maximum potential hardness. Steel with a low carbon content is soft but easily shaped. High-carbon-content metal becomes harder and stronger but is more difficult to work.

Performing the heat-treating and tempering process correctly is the second thing that affects blade quality. Heat-treating is a very complex process that generally consists of heating the steel to a very high temperature, and cooling it quickly (called quenching) in water or oil to give the steel hardness. The steel is then tempered (reheated to a lower temperature and cooled) to reduce the brittleness that the heat-treating process creates.

The easiest way to determine the quality of a tool is by looking at the hardness, which is usually graded by a standard called the Rockwell scale. Three distinct scales (a, b, and c) are used in the Rockwell standard. The small letter "c" is the scale for hard steel, such as steel used for cutting tools. The Rockwell "c" scale runs from the low 40s (unhardened steel) to the upper 60s (the hardest steel can get). If hard steel, for example, has a Rockwell hardness of 58, it is usually written as R58c or Rc58.

When purchasing carving knives, look for a notation of Rockwell hardness in the tool's specifics. The softer the steel, the lower the Rockwell number. Steel less than R58c is too soft for a carving tool and will not hold a sharp edge; steel over R63c is too brittle and will chip easily.

You can slowly heat a tool for tempering by passing it quickly through a torch flame.

To normalize the steel, allow the tools to cool slowly in a bucket of insulation.

From Make Your Own Woodcarving Tools, by Mike Burton, 2006, Fox Chapel Publishing, Inc.

From Make Your Own Woodworking Tools, by Mike Burton, 2006, Fox Chapel Publishing, Inc.

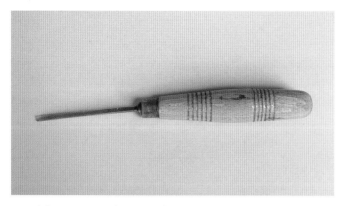

A tool that is set crooked within its handle will not cut correctly.

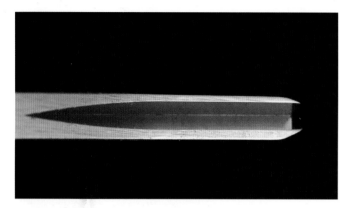

Both wings of a V-tool need to be the same thickness to cut properly.

Sand down the handle of your tool until it fits your hand comfortably.

PHYSICAL CHARACTERISTICS

When you've determined what type and brand of tool you want to buy, it's time to consider physical characteristics. Some characteristics are a matter of personal preference; others are important for comfort, safety, and ease of carving.

❏ Is the handle straight with the blade?
  ❏ Yes ❏ No
  If the handle is not straight with the blade, the tool will tend to skew, or not cut straight, through the wood. This trait is even more obvious if you use a mallet.

❏ Is the metal across the cutting edge the same thickness from one side to another?
  ❏ Yes ❏ No
  It doesn't happen often, but once in a while, you'll find a tool that has more metal mass on one side of the blade than the other, making the tool difficult to sharpen. Keep an eye out for this defect, particularly with V-tools. The metal must be the same thickness on both wings; otherwise, sharpening this already difficult-to-sharpen tool will become even more complicated.

❏ Does the handle feel comfortable in your hand?
  ❏ Yes ❏ No
  You will spend many hours holding the tool as you carve, so it should feel comfortable. Modify the handle if it doesn't.

❏ Does long handled or palm handled make more sense?
  ❏ Yes ❏ No
  If you hold the wood in one hand while you carve with the other hand, you'll normally use palm-handled tools to give you more control. You can also use long-handled tools if you find them more comfortable. Long-handled tools are excellent for carving with a mallet and when the work is in a vise.

❏ Does the tool need to be returned?
  ❏ Yes ❏ No
  If you buy a tool and it's not the quality it should be, return it to the supplier and get a replacement. Most suppliers will be very helpful if you point out what the defect is.

Whatever characteristics you choose for your tools, I recommend the following tools as a good starter set:

- Carving knife with a straight-edge blade no more than 1½ inches long

- ⅜ inch (10 mm) #9 gouge

- ½ inch (13 mm) #5 gouge

- ¼ inch (6 mm) 60 degree V-tool

The next two tools you will find helpful are:

- ³⁄₁₆ inch (5 mm) veiner

- ⅜ or ½ inch (10 mm or 13 mm) #3 gouge

As you can see, you don't need a large number of tools. Start with this basic set of four to six tools, and then add to your collection as you carve and find you can't make "that specific cut" with the tools you have. Always buy the best-quality tools you can afford. Quality tools will last for generations and be a pleasure to use.

Keep in mind that the type of carving you do will also be a factor when you're buying tools. When I carve, I start with larger tools to remove the major amounts of waste wood, and I go to smaller tools as I progress to the finer details. If you carve only small items, you'll need tools that have narrower widths at the cutting edge.

Finally, I don't recommend buying kits of tools. Kits usually include some tools that you will rarely, if ever, use. That money can be better spent on individual tools that you will use.

Basic palm-handled tool set.

Basic long-handled tool set.

TOOL SAFETY

The pleasure you'll get out of your carving tools depends not only on the quality of the tools but also on how safely you use them. Follow these tips and throw in a healthy dose of common sense to get the most out of your new tools. I always begin with these two rules:

■ First, keep your tools razor sharp. While this sounds contrary to safety, it's actually one of the best safety rules. As it slices through the wood, a sharp tool is easier to control than a dull one.

■ Second, think. Keep focused at all times and make sure you know where your body parts are in relation to the tool blade. Never put anything that can bleed in front of the blade.

HOLDING THE TOOL

If you hold your carving in one hand and a tool in the other, odds are that the hand holding the carving will be in the path of the blade at some point. Properly holding the tool and protecting your hand (see Protecting Your Hands on page 64) are essential.

If you hold the item you're carving in your hand and use a long-handled tool, there are two different ways to hold the tool.

Note: If it's possible to clamp the piece you're carving, I recommend using long-handled tools. With the piece clamped, you can have both hands on the tool and never expose either of your hands to the cutting edge.

> "*Properly holding the tool and protecting your hand are essential.*"

Palm-Handled Tool Grip

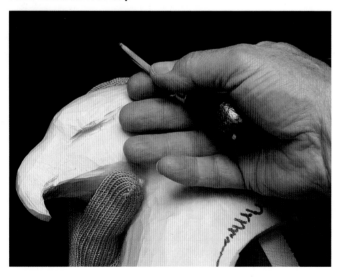

1. Lay the tool in your hand and wrap your fingers around the handle with your fingers on the blade of the tool.

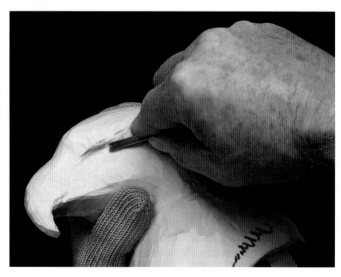

2. Push the tool through the wood, as shown.

Long-Handled Tool Grip, Method One

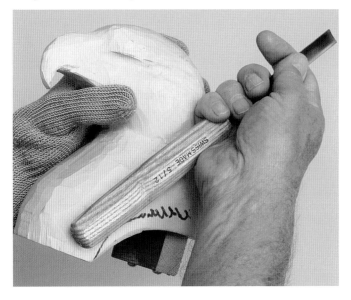

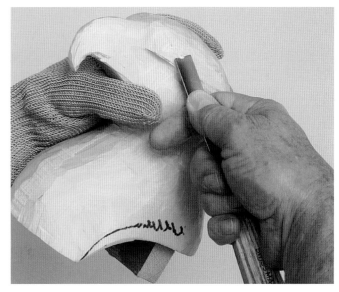

1. Lay the tool in your hand, as shown, with your fingers wrapped around the blade of the tool.

2. Carve by pushing the tool through the wood.

Long-Handled Tool Grip, Method Two

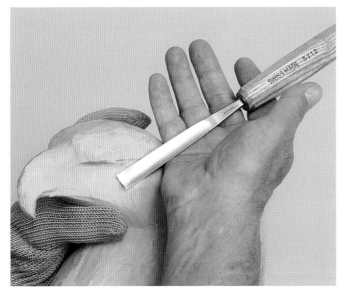

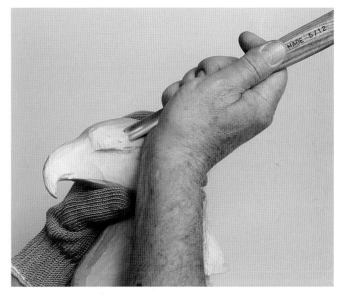

1. Lay the tool in your hand with the blade over the pad of your hand.

2. Use wrist action to drive the tool through the wood.

PROTECTING YOUR HANDS

If you hold the wood in your hand as you carve, you can wear two protective items to help keep you safe: a carving glove and a thumb guard.

Carving gloves are ambidextrous; they can be worn on either hand. You need only one carving glove because it's always worn on the hand that is holding the wood.

A popular glove is made of Kevlar, the same material from which bulletproof vests are made. A Kevlar glove will give you protection, but it will not shield you from heavy slashing or stab cuts.

A better glove is one made for people who handle glass panes, pick up sharp metal sheets, or fillet fish. This glove has stainless-steel wire in the middle of each fiber, so the glove is actually woven with stainless-steel thread. These gloves are available in many sizes from extra small to extra large. A woven stainless-steel glove will protect you from slashing cuts, but be aware that the tip of a knife can go between the weave of any glove—no glove will protect you from stabbing cuts. Whatever type of glove you buy, make sure it fits snugly on your hand.

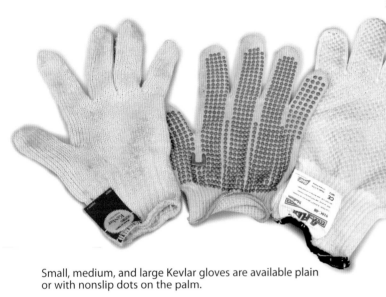

Small, medium, and large Kevlar gloves are available plain or with nonslip dots on the palm.

A stainless steel glove will protect your hand from slashing cuts.

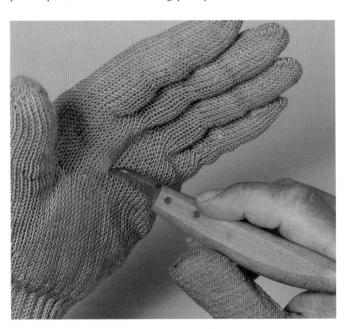

No glove can protect your hand from stabbing cuts.

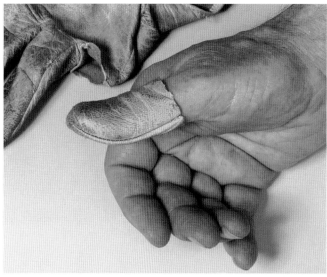

One of the more popular thumb guards is made of leather, with an elastic band that grips the guard to your thumb.

The fingers from leather gloves also make good thumb guards.

Another protective item is a **thumb guard** worn on the hand that holds the knife. It protects your thumb as the knife exits the wood at the end of a cut. Thumb guards are available in many sizes, from extra small to extra large, so you can find one to fit snugly and comfortably. You can also make a thumb guard by cutting off the thumb, or one of the fingers, of an old leather glove.

Another thumb guard I find effective is one you make yourself from a material called Vetrap. Vetrap is a bandaging tape originally developed to wrap horses' ankles, but it's now used for other medical applications as well. You can buy Vetrap from any business that sells horse supplies, and it is also available at some pharmacies. Vetrap is made of stretch cloth impregnated with latex. When wrapped, it will adhere to itself but not to your thumb. Vetrap conforms to your thumb and, if carefully removed, can be used multiple times. If you develop small cuts in the surface, wrap a couple more layers over the original wrap or make a new one.

Vetrap is a commercial tape used by veterinary doctors that is great for protecting your thumb from cuts.

Chapter Five

CARVING ACCESSORIES

You don't need an elaborate setup to start carving.

Once you've chosen wood and carving tools, you'll want to set up a carving area that meets your needs for working ergonomically and includes any helpful accessories. Like the wide variety of carving tools, a large number of shop accessories are available. They range from very helpful to nice-to-have and carry price tags of several dollars to several hundred dollars. Ultimately, your choice of accessories should be governed by your working style and your budget—if something helps you achieve your goals and fits your budget, use it. Let's take a look at some commonly available items and their relevance to the various types of carving.

WORK SURFACE

Your work surface can be a table, a bench, or whatever you have on hand to use. There are also a number of commercial workbenches available, or you can make your own. You don't, however, need an elaborate setup to start carving. My first carving bench had two-by-fours for the legs and a couple of wide two-inch-thick boards for the work surface. Clamps between the surface boards could hold flat carvings, and drilled holes for screws could hold larger pieces. The base held cement blocks to stabilize the bench and to keep it from moving as I carved. This simple bench served me well until I built a permanent bench in my basement shop (see the photo on page 70).

When you start carving, try a simple carving table. My first one had plenty of space for small carvings, spaces for clamps, and drilled holes for screwed-in items.

Because I now travel to many woodcarving shows, I made this bench, which comes apart easily and doesn't take up much space when traveling.

Think about whether you'll sit or stand to carve. What you're carving may determine which one is more comfortable. If you hold the object you're carving, you can easily sit. However, if you're carving something that is difficult to hold, you may want to clamp the piece and stand while carving. If you decide to sit at your bench to carve, get a stool that puts you at a comfortable height next to the work surface.

If you decide to stand while carving, consider adding some type of pad to alleviate foot pain. I glued ¾-inch-thick dense particleboard over the cement floor in my work area because it is easier to stand on than concrete and tools that fall will hit wood rather than concrete. A cushioned floor mat is also a nice addition to your carving area.

Whatever type of work surface you choose, make sure it fits you ergonomically. Ensuring your surfaces are the proper height allows you to work with minimal bending or stretching. If you stand to carve, the height of your work surface should be about one hand's width below your elbow. If you sit to carve, get a comfortable stool that puts you at the same height as if you were standing.

All my work surfaces are this height, including my table saw and lathe. If you buy a commercial bench, extend or shorten the legs to conform to your height. If you make your own bench, build it so it suits you.

To find the proper height for your work surface, stand and bend your elbow, keeping your arm relaxed next to your body. Place your other hand vertically under your elbow. Your work surface should be at the bottom of your hand.

CARVING TABLE

A carving table, also called a bench hook table, gives you a portable work surface and can make a good beginner's workbench. If you like to sit while carving, you can make one that fits on your lap. If you are worried about getting chips on the floor, center an old sheet on the floor under your work area. As you carve, the chips will fall on the sheet. When you have completed your carving session, simply fold up the sheet and dump the chips in a waste area.

A good work surface is about 9-inches deep by 12-inches wide. Carving tables should have a stop that hooks over the edge of a table, along with a side stop and a back stop that hold the carving as you carve. If you're right-handed, the side stop is on the left side; if you're left-handed, it's on the right. Leave about one inch of space between the back stop and the side stop. This space makes it easy to flick any chips from the work surface. If the two stops are butted against one another, the chips collect in the corner and are difficult to remove.

To keep the work surface free of any exposed metal, recess the screws that hold the tabletop to the stops, and glue part of a dowel in the recessed area. This measure gives you a work surface devoid of any metal that could potentially damage the cutting edge of a tool.

Placing nonslip tread material, such as the type used on wooden steps, under the carving table keeps it from moving and protects the surface the table sits on. Nonslip tread material is available from most hardware stores, can be bought in short lengths, and has adhesive on the back so it can be easily applied to the bottom surface of the carving table.

> **"A carving table, also called a bench hook table, gives you a portable work surface and can make a good beginner's workbench."**

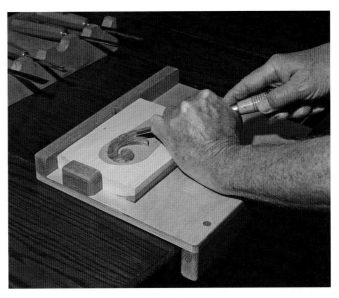

If set up correctly, a bench hook table with stops works well for carving and collecting chips.

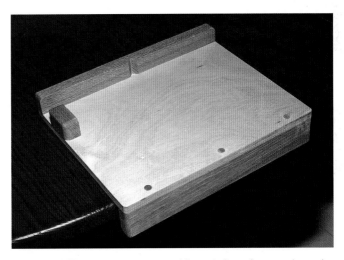

Recess and fill any screws so your tabletop is free of exposed metal.

Place nonslip material under your carving table to keep it from sliding.

LIGHTING

Good light is a necessity when carving and finishing. The optimum light source for true colors is natural sunlight. Because the majority of us don't have the luxury of natural light in our shops, we need to create our own light source. All types of light can be useful, depending on the work you're doing. Let's take a look at the three different types.

Over my work area, I have stationary, high CRI, fluorescent lights (*1*), which flood the area with light. To the sides are swivel incandescent lights (*2* and *3*) that adjust to shine across the surface of a carving. The mounted swivel magnifier lamp (*4*) is helpful for detailed work. The permanent workbench I built includes lighting, clamps, storage, and everything else I need. The top of the bench is an old solid-core door with a sheet of ¾-inch particleboard. The legs are four-by-four posts, around which I built a shell with doors and drawers. A woodworker's vise is mounted on the front edge.

Incandescent lighting. Most people use standard bulb lighting, also known as incandescent lighting, which you can buy at your local hardware or lighting store. This type of light is sufficient for most projects, but it's particularly useful for relief carving because it creates shadows. Shining incandescent light over the surface of a carving at about a 45-degree angle creates shadows to see depth.

Full-spectrum lighting. Full-spectrum lighting is not a necessity, but it's extremely useful if you plan to paint a carving because, like sunlight, it contains all true colors of the rainbow in equal amounts. Because a lighted object reflects its natural color and absorbs all other colors, a light source must contain the natural color or we'll see the object as something other than its true color. A red apple, for example, absorbs all colors except red, which is reflected from the apple. This phenomenon explains why objects' colors look different in artificial indoor lighting than in sunlight.

While it cannot replace natural sunlight, full-spectrum lighting can produce color similar to natural sunlight. Two terms specify light-source color: color rendering index (CRI) and color temperature (given in degrees Kelvin). CRI rates a light source's ability to replicate colors in a natural way, based on a scale from 0 to 100. (Natural sunlight has a CRI of 100, with a color temperature of 5500K.) To replicate natural sunlight, a light source must have a CRI over 91 and a color temperature near 5500K.

Fluorescent lighting. Fluorescent lighting is excellent for providing general illumination to a large area. Due to its inherent nature, however, fluorescent light creates minimal shadows, so it cannot be used alone for relief carving.

MAGNIFIERS

A lighted magnifying glass aids in working detailed areas of a carving. Ideally, a magnifier uses a 60-watt bulb and has a flexible arm so you can position the magnifying lens over your carving. Magnifying lamps are also available with fluorescent bulbs.

Another popular magnifier is one that fits on your head and has a magnifying lens in a pivoting visor. This type of magnifier is also available with a light attached to the visor.

DUST COLLECTION

If you sand or cut and create fine dust, you need to control your intake of the dust. Base the method you choose on the amount of carving you do and the type of dust you make.

Dust mask. Remember that a dust mask is necessary when working with any type of wood dust. Breathing fine dust particles not only is a nuisance but also can create health problems. Get a mask that is NIOSH (National Institute for Occupational Saftety and Health) approved, with a rating of at least N95. The N designates that the mask is nonoil resistant (an R indicates oil resistant; a P indicates oil-proof). The number indicates the filter efficiency. A 95 designation is guaranteed to filter 95 percent of the dust particles down to a minuscule diameter of 0.3 microns. Human hair, in contrast, ranges from 40 to 120 microns in diameter. If you have a beard or mustache, make sure the mask is designed to cover facial hair.

Central vacuum system. If you frequently create large amounts of dust, a central vacuum system connected to each of your major tools, such as table saws, band saws, and sanders, is ideal. A vacuum system filters the dust from the air as it is created. Remember, if you install a central vacuum, make sure it's properly grounded to eliminate the possibility of static sparks. Dry sawdust flowing through a pipe can create static electricity that can ignite the sawdust. To transport sawdust from the source to a receptacle, use metal pipe and ground it at one end. If you use plastic pipe, run a bare wire (one without a protective cover) through the inside of the pipe and ground the wire at one end. Either of these techniques will eliminate the potential of static buildup.

Magnifying lamps and visors can illuminate and enlarge small items as you are working.

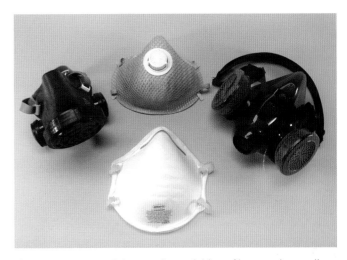

There are a variety of dust masks available to filter out the small particles in the air.

Dust Mask, Earmuffs, and Goggles

These are three items any work environment should have:

- **Dust mask**—when doing a project where you're creating any type of dust, such as when sanding or grinding.

- **Earmuffs**—for noise abatement if you're using any noisy equipment, such as sanders, portable shop vacuums, or grinders.

- **Goggles**—for any time that objects could fly toward your eyes, such as when grinding or using a mallet to remove large chips.

Air filtration systems such as this one clean the air in a room every 10 minutes. Notice the track lighting in the upper left.

Shop vacuums. Shop vacuums are another good source for removing sawdust and are much less costly than a central vacuum system. A shop vacuum will not have the capacity that a central vacuum has, but it can be wheeled to the source of the dust. If the shop vacuum is noisy, wear earmuffs to protect your hearing.

Air filtration system. To remove microscopic airborne dust particles in your work area, use an air filtration system. Systems such as the one I put in will clean the air in a room 20 feet by 20 feet by 8 feet every 10 minutes; smaller rooms are cleaned even faster.

Tabletop dust collectors. If you're removing wood with a small handheld grinder, consider a tabletop or an in-lap dust collector. A tabletop collector filters the air and a laptop pulls dust away from your work area by drawing air through a tube and into a collection bag. You can make your own tabletop or in-lap dust collector by attaching a dust collection bag to the output of a blower from a discarded clothes dryer.

A laptop dust collector pulls dust particles you're creating into a bag.

A tabletop dust collector is ideal for a small shop where carvings are done in one general area.

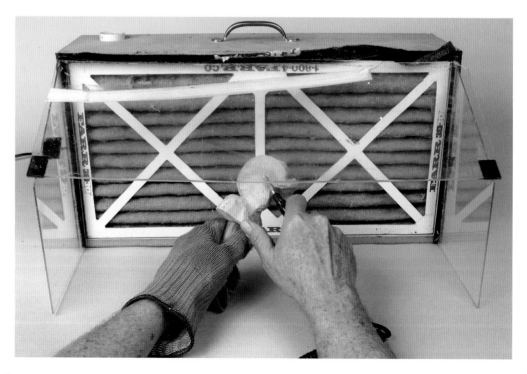

Hand Tools

While browsing through the hand tools at the store, check out the following accessories. While they won't be used as heavily as your carving tools, these items will get frequent use during carving sessions and are a welcome addition to any shop.

Carving Mallet

Carving mallets are helpful for carving hard woods or for working with large tools, but they can be used on any type of wood and will give you a tremendous amount of control as you drive a tool through wood depending on how hard or soft you strike the tool handle. If you use a mallet, the object you are carving should be clamped to hold it stationary.

Look for a mallet with a face that tapers slightly toward the handle. This angle allows the face of the mallet to strike the tool handle flat. If the face of the mallet is not angled, the mallet will tend to drive the tool into the wood at an angle. The tapered face also helps keep your wrist parallel to the rest of your arm, which is the most comfortable position for your arm and wrist.

Commercial mallets are available with wood, brass, or urethane heads. I prefer urethane heads because they are quieter and gentler when striking the handle of the tool. Urethane mallets typically come in weights of 12, 18, 20, and 30 ounces. Select a mallet that fits your size and strength. Larger tools and denser woods may require the heavier mallets.

Mallets are available with wood, brass, or urethane heads and come in a variety of weights and sizes.

A tapered head keeps your wrist and arm in the most comfortable position.

Handsaw

Handsaws, those that run just on human power, are ideal for smaller carvings. You won't actually carve with a handsaw, but this tool can remove a lot of excess wood in little time, making your carving experience that much more enjoyable. There are a variety of saws available.

To cut large pieces of wood in preparation for making a carving blank, choose a larger handsaw with fine teeth. These saws work well for stop cuts and removing small sections of wood. A coping saw is also useful for cutting out blanks and for other detailed work because its thin blade can cut tight radiuses. Coping saws do not generate the cutting power of larger handsaws, but they do a nice job.

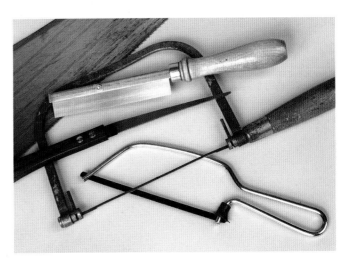

Fine-tooth handsaws are handy for removing excess wood quickly, making stop cuts, and preparing blanks for carving.

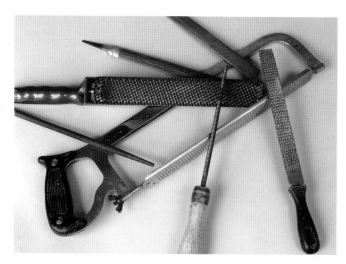
Rifflers excel at cleaning undercuts and hard-to-reach places.

RIFFLERS

Rifflers are small files curved and angled to work in hard-to-reach places, such as cleaning out undercut areas in a carving. They normally have a different-shaped cutter on each end of the tool and are available with coarse and fine metal or diamond-grit teeth.

RASPS

The surface of a rasp is made up of individual teeth that cut wood or metal. Rasps are available in coarse, medium, or fine grades and come in a number of shapes and sizes. Many rasps are round on one side and flat on the other; some have coarse teeth on one side and fine teeth on the other. They are available in frames designed to fit the blade, or the blade can be mounted in a hacksaw frame.

Another type of rasp, called a surform file, is based on the principle of a cheese grater, where the teeth are stamped in a tempered metal plate. A hole in front of each tooth allows the wood chips being removed to flow through the rasp, making it a self-cleaning tool.

Rasps come in a variety of grades, shapes, and sizes.

STAMPS

Stamps are primarily used for making background patterns in relief carvings; however, they should not be used to cover up poor carving. They can be bought from carving supply stores, or you can make your own using a file or a hacksaw to cut patterns in the ends of nails, bolts, or metal rods. Some relief carvers use stamps made for leather tooling.

Make sure the area you wish to stamp is smooth before you begin. When you're ready to stamp the pattern into the wood, use a mallet or a hammer to apply force to the handle of the stamp.

You can make your own stamps or buy them from carving supply stores. Relief carvers often use stamps to detail the backgrounds of their carvings.

DENTAL TOOLS

It may sound like they have no place on a woodcarver's bench, but dental tools make excellent tools for cleaning out undercut areas. Available in a variety of shapes and sizes, these tools can get into the most detailed areas. If you get a set of dental tools made from good-quality steel, they can actually be sharpened and used as detail knives.

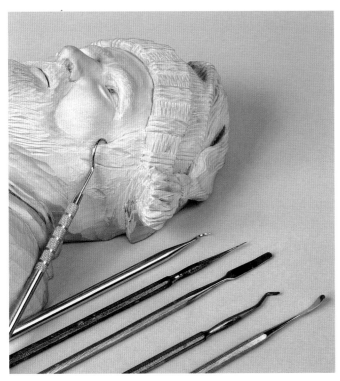

Though they don't seem as if they belong on a carving table, dental tools are great for getting into detailed areas.

BRUSHES

Brushes aren't only for painting. A used or new toothbrush is helpful for cleaning loose chips from a carving. The bristles are stiff enough to get into tight areas but not abrasive enough to mar the carving. Try using a wide paintbrush for brushing dust and chips from your work area.

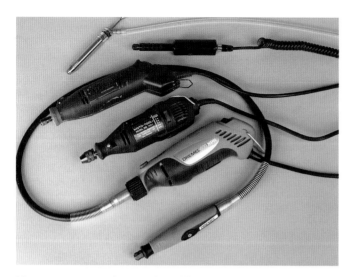

Most power carvers have replaceable collets to fit various-size bit shanks from 1/16 inch to 1/4 inch.

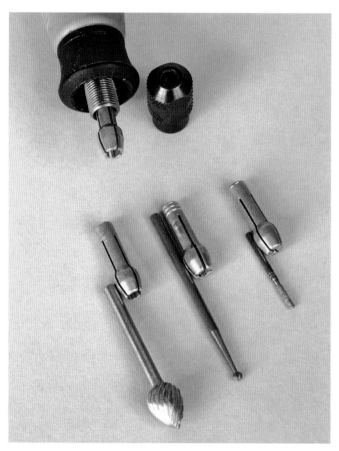

The collet attaches directly to the handheld unit, or is in the handpiece on flexible shaft units. The various bits and cutters inserted in the collet remove the wood.

POWER CARVING

Power carving can be used in addition to, or as an alternative to, hand carving.

There are two types of rotary power carvers. One is a variable speed handheld power tool, and the second has a flexible shaft between a motor and a handpiece. Both types remove wood.

Most rotary carvers are variable speed, with the speed controlled by either a hand-activated speed control or a variable speed foot petal. Many rotary carvers have the capability of switching to run clockwise or counterclockwise. The capability of running counterclockwise is a useful feature for left-handed people. Be aware that if the rotary carver runs counterclockwise, the bit must have the ability to cut that way. Many bits cut only in the clockwise direction.

Power carvers driven by motors or air (turbine) are available. Most motor-driven units have a maximum speed of about 35,000 rpm. Air turbine carvers are capable of much higher speeds, with some capable of speeds up to 500,000 rpm.

Air turbine carvers have less torque than motor-driven units but are capable of much higher speeds. You also will find that, at these high speeds, vibration is almost totally eliminated, which allows you to do ultrafine detail on wood and other mediums such as eggshell, bone, and glass. The amount of air flowing through the unit to turn the air turbine determines the unit's speed. The air to drive the

> *"Many carvers use power carvers as an adjunct to their hand carving to assist them in activities like getting into tight areas, for clean-up and texturing."*

turbine is generated by an air compressor, with the amount of airflow through the unit normally managed by a foot-controlled valve mechanism. The specifications on most units recommend a maximum airflow at about 40 psi. Being driven by an air turbine, rather than an electric motor, makes the air turbine carver lightweight and not much larger in diameter than a pencil.

If you use an air turbine carver, be certain the bits you use are intended for speeds compatible with your unit. Many bits are not made for high speeds and actually may fly apart at high speeds, creating a dangerous situation.

Many carvers use power carvers as an adjunct to their hand carving, to assist them in activities like getting into tight areas for cleanup and texturing. Some carvers use power tools as the principle means of creating their works of art, and rarely or never use any hand tools. Power carving may require less physical effort than hand carving, so someone with arthritis or other hand conditions may find this style of carving to be less stressful than using knives or gouges. Make sure you test a unit to determine whether it will affect your condition.

Manufacturers of Power Carvers:

- Dremel
- Foredom
- Gesswien & Co.
- Master Carver
- N.S.K.
- Optima
- Pflingst
- PJL Enterprises
- Proxxon
- Ram Power Micromotor
- Sears
- Turbo Carver
- Wecheer Industrial Co.

Manufacturers of Air Turbine Carvers:

- Power Carver
- Powercrafter
- Turbo Carver
- Ultra Carver

An air turbine carver.

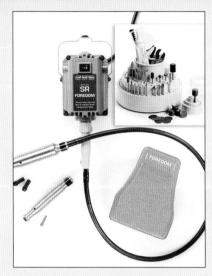

Variable speed foot control is available for some units.

Various brushes, buffers, sanding drums, shaping stones, cutting stones, and mandrels upon which you can attach various pads and disks.

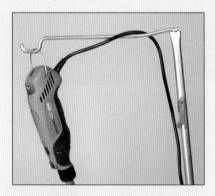

If you use a flexible shaft grinder, use some type of hanger from which you can suspend the motor.

Base upon which to set the handheld unit or handpiece. Some power carvers come with a base.

Some units, like this one from Foredom, come with a hanger for the grinder motor and the handpiece.

A variety of commercial bit holders are available. You can also make your own.

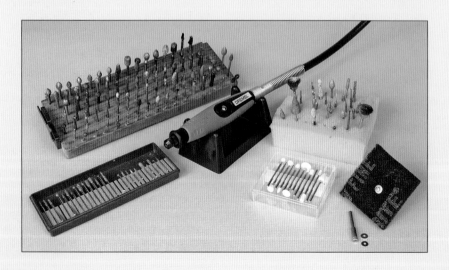

CARVING BITS

Bits are made from a variety of materials, from real or artificial diamond chips to solid tungsten carbide. Again, there are probably more available than an average carver will need. The key is to learn which types of bits work best for specific types of carving.

If you use any cutter with a sharp 90-degree corner, use it with caution, because they can be difficult to control. If the corner catches in the wood, it will kick back and you can easily lose control of the cut you are attempting to make.

Most Useful Bits

One of the most versatile cutters is the flame with a curved bottom. With the flame, you can remove wood quickly or do detailed cuts using just the one bit.

Bit Care

As you carve, keep an eye on the bit to make sure it's not loading up with wood residue or pitch. There will be times, no matter how careful you are, that the bit will load up with pitch and won't cut properly. When a bit gets loaded, it will burn the wood rather than cut it.

To remove the pitch, take these measures:

- Brush the bit with a stiff toothbrush or a small brass brush.
- To remove pitch from any type of bit, soak the bit for about an hour in oven cleaner. Remove the loosened pitch with a brass brush.
- For ruby and diamond bits, either soak them or use the same type of eraser you use to clean pitch buildup on your belt or disk sander. Run the bit at a slow speed as you place it on the eraser. If you see any minor buildup as you are carving, use the eraser from time to time as you carve.
- You can remove pitch in your carbide bits by soaking them, or you can do it quickly by burning it out using a propane torch. Grip the bit shank with pliers and hold the bit in the flame. When the trapped wood turns to ash, brush the ash from the bit, and you are ready to carve.

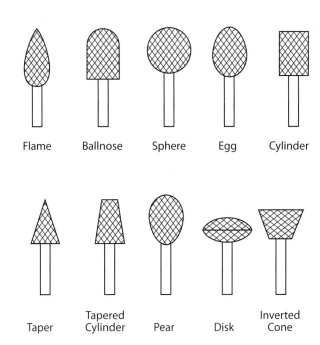

Flame Ballnose Sphere Egg Cylinder

Taper Tapered Cylinder Pear Disk Inverted Cone

Bits are available for your power carver in a number of different shapes, sizes, and constructions. These are a few of the various shapes available. You have more choices than you'll ever need.

" The key is to learn which types of bits work best for specific types of carving. "

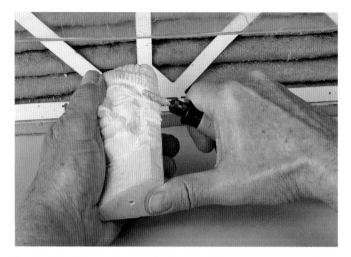

Paring Grip. This grip is used when roughing out a carving. Hold the power carver the same way you hold a carving knife when you do a pull cut. Place your thumb in a position on the wood where you pull the cutter toward it, and pull the tool through the wood by closing your hand. This grip is used mainly to remove large amounts of wood.

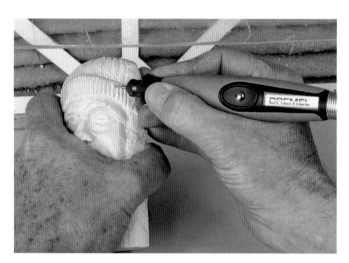

Pencil Grip. The pencil grip provides the most control while carving and allows you to carve as if you were doing it with a pencil. Place your thumb and pointer finger on the sides to control the tool as you use a stroking motion to remove wood.

Your dust mask should have a NIOSH approved rating of at least N95, and if you have a beard or mustache, make sure the mask seals properly to prevent dust from seeping around it (see Dust Collection on page 71 for the definition of a NIOSH rating of at least N95). Goggles and ear muffs, too, are valuable additions to your protective gear.

HOW TO HOLD A POWER CARVER

The bit should always spin in the direction in which the wood being removed is coming toward you. This rotation allows you to see the cut as it's being made and gives you control of the tool.

Depending on the type of cut you're making, either your thumb or little finger should be in contact with the wood at all times.

There are two basic grips used for carving with a power carver: the paring grip and the pencil grip, described at left. Which one you use depends on the type of cut you are making.

SAFETY

Always wear eye and breathing protection items when doing power carving. The bit rotates in a direction in which it throws chips and ultrafine dust toward you, so it is imperative that you use proper protection. Wear goggles, or if you wear glasses, use side shields on your glasses.

For your own safety, and to minimize dust circulating throughout your house, I highly recommend a dust collection system. This can be a tabletop or an in-lap dust collector.

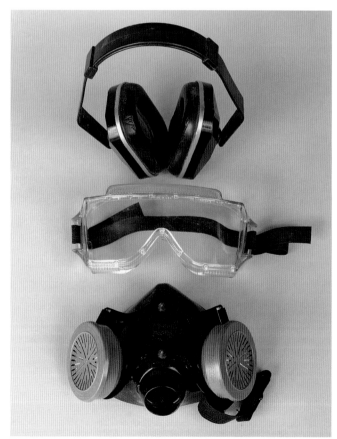

OTHER POWER TOOLS

Using power tools is purely a matter of personal preference. Some carvers shy away from power tools completely; others use them frequently. These additions to your workshop, if you choose to incorporate them, can be real time-savers. Power tools can remove waste wood much faster than hand tools can, but dust, noise, and vibration can cancel out the timesaving benefits. Detail work with power tools, while less noisy, can create superfine dust. Weigh your options carefully and always protect your lungs, eyes, and ears.

BAND SAW

A band saw is one of the most useful saws a carver can own. Its price tag is quite high, but its versatility can easily make up for the cost. I use my band saw more than any other power tool I own because it makes cutting blanks easy. There are small band saws, but if you have the space, I recommend you purchase one with a throat depth of at least 12 inches and a cutting depth of at least 5 inches. The minimum radius you can cut depends on the width of the blade installed.

SCROLL SAW

A scroll saw is another powered saw, but it uses a much narrower blade than a band saw. The top end of the blade can be easily disconnected and fed through a hole that has been drilled through the wood. This feature makes the scroll saw helpful for cutting out internal pieces in a board, such as those for pierced relief carving. The narrow blade allows the saw to cut tight, intricate curves.

SABER SAW

A saber saw, or jigsaw, is a handheld saw that works well for cutting curves and straight lines. Capable of cutting material up to an inch thick, it often comes with interchangeable blades for different functions and materials. It can be used to cut out small blanks and both internal and external pieces in a relief carving. Look for a saber saw that features variable speeds, long strokes, and up to 3000 strokes per minute.

DRILL

Drills are used to remove wood in selected areas for pierced relief carving, to make holes for inserting carver's screws, or to make holes in general. Thoroughly investigate the types of drills on the market—including stationary drill presses, portable drills (which plug into a 120-volt outlet), or battery-operated drills—to make sure you are purchasing the right tool for the type of carving you plan to do.

ROUTER

Routers are extremely useful tools for removing wood to make a border around a carving or for removing various levels of wood as in a relief carving. A router consists of a motor in a housing with handles that allow you to control the router. Various shaped cutters, or bits, can be inserted in a collet, which is attached to the motor. As the motor spins, the bit cuts the wood as you move the router across the wood's surface.

With a **fixed router** (right), the bit is extended to the depth you want to cut. To start the cut, set the router at an angle on the wood, and as the bit is spinning, slowly set the bit into the wood.

The **plunge router** (left) gives you more versatility and control for removing wood. Simply preset the depth, set the router flat on the surface of the wood, and turn on the router. As the bit spins, it is slowly lowered into the wood.

Note: With both types of routers, never attempt to make cuts more than ¼-inch deep at a time. For deeper cuts, make multiple passes.

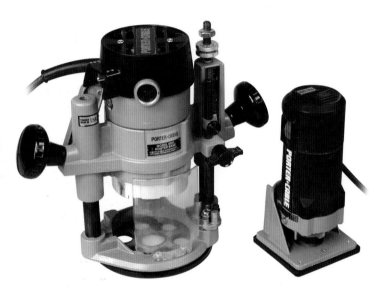

"Using power tools is purely a matter of personal preference. Some carvers shy away from power tools completely; others use them frequently."

CLAMPING DEVICES

It's almost always safest to immobilize the object you're carving so you have both hands on the tool as you carve. If both hands are on the tool, theoretically they should never be exposed to the cutting edge of the blade. While it may not be possible to clamp the piece you're carving at all times, secure the piece in a clamp whenever you can.

NONSLIP MATERIAL

Nonslip material works great to hold a flat object, such as a relief carving. You can find nonskid material in the housewares section of department stores. It normally comes in rolls, so you can easily cut it to fit the space under the piece you're carving.

STICKS AND SCRAP WOOD

If you are carving a small object, a grip stick helps hold the piece. To make a grip stick, drill a hole big enough to accept a hanger bolt in the end of a round piece of wood or a dowel. Glue or epoxy the bolt into the hole so the screw threads are exposed. Gently twist the screw into the bottom of the piece, and you have a larger gripping area.

Another way to handle small, irregularly shaped, or delicate items is to cut out the piece you're going to carve and then glue cardboard or heavy paper between a scrap board and your carving piece. When you've completed the carving, carefully pry it off the cardboard with a flat carpenter's chisel and sand away the cardboard residue.

Nonskid material can be cut to shape and is perfect for holding flat carvings in place.

You can make your own grip stick by simply adding a hanger bolt to the end of a stick or dowel. These sticks are great tools for handling small or irregularly shaped items.

Use glue to adhere delicate carvings to cardboard. Once you've finished carving, you can pry the carving off the cardboard and simply sand away any residue.

CLAMPS, DOGS, AND VISES

C-clamps, bar clamps, quick-grip clamps, and wood clamps are effective and relatively safe ways to hold items you're carving. If you use a metal clamp, place pieces of wood between the jaws of the clamp and the piece you're carving so if the tool ever slips, it hits wood rather than metal. Drilling holes in your bench top and inserting "dogs," a type of wooden peg, in the holes makes a versatile clamp for various-shaped objects. Vises are also a good way to hold your project as you carve. They come in a variety of designs, but some are more user-friendly than others. If you buy a vise, it should have the following characteristics:

- Be sturdy enough to firmly hold the piece you're going to carve.
- Allow you to reposition the carving quickly.
- Have a range of motion allowing you to easily position the piece where you want it.
- Not be so large that it gets in the way as you carve.

Have a variety of clamps available for effective ways to hold carvings in place.

If you use a metal clamp, place wood between the jaws of the clamp and your carving.

I almost exclusively use hanger bolts to mount my carvings to a vise or other holding device. Hanger bolts are available in a variety of sizes from any hardware store. Use hanger bolts to mount a carving in a vise by drilling pilot holes that match the mounting holes in the vise's mounting plate in a nonviewed area of your carving. Then, screw in the hanger bolts using lock pliers, and mount your carving to the vise plate. Upon completion of your carving, remove the hanger bolts or use them to mount the carving to a base.

Hanger bolts also come in handy when you are carving relief pieces. Simply glue a scrap piece of wood to the back of the piece you're going to carve. Then, mount the hanger bolts only in the scrap piece, and you never have to worry about your tools hitting metal. When the carving is completed, carve off the attached piece.

Another way to clamp a piece is to leave excess wood on a waste area of the piece. Use this waste wood for clamping. When the rest of the carving is completed, remove the excess wood and finish the carving.

Dogs make a versatile clamp for irregularly shaped objects.

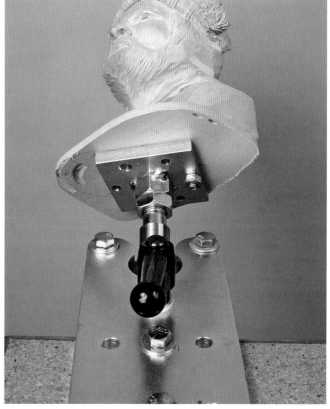

There are other specially made holding devices that allow you to move the carving in any direction you wish.

MEASURING DEVICES

Measuring devices are small but important tools. They ensure that carvings are straight and square when they need to be and that the proportions of a carving are just right. Take some time to browse through these tools and find the ones that best suit your needs.

Dividers.

Compass.

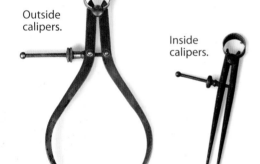
Outside calipers.

Inside calipers.

Vernier calipers.

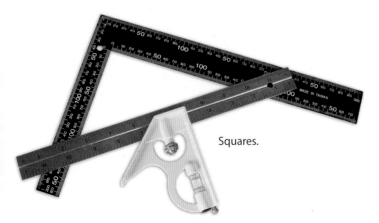
Squares.

DIVIDERS

Dividers have two hinged legs with sharp points at the ends and are used to transfer dimensions from a model to a carving or to transfer measurements from a ruler to a carving or vice versa. Dividers are available with a friction hinge to hold the setting or with a thumb wheel adjustment between the legs.

Proportional dividers have an adjustable pivot point allowing a ratio to be set between the opposite ends of the divider points. This measuring device allows you to enlarge or decrease the size from a model to the carving.

COMPASS

A divider that has a sharp point at the end of one leg and a pen or pencil at the end of the other leg is called a compass. The key to making perfect circles, a compass is an extremely useful tool when laying out chip carvings.

CALIPERS

This handy tool measures inside or outside dimensions of an object. Both legs are hinged from one end. The ends of the legs on inside calipers are bent out to measure the internal size of an object; the ends of the legs on outside calipers are bent in to measure the external dimension.

Vernier calipers measure both inside and outside measurements on the piece you're measuring. The top jaws measure inside dimension, and the bottom jaws measure outside dimension. Most vernier calipers also have a probe that measures depth.

SQUARE

A square consists of two straight legs that intersect at a right angle to one another. This tool is useful for laying out patterns, squaring up a board, or marking an area 90 degrees from the edge of a board. A combination square is a very useful tool, with a shoulder that lies on the edge of a board. In addition to a 90-degree angle, it also has a 45-degree angle. You can loosen a knurled nut to reposition the square's head.

ADHESIVES

A few different adhesives are good to have on hand, whether you're assembling a project, repairing a carving, or gluing up wood to make a larger carving blank. Cyanoacrylate glue and wood glue are the two most common types.

CYANOACRYLATE GLUE

For immediate bonding, use Specially Formulated Super Glue or Bondini, which are water-activated cyanoacrylate glues. Moisture causes these glues to bond instantly. Look for the words "specially formulated for leather and wood" on the label.

> *"A few different adhesives are good to have on hand, whether you're assembling a project, repairing a carving, or gluing up wood to make a larger carving blank."*

Be careful you don't get any specially formulated glue on yourself. The moisture in your skin will activate this glue, causing it to set up immediately if another part of your body comes in contact with it. To unattach body parts from one another, use a specially designed remover or acetone nail polish remover.

WHITE AND YELLOW GLUES

If you're gluing up pieces for a carving, white or yellow glue is the recommended adhesive. White glue starts to set up in about five minutes; yellow glue gives you about ten minutes to get the parts together before it begins to get tacky. Elmer's also has stainable glue, which contains real wood fibers, so if you stain the wood, the joint should be less noticeable.

If you should ever break off a piece as you're carving, you can glue the pieces back together by using white glue and holding them in place for about ten minutes. White and yellow glues require no special safety measures.

Many glues will hold wood; however, yellow, white, and water-activated cyanoacrylate glues are best for woodcarving purposes.

Chapter Six

Sharpening Your Tools

I'm convinced more people stop carving because of dull tools than for any other reason.

Keeping your carving tools in their best working condition involves some detailed care. The two major steps in sharpening your carving tools are shaping them to the proper cutting angle using sharpening stones and then polishing them to a razor-sharp edge on a strop. If you purchase good-quality steel tools and keep the blades protected when they're not in use, you can look forward to more time carving and less time sharpening.

In this chapter, we'll take a look at the different types of materials available for sharpening your tools before we address sharpening techniques.

SHARPENING MATERIALS

There are a number of sharpening materials available, most of which are sharpening stones. You can choose from oilstones, diamond stones, water stones, ceramic stones, and Arkansas stones, to name a few. Sandpaper can also be a great way to shape and sharpen your tools. Any of these materials work, but the way they get the job done differs widely. Some cut faster than others; some require oil, some water, and some nothing; and some give you better results depending on your tool.

A very useful type of oilstone is an India combination stone, which has coarse grit on one side and finer grit on the opposite side.

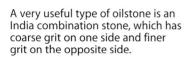

CHARACTERISTICS OF A SHARPENING MEDIUM

All sharpening mediums consist of abrasive particles, called grit. Grit abrades metal from your carving tools to shape and sharpen them. The larger the grit size, the faster it removes metal. Large grit leaves deep abrasions in the tool blade that must be removed with a finer-grit abrasive. Once tools are honed and polished, no abrasion lines should be visible.

Grit size is designated with a numeric value. The smaller the numeric value, the larger the physical size of the grit particle. For example, grit in a 100-grit stone is coarser than grit in a 600-grit stone.

The size of the sharpening medium is also an important element. Stick with something at least six inches long and two inches wide. Smaller sizes work, but you are limited when sharpening larger tools.

OILSTONES

Oilstones have been the old reliable sharpening stone for over 75 years and are very efficient at removing metal. They are reasonably priced and are relatively low maintenance. Because the finest-grit oilstone is 320, you need to use another type of stone for the final finishing.

Composition. Oilstones can be aluminum oxide, silicon carbide, or certain natural stones for grit.

How they work. As their name implies, oilstones require lightweight oil (called honing oil) for sharpening. As the stone removes metal from the tool, the oil keeps the metal particles in suspension so they don't become embedded and clog the stone's pores. When metal particles clog the pores, it is called glazing. Glazing can ruin the stone.

OILSTONE PROS AND CONS

Pros
- Is reasonably priced
- Cuts relatively fast
- Is available as a combination stone
- Is low maintenance

Cons
- Is not available in fine grit
- Cups over time
- Can stain wood if tools are not wiped clean after sharpening

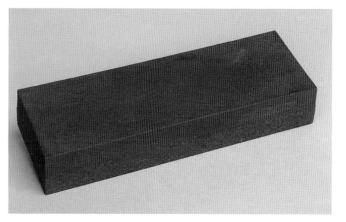

Honing oil is used on the surface of sharpening stones to keep the metal shavings in suspension. Commercial honing oil and lightweight mineral oil, which is odorless and nontoxic, work well.

When fine bits of metal abraded from sharpening become embedded in the stone, the effect is called glazing.

Almost any lightweight oil works as honing oil. I prefer lightweight mineral oil. Do not, however, use vegetable oil or motor oil. Vegetable oil clogs the pores of the stone; motor oil does not allow a tool enough contact with the grit. Commercial honing oils work well.

Care and maintenance. Always wipe the oil from the stone's surface with a soft cloth or paper towel to remove the metal particles once the sharpening is complete. When purchasing an oilstone, beware of cheap oilstones that won't keep oil on the surface. As a preventative measure, buy an oilstone that is presaturated or preloaded with a medium about the thickness of petroleum jelly. The preloaded medium forces the honing oil to remain on the surface.

Because some grit is removed from the oilstone's surface every time you sharpen, a slight hollowed area can form. This is called cupping, or dishing. To minimize cupping, move the tool around the surface as you sharpen so the stone wears more evenly.

If cupping does develop, you'll need to flatten your stone. One method is to spread about a teaspoon of 70-grit silicon carbide powder on a flat metal plate, add some water, and rub the stone in the slurry (a watery mix of silicon carbide and the stone's grit) using a circular motion. I flatten my oilstone with no lubricant by rubbing it in a circular motion on my concrete driveway or sidewalk. Check the flatness of the stone by placing a straightedge on its surface.

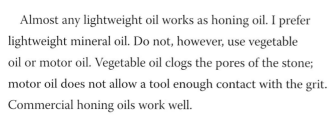

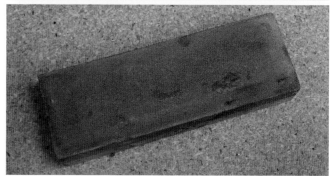

When purchasing an oilstone, beware of cheap stones that allow the honing oil to bleed through the stone, therefore not keeping the metal particles in suspension and making them ineffective. (This sequence was shot in one minute.)

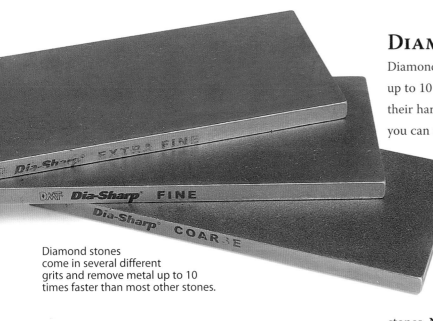

Diamond stones come in several different grits and remove metal up to 10 times faster than most other stones.

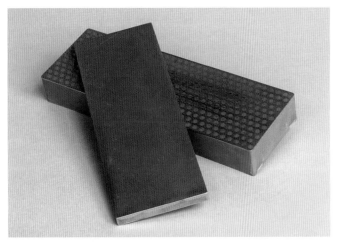

Diamond stones come in uninterrupted (diamonds are plated over the entire surface) and interrupted (diamonds are plated on a perforated metal plate) types.

DIAMOND STONE PROS AND CONS

Pros
- Cuts faster than any other stone
- Has a wide range of grits available
- Stays flat within ± 0.002 of an inch forever
- Does the job with light pressure
- Has the lowest maintenance of any stone available
- Can be used dry, with water, or with honing oil
- Will not break

Cons
- Is expensive
- Requires the user to learn to apply light pressure

DIAMOND STONES

Diamond stones are extremely efficient and remove metal up to 10 times faster than most other stones. Because of their hardness (diamonds are the hardest known substance), you can use far less pressure with diamond stones than with other stones. Diamond stones come in four different grit categories: extracoarse (220 grit) for changing bevel angles or surface flattening, coarse (325 grit) for tool repair, fine (600 grit) to refine the cutting edge, and extrafine (1200 grit) to polish the cutting edge of the tool. Their high efficiency and makeup cause diamond stones to be the most expensive stones. **Note:** Be aware that there are some poorly made copycat diamond stones out there. Stick with quality, name-brand, reputable manufacturers.

Composition. The diamonds are grown, then milled and sorted by micron size. They are also purer than natural diamonds, which can have foreign inclusion within the crystals that can weaken the diamond. For stones, there are two types of synthetic diamonds used: monocrystalline and polycrystalline. Monocrystalline diamond stones are slightly more expensive than polycrystalline stones, but monocrystalline diamonds wear less. If you buy diamond stones, invest in the monocrystalline diamonds.

You can also select two types of plates: uninterrupted and interrupted. In uninterrupted diamond stones, diamonds are plated over the entire metal plate; in interrupted, they are plated on a perforated metal plate. Uninterrupted stones are best for carving tools. Interrupted stones are difficult to use with small tools.

How they work. Like an oilstone's grit, a diamond stone's grit abrades a tool's metal, but a diamond stone can be used with or without honing oil or water. I use a lightweight mineral oil on my diamond stones. **Note:** Interrupted-surface diamond stones should never be used with a petroleum-based honing oil. Petroleum can soften the materials the stone is molded in.

Care and maintenance. Good-quality diamond stones require very little maintenance. They remain flat within ± 0.002 inch for their entire life and never need to be resurfaced. If you use a honing oil or water, wipe the stone clean with a soft cloth or paper towel when sharpening is complete to remove the metal particles in suspension. If you wipe your stone after sharpening, the stone will be ready for the next sharpening session.

> *"Diamond stones are extremely efficient and remove metal up to 10 times faster than most other stones."*

If no medium is used to keep the metal particles in suspension, clean the stone with warm, soapy water and a scrubber pad or brush. Because diamond stones do not have open pores like oilstones, the metal particles do not become embedded and can be removed by a simple washing. Make sure the stones are completely dry before storing them.

Water Stones

Water stones do a great job sharpening, and a complete set allows you to go from shaping your tools to putting a polished edge on them, something to consider when looking at price because they are relatively expensive. They are available in four categories of grit: coarse (220 grit) for tool repair, medium (1000 grit) for establishing an edge, fine (4000 grit) for refining the edge, and extrafine (8000 grit) for polishing the edge.

Composition. Natural Japanese water stones are sedimentary and consist of fine silicate particles in a clay matrix. As the sources of the natural stones are gradually becoming exhausted, man-made water stones are becoming more popular.

How they work. As the name implies, water stones need water for sharpening. As the stone removes metal from the tool, the water keeps the metal particles in suspension and develops a slurry, a watery mixture of grit from the stone's surface and the suspended metal particles. This process of creating a slurry exposes new, sharp abrasive, helps speed up the sharpening process, and polishes the blade while it is being sharpened. All of this action accounts for the fast sharpening characteristic of water stones.

The three coarsest grits require soaking for about 10 minutes prior to use, and water must be kept on the surface during sharpening. The finest stone does not require

Water stones can be natural or man-made and use water on the surface.

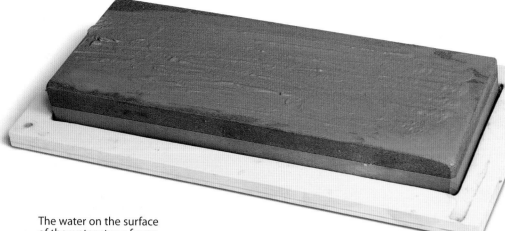

The water on the surface of the water stone forms a slurry that helps abrade the blade.

soaking, but water must be present on the surface while sharpening. You can also use a Nagura stone, a fine-grained chalk stone, on the surface of the two finest water stones. In combination with water, the Nagura stone makes a polishing solution that polishes the tool's cutting surface as you sharpen using the water stone. Additionally, the Nagura stone makes the water stone's surface slipperier and prevents the tool from sticking to the water stone during sharpening.

Care and maintenance. Water stones can be messy. The slurry won't damage anything, but it does take time to clean up. To contain the mess, make a base for the stone to rest in as the tools are sharpened.

When you've completed the sharpening process, wipe all the water off the tools with a soft cloth or paper towel. Any water remaining on the tools could cause rust spots. If you live in an area that gets cold enough to freeze, make sure your water stones are completely dry before being exposed to freezing temperatures. If a wet water stone freezes, it will shatter.

WATER STONE GRITS

If you are used to working with another sharpening medium and then switch to water stones, the water stone grits can be misleading. Because water stones originally came from Japan, most are graded by the Japanese Industrial Standard (JIS). In contrast, the Federation of European Producers of Abrasives (FEPA) is the standard used for almost all other sharpening stones. To help eliminate confusion, compare the micron size of the grit.

If you see a water stone labeled JIS:	It is equivalent to a FEPA grit of:
220 grit	200
1000 grit	525
4000 grit	1200
8000 grit	1600

The Norton Company makes a container that protects the water stone when not in use and serves as a base while you sharpen.

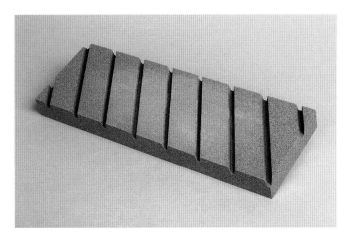

Flattening stones must be used occasionally to flatten a stone's surface. To use the flattening stone, soak the water stone until it is saturated with water, lay the water stone on the grooved side of the flattening stone, and rub it in a circular motion until it's flat.

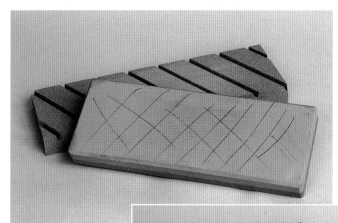

To make sure a stone is flattened evenly, draw a grid across its surface. When all the lines are removed, the surface is sufficiently flat.

A water stone's tendency to break off and expose new grit is sort of a double-edged sword: It removes metal quickly, but it also means that the two coarser water stones wear quickly and need to be flattened often. Flatten a water stone by rubbing it in a circular motion on wet, 220-grit wet/dry sandpaper or flat concrete, or by using a flattening stone developed for this specific purpose.

Make sure your sharpening stones are flattened correctly by penciling a grid on the surface to be flattened. As you work, check the grid lines. When they all disappear, your stone is flat.

WATER STONE PROS AND CONS

Pros

- Is available in coarse to extrafine grits
- Cuts fast
- Shapes, sharpens, and hones tools with one set of stones
- Polishes blades using the finer grits

Cons

- Is relatively expensive
- Wears rapidly in the coarse grits
- Must be flattened often
- Must be soaked in water
- Can rust tools with its water
- Can't be allowed to freeze when wet

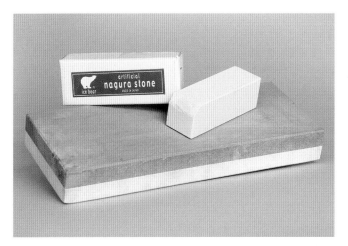

Rubbing a Nagura stone, a fine-grained chalk stone, on the surface of a wet water stone creates a polishing solution.

Ceramic sharpening stones are not made to remove large amounts of metal. They come in two colors: white and black.

CERAMIC STONES

Ceramic stones are more expensive than diamond stones of the same size and are not made to remove large amounts of metal. Their grit is too fine. Instead, they are for final sharpening or for maintaining a sharp edge on your tools. White stones (1200 grit) put a mirror finish on a sharpened edge. Black ceramic stones (600 grit) keep a tool properly shaped and sharp. The black stone is as hard as the white, but the bonding matrix is softer, giving it a quicker cutting ability. Ceramic stones are popular with chip carvers who need to keep their chip carving knives correctly shaped and very sharp.

Composition. Ceramic stones are synthetic man-made stones fabricated of alumina (aluminum oxide) or silicon carbide in a ceramic bond. This type of silicon carbide is the hardest material next to diamonds, even though it is several orders of magnitude softer than diamonds. Ceramic stones are made of the same material as water stones, but the grit in ceramic stones is bonded together into a harder mass.

How they work. Ceramic stones work the same as the other stones and can be used dry, with water, or with honing oil.

Care and maintenance. The tight bond between the grit and the stone means that cupping is rare in ceramic stones. They stay flat and require very little maintenance. If used dry, they should be washed from time to time with warm, soapy water and a scrubber pad to remove any metal particles trapped between the grit.

ARKANSAS STONES

Arkansas stones do a wonderful job of putting the final edge on your tools, but start with a coarser-grit stone of a different type if you need to remove a great deal of metal or shape a tool. Arkansas stones range from white to black, and many are mottled with different colors. The soft white stones cut faster than the black because of their coarser grain characteristics; however, no Arkansas stone cuts ultrafast. Due to their unique crystalline structure, Arkansas stones polish as they sharpen and leave a smooth surface on your tools, but they are expensive.

Composition. Arkansas stones are natural, quarried mineral stones mined in the Ouachita Mountains near

Hot Springs, Arkansas. The abrasive material is novaculite, a white quartz rock composed mainly of silicon dioxide. Arkansas stones are related to flint and have a hardness just a bit greater than a steel file.

How they work. Arkansas stones operate in the same manner as the other sharpening stones. Use a few drops of lightweight mineral oil to prevent glazing while sharpening.

Care and maintenance. Wipe all of the mineral oil and metal particles from the stone with a soft cloth or paper towel when sharpening is complete. Do not use petroleum-based honing oils on Arkansas stones. An Arkansas stone should never need to be flattened; however, if it does, it should be done only by a professional who has special polishing equipment.

Types of Arkansas stones.

- **Soft Arkansas** (extrafine, 600 to 800 grit) stones are the coarsest grained and least dense of the natural stones. They are used to sharpen and upgrade tool and knife edges to an even, polished surface, frequently after sharpening with synthetic stones. Soft Arkansas stones are opaque to milky white in color.

- **Hard Arkansas** (superfine, 800 to 1,000 grit) stones are finer grained and denser than soft Arkansas stones. Hard Arkansas stones impart the fine edge necessary for most cutting tools and knives.

- **Hard translucent Arkansas** (ultrafine, 1,000+ grit) stones are the finest grained and most dense natural stone available. They produce the keenest, most precise finish possible. Hard translucent Arkansas stones may contain shades of red, yellow, and gray, but they are translucent white in their purest form.

- **Black Arkansas** (ultrafinish, 1,200+ grit) is an ultrafinish stone. Some carvers feel the black Arkansas puts the optimum edge on tools, even better than the hard translucent. Because of their ability to put on that "ultimate edge," they have been nicknamed "surgical black Arkansas."

- **Ouachita stone** is a second grade of Arkansas stones. It comes from the area around the Ouachita River and is softer and coarser in structure than the best Arkansas. It's a good intermediate stone.

"Arkansas stones are natural, quarried mineral stones mined in the Ouachita Mountains near Hot Springs, Arkansas. They are related to flint and have a hardness just a bit greater than a steel file."

ARKANSAS STONE PROS AND CONS

Pros
- Polishes while sharpening
- Puts on a near-mirror finish
- Wears very slowly
- Is used for final honing
- Is available in four grades
- Is a natural stone

Cons
- Does not cut rapidly
- Is expensive
- Is available in fine grits only

Specific jobs require a specific grit. Here are my recommendations:

Job	Grit recommended	Results
Shaping	100 grit to 220 grit reshape a tool	Removes large amounts of metal and performs major rework
Honing the edge	320 grit	Reworks and sharpens most tools, hones the edge, and removes abrasions from the coarser stones
Final sharpening	600 grit	Produces a keen edge and begins to polish the blade
Achieving the sharpest edge	1000 grit	Polishes the blade and shapes the razor edge (the last step before stropping)

SANDPAPER PROS AND CONS

Pros
- Costs little
- Is available in multiple grits
- Is a good way to get started
- Can be found in most hardware stores

Cons
- Wears out quickly
- Must be adhered to a flat surface

ALUMINUM OXIDE OR SILICON CARBIDE SANDPAPER

Sandpaper is a reasonably quick and cost-effective sharpening medium, especially for beginners who want to limit their expenses to good-quality tools until they have more experience in the art form. Once you've gained experience, however, you may want to consider adding permanent sharpening stones to your tools. Sandpaper comes in a variety of grits, but I have found 220, 320, P400, P600, and P1200 to be the best grits for sharpening tools.

Composition. Aluminum oxide or silicon carbide particles are attached to a paper backing for this medium.

How they work. Aluminum oxide sandpaper is normally a yellowish color and is always used without a lubricant. Silicon carbide sandpaper can be distinguished by its shiny black color and is a wet/dry sandpaper that can be used dry or with water.

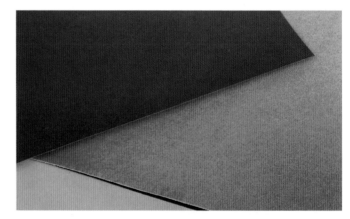

Aluminum oxide and silicon carbide sandpaper sheets in varying grits can be used to sharpen tools.

A grit size on the back of a piece of sandpaper without a letter designation means that the sandpaper grading is from the Coated Abrasive Manufacturers Institute (CAMI).

To use sandpaper for sharpening, cut a standard 9-by-11-inch sheet of 220-grit sandpaper in half so it is 4½ by 11 inches. Use a temporary glue to attach the half sheet of sandpaper to fiberboard or granite tile. Sandpaper does not last as long as a regular sharpening stone, but by using temporary glue, the sandpaper can easily be peeled off and be replaced. Plate glass also works well as a base; just make sure you use tempered glass so it doesn't break easily. Cut the other grits in half also, so they fit the surface of the board.

Try attaching sandpaper to fiberboard with a spray or stick adhesive to make a sanding block.

SANDPAPER GRITS

If you're going to use sandpaper, be aware that there are three different grading systems used to designate the grit size of sandpaper:

- **JIS** (Japanese Industrial Standard)
- **CAMI** (Coated Abrasive Manufacturers Institute)
- **FEPA** (Federation of European Producers of Abrasives)

Sandpaper is labeled on the back of the sheet with the grit size. If there is no alpha designation before the numeric value, it is CAMI. If you see a P prefix before the grit size, it is the FEPA grading standard. I have not included information on the JIS standard because it is rarely used outside Japan.

The scratch patterns between the CAMI and the FEPA grading through 240 grit are very similar. After that, you see some variation between the two standards. (If you see a sheet of sandpaper labeled 180 grit, it is equivalent to P180 grit, and each has basically the same scratch pattern. However, if you see a sheet labeled 600 grit, it has the same basic scratch pattern as a sheet of P1200 grit.) Use the following chart to compare the CAMI and FEPA grit designators to the actual grit micron size of the abrasive used in both grading systems. This way, you can make substitutions between the two systems and know you're getting the correct grit.

CAMI grit	FEPA grit	Grit micron size
60	P60	260
80	P80	197
100	P100	141
	P120	127
120		116
	P150	97
150		93
180	P180	78
	P220	65
220		60
	P240	58
240		53.5
	P320	46
320		36
	P400	35
	P600	25.8
400		23
600	P1200	16
800	P1500	12.6
	P2000	10.3
1000		9.2

As the sandpaper wears, it is easy to remove and replace.

If you need to remove a large amount of metal, lay a coarser sheet of sandpaper on the surface of the 220 grit. The abrasive properties of the 220-grit sandpaper keep the coarser sheet in place, without gluing, while you sharpen. Continue to use the 220 grit to hold the other grits in place until the tool is sharp. The series of 220, 320, P400, P600, and P1,200 grits is sufficient for most sharpening requirements. If you want individual sharpening surfaces of various grits, glue each grit to individual pieces of fiberboard.

Care and maintenance. Because sandpaper is easily replaced, little to no maintenance is needed for this sharpening material. From time to time, wipe the metal particles from the sandpaper with a soft cloth or a brush.

STONE TYPE AND FEPA/JIS GRIT SIZES

The following chart shows the various sharpening mediums, what grit size they are, and how the grit size correlates FEPA to JIS. **Note:** You can find grits of sandpaper that correspond to all of the grits in the list.

Stone type	FEPA	JIS
Coarse India	100	150
Medium India	180	220
Coarse water stone	180	220
Extracoarse diamond	220	240
Fine India	280	360
Coarse diamond	325	500
Washita	350	600
Medium water stone	525	1000
Soft Arkansas	600	1200
Fine diamond	600	1200
Medium black ceramic	700	2000
Ultrawhite ceramic	900	2500
Hard white Arkansas	1200	4000
Fine water stone	1200	4000
Extrafine diamond	1200	4000
Extrafine water stone	1600	8000
Hard black Arkansas	3000	8000+

SLIP STONES

Small contoured stones called slip stones are made to remove metal from the inside contour of tools. I recommend the India taper triangle, which has a 60-degree angle and is used to remove the burrs, or wire edges, from the insides of V-tools with angles 60 degrees or greater. For V-tools with angles less than 60 degrees, I recommend a slip stone called a tight taper shape stone.

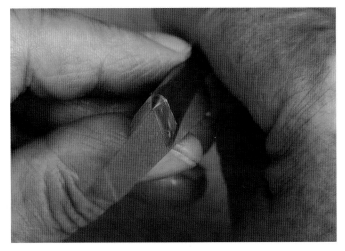

An India taper triangle is a type of slip stone used to remove burrs from the inside of a 60-degree V-tool.

Use a tight taper for V-tools with less than a 60-degree angle.

PROS AND CONS OF VARIOUS SHARPENING STONES AND SHARPENING MATERIAL

Medium	Lubricant	Price	Grit	Maintenance
Oilstone	Oil	Moderate	Up to 320; does not come in fine grit	Must be flattened; oil can stain wood if tools are not wiped clean
Water stone	Water	Moderately expensive	Coarse to extrafine	Wears rapidly; must be flattened often; water can rust tools; can shatter if freezes when wet
Diamond stone	Water, oil, or none	Expensive	Coarse to extrafine	Stays flat within ± 0.002 of an inch forever; will not break
Ceramic stone	Water, oil, or none	Moderately expensive	Fine only	Is fragile; does not wear quickly; does not need to be flattened often
Arkansas stone	Mineral oil	Expensive	Fine only	Wears very slowly
Sandpaper	Water or none	Inexpensive	Coarse to extrafine	Wears quickly

STROPS AND HONING COMPOUND

A strop and honing compound are used together to put the final cutting edge on your tools and to polish the blade. Stropping does not reshape a blade the way sharpening does. Ideally, if the cutting edges of your tools do not become extremely dull or damaged, you should be able to simply strop your tool when it becomes dull to hone the edge back to its razor sharpness about five to six times before you need to go to your fine stone.

> *"A strop and honing compound are used together to put the final cutting edge on your tools and to polish the blade."*

A strop can be made of leather, cardboard, cloth, or even wood and acts as a binder to hold the honing compound. For my carving knives, I use a homemade leather strop that consists of a ⅛-inch-thick-by-2-inch-wide-by-10-inch-long piece of leather glued to a ¾-inch-thick piece of wood the same length and width as the leather. Size can vary, but I feel this size accommodates my knives well. I glued the leather to the wood with contact cement.

Honing compound is a fine abrasive compound that is rubbed into the strop. This step is called loading the strop. The honing compound does the actual work of creating the ultrasharp cutting edge and polishing the blade.

Strops are used to put a final polished edge on your knife.

Many strops, like mine, are made of a piece of leather glued to a board.

Honing compound is available in powder, paste, or stick form. I prefer the stick form because it's easy to apply and stays where you put it. If you get buildup over time, simply scrape it off your strop with the back of your knife. Powder tends to drift off the strop and onto the work surface. Paste builds up and becomes gummy on your strop.

Of the stick honing compounds, I primarily use the white variety. It cuts fast and gives your tools a mirror polish. The white color is also useful when sharpening micro tools because, as I pull the tool through the compound, it's easy to see the track where the metal is being removed.

HONING COMPOUND COLORS AND GRIT SIZES

Honing compound comes in a variety of colors. Generally, but not always, the color of the honing compound relates to the grit size.

Color	Grit	Purpose
Black (gray)	Extracoarse	Fast cutting
Green (dark)	Coarse	All-purpose fast cutting
White	Medium to fine	Good all-purpose
Brown	Fine	Slower cutting
Green (light)	Extrafine	Polish only
Yellow	Ultrafine	Polish only; leaves little residue

Honing compound is placed on the strop to polish the edge of the blade.

A buildup of honing compound can be quickly removed with the back of a knife blade.

SHARPENING TECHNIQUES

I'm convinced that more people stop carving because of dull tools than for any other reason. Once you carve with a sharp tool, you will never be satisfied with anything else. A sharp tool allows you to concentrate on the cut you want to make. Use a dull tool and you'll find yourself concentrating on how much force is required to drive the tool through wood. In this section, I will show you how to get your tools sharp each and every time you attempt to sharpen them, no matter what medium you use.

The method presented here is not the only way to sharpen carving tools, but I've developed these techniques by talking with numerous experienced carvers and by doing a tremendous amount of research and experimentation over my 30-plus years of carving. These techniques have worked well for me and for the thousands of carvers I've taught through my classes and my very popular video *Sharpening Simplified*.

There are two very important fundamentals to getting your tools sharp: 1) know what a tool looks like when it's properly sharpened so you know what to achieve, and 2) make sure each sharpening step is specific and

> **" *Sharpening tools is like learning to play an instrument. The more you do it, the better you get.* "**

repeatable. Focus on the fundamentals and then practice until they become second nature. Master the fundamentals, and you master sharpening.

Sharpening tools is like learning to play an instrument. The more you do it, the better you get. Sharpening may feel cumbersome at first, but each time you sharpen, it will become easier until it will be fun to see how sharp you can get a tool. The key is practice, practice, practice.

Tip: *When to Sharpen*

When your tools are properly shaped and sharpened, it will take you very little time to keep them sharp.

All woods contain some natural abrasive materials, and as you carve, these abrasive materials will take off the ultrasharp edge to where you will need to go back to a stone from time to time. When your tools don't flow through the wood and don't leave a smooth, shiny surface where you cut, you need to put that razor-sharp edge back on the tool. Stropping will normally put it back on; but if it doesn't, go to your fine stone to reshape the blade and then to your strop, and you'll be back carving in very little time with a sharp tool.

Tip: *Test for Sharpness before Carving*

Before I begin a carving session, I select all the tools I will be using for that session and test each of them on a piece of wood similar to the type I'll be carving. Any tool that is not ultrasharp is sharpened. By doing this, I know that when I pick up any of the tools, they will cut the way I want them to. After all the tools are sharp, I wash my hands to get off any dirt or grime so I won't get my carving dirty—and I'm ready for a relaxing carving session.

Sharpening Straight-Edged Carving Knives

In this section, we'll look at evaluating and sharpening knives. You need to sharpen your knife when you first purchase it or if you nick or otherwise damage the blade. Under normal conditions, you won't have to go through the entire sharpening process every time your knife gets dull. If your knife has a good edge but seems dull, use your strop to hone the blade.

Evaluating the Blade

Before you begin sharpening your knife, determine what needs to be done. You can easily check the condition of the blade by doing a quick visual and physical check. If the answer to any of the following questions is no, your knife needs to be sharpened.

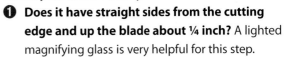
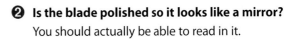

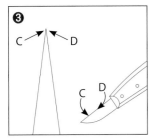

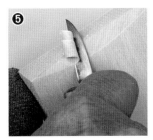

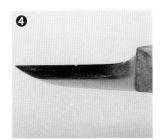

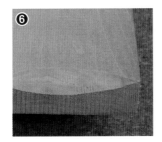

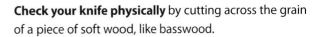

Check your knife visually.

❶ Does it have straight sides from the cutting edge and up the blade about ¼ inch? A lighted magnifying glass is very helpful for this step.

❷ Is the blade polished so it looks like a mirror? You should actually be able to read in it.

❸ Does it have a small secondary angle (called a microbevel), about the thickness of a fine hair, along the total cutting edge of the blade? To see the microbevel, tilt the blade back and forth in bright light, and look for a small reflection of light, about the thickness of a fine hair, on each side of the cutting edge of the blade.

❹ Is the cutting edge of the blade free from nicks or flat spots? A nick looks like a small sparkling diamond on the cutting edge. A flat spot looks like a shiny line. When your knife is sharp, you can't see the cutting edge.

Check your knife physically by cutting across the grain of a piece of soft wood, like basswood.

❺ Does it cut through the wood easily?

❻ Does it leave a smooth, shiny surface where you cut?

❼ Is the cut free of small lines? If you see any lines, the blade has a nick in it.

✓ Visualizing the Final Form

❑ Your knife should have straight sides from the cutting edge and up the blade about ¼ inch.

❑ The blade should be polished so it looks like a mirror.

❑ There should be a small secondary angle (called a microbevel), about the thickness of a fine hair, along both sides of the cutting edge.

❑ The two surfaces should meet at a single point.

❑ The knife should be so sharp you can't see the cutting edge.

❑ The blade should be properly contoured to minimize the metal mass going through wood.

❑ The blade should be polished to cut down the resistance of the blade going through wood.

❑ The blade should have a razor-sharp cutting edge to cleanly slice the wood fibers, leaving a smooth, shiny surface where you cut.

KNIFE RESCUE

Cutting a carving knife in half is not a practical way to determine whether your knife needs to be sharpened, but it is a good aid in visualizing the proper shape of a knife blade.

By cutting a knife blade in two, we can see the shape and bevel of the blade.

If you look into a cross section of the blade it should look like A. If your knife looks like B, you need to remove all the metal shown in red so it looks like A. Unfortunately, if your knife looks like B, no matter how sharp you get the cutting edge, the knife will not go through wood easily.

Think of your knife as nothing more than a sharp little wedge, and as the wedge goes through wood, it's displacing the wood. The more mass the blade has, the more wood must be displaced and the harder it is to drive the tool through wood. When a blade looks like B—even if it's sharp—it tends to tear the wood fibers before it cuts them.

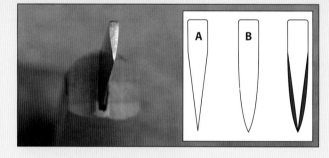

If you don't want to get rid of your knife, follow the knife sharpening techniques in this section with the following adaptations:

Lay the knife on the sharpening stone, as shown, with the apex of the high spot on the stone. *You need to remove all the metal in red to attain a flat surface on the blade.* When your knife is sharpened properly, it will be straight on both sides of the blade.

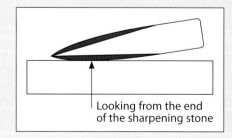

Looking from the end of the sharpening stone

Let's Sharpen

Before you begin, decide what grit of sharpening stone to use based on your evaluation of the blade. In the demonstration, I will start with a coarse stone and take you through the full sequence from shaping the knife to sharpening to stropping. You can start with any type of stone. I am using an oilstone. Please note that the instructions are given for a right-handed carver. Simply transpose the instructions if you are left-handed.

■ Use a coarse-grit stone to reshape a tool. (Don't use this unless the tool needs major work.)

■ Use a medium-grit stone for normal sharpening.

■ Use a fine-grit stone for slight tune-ups.

■ Use an extrafine-grit stone to prepare the blade for stropping.

1 Place the sharpening stone on a piece of nonskid material, and treat the surface of the stone accordingly in preparation to sharpen. If you use sandpaper, use it dry.

2 Lay your knife on the left end of the coarse sharpening stone, with the blade's cutting edge facing to the left (away from the direction you are going). Never run the cutting edge into the abrasive.

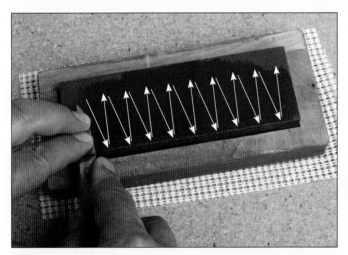

3 Hold the handle in your right hand, and place the first one or two fingers of your left hand on the blade. Pull and push the blade back and forth, using long sawing strokes, from the left to the right end of the stone.

Each sawing stroke should be about ⅛ inch apart. Keep enough pressure with your left-hand fingers to have control of the knife. The sawing motion keeps the blade in contact with the stone and removes metal with each stroke.

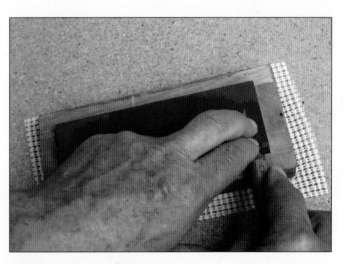

4 When you reach the right end of the stone, flip the blade over so the blade's cutting edge is facing to the right.

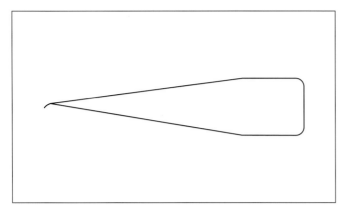

5 Repeat the same sawing motion from the right to the left end of the stone. Continue this sawing motion until the waste metal has been removed from both sides of the blade and the abrasions on the blade are uniform along the entire surface. A small burr should form along the entire cutting edge on one side of the blade. If you had a nick in the blade, the burr must go past the nick.

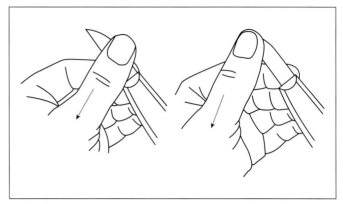

6 To test for a burr on the left side of the blade, hold the knife handle in your right hand, and turn the knife so the cutting edge of the blade is facing toward the palm of your left hand. Slide your left-hand thumb pad from the top of the blade down across the cutting edge, as shown. If a burr has formed, you will feel a drag on your thumb pad. **Caution:** Never run your thumb or fingers into the cutting edge.

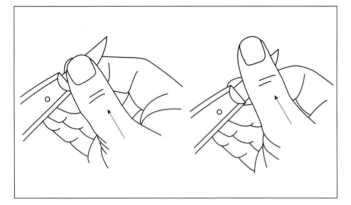

7 To test for a burr on the right side of the blade, hold the knife handle in your right hand, and turn the knife so the cutting edge of the blade is facing away from the palm of your left hand. Slide your left-hand thumb pad in the direction shown. Again, if a burr has formed, you will feel a drag on your thumb pad.

Troubleshooting

■ If you can't feel a burr on either side of the blade, continue the left-to-right, right-to-left sawing motion until you feel a burr.

■ If the burr is formed in one area on the blade and not another, you need to move your left-hand fingers over the area that does not have the burr and continue the left-to-right, right-to-left sawing motion until you have a burr along the total cutting edge.

8 When the blade is properly contoured, with straight sides, and a burr is formed along the total cutting edge, wipe the honing oil from the coarse stone and go to the next finer stone. Lay the blade flat on the surface of the finer stone. Using the sawing motion, work the blade across the stone until you have removed the coarse abrasions on both sides of the blade and left finer stone abrasions. Watch for the burr to roll from one side of the blade to the other in just a couple of strokes.

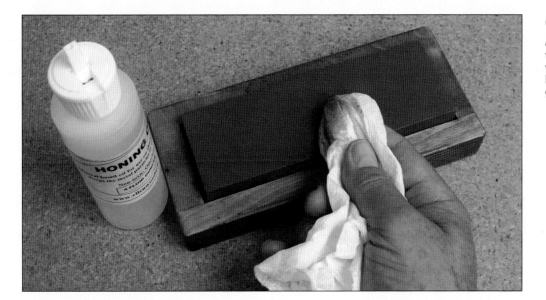

9 Wipe the surface of the finer stone with a soft cloth or paper towel to remove the fine metal particles that were abraded from the knife blade, and go to the next finer-grit medium.

10 With the finer-grit stone, start with the burr side down on the stone. If you were using an oilstone, you need to switch to a diamond stone, a water stone, an Arkansas stone, or sandpaper for the fine stone. When you've removed the abrasions left by the fine-grit stone and the burr flips from one side to the other with just a couple of sawing strokes, go to an extrafine stone and do the same procedure as with the other stones.

When both sides look polished, you're ready to strop. **Note:** It is important that the burr roll from one side of the blade to the other with just a couple of sawing strokes. This way, any remnants of a burr on the blade should fall off during stropping.

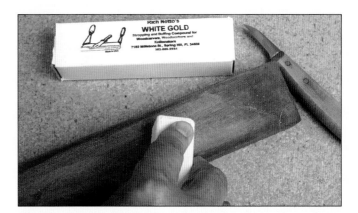

11 Rub honing compound onto your strop.

12 Lay your knife blade flat at the top end of the strop (with the blade's cutting edge facing the top). Never run the cutting edge of the blade into the leather. With your finger putting controlled pressure on the blade, pull your knife through the honing compound about eight to ten times. Keep the blade flat on the strop at all times during the stropping stroke. **Note:** Each time you reach the end of the pull, *raise the blade straight up* and move it back to the top end of the strop. *Never roll the blade when you come to the end of the strop.* If you roll the blade, you will round the blade. You want the blade to remain flat from the cutting edge to the top of the bevel.

13 After stropping the blade on that side, lay the other side of the knife blade at the bottom end of the strop (with the blade's cutting edge facing the bottom), and pull it through the honing compound about eight to ten times. Be sure to keep the blade flat on the strop through the entire stropping stroke.

14 Do a couple more light strops on both sides of the blade and you should be ready to carve. Your knife blade should be so polished that it looks like a mirror. This technique should also automatically form a small microbevel.

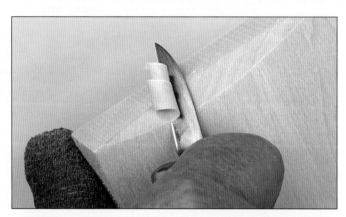

15 Wipe the blade clean with a soft cloth or paper towel, and wash your hands so you don't get metal filings, honing oil, or honing compound on the wood you will carve. Test your knife by cutting across the grain of a soft wood, like basswood. Your knife should flow through the wood easily and leave a smooth, shiny surface where you cut. Your knife should also be so sharp that you can cut a shaving thin enough to read through.

Troubleshooting

- If after sharpening, your knife doesn't flow through wood easily, tears the wood fibers, or leaves little lines in the wood, check to make sure you've removed the entire burr while stropping.

- If after stropping, it still doesn't cut properly, the microbevel is too wide, creating too much metal mass on the cutting edge of the blade. If the microbevel is wider than a fine hair, go back to your *fine* stone and sharpen the blade until the microbevel disappears. (You don't need to form a burr again.) Then, strop the blade again.

- If you nick the blade, you'll need to use the coarse stone to remove enough metal from the blade to where the nick has disappeared; then, go through the entire sharpening sequence.

- Over time, the abrasive properties in the wood take off the ultrasharp edge. If your knife doesn't leave a smooth, shiny surface where you cut, strop it again and the razor edge should be put back on.

Quick Ref: Sharpening Starters

If	Then
The blade has nicks or needs to be reshaped	Start with a coarse stone
The knife tears the wood fibers or does not cut smoothly	Start with a fine stone
The blade needs to keep an ultrasharp cutting edge	Strop
The knife cuts properly	Do nothing

KEEPING THE BLADE FLAT PRESERVES THE CONTOUR

If you always keep the blade flat on each of the sharpening mediums, the blade will always retain a shape that is easy to maintain. The blade will wear back, but it will always maintain the correct contour.

SHARPENING CURVED-BLADE CARVING KNIVES

Carving knives with a curved blade along the cutting edge are not as popular as those with a straight-edged blade, but many carvers prefer these tools. The sharpening technique differs just slightly.

 Evaluating the Blade

The same criteria used to determine what needed to be done to sharpen a straight-blade knife apply to the curved-blade knife (see page 105). Then, decide which stone you need to start with (see page 110).

 Visualizing the Final Form

❑ Your knife should have straight sides from the cutting edge and up the blade about ¼ inch.

❑ The blade should be polished so it looks like a mirror.

❑ There should be a small secondary angle (a microbevel), about the thickness of a fine hair, along the total cutting edge of the blade.

❑ The blade should be properly contoured to minimize the metal mass going through wood.

❑ The blade should be polished to cut down the resistance of the blade going through wood.

❑ The blade should have a razor-sharp cutting edge to cleanly slice the wood fibers, leaving a smooth, shiny surface where you cut.

Let's Sharpen

The only difference when sharpening a curved-blade knife is the motion you make across the sharpening stone.

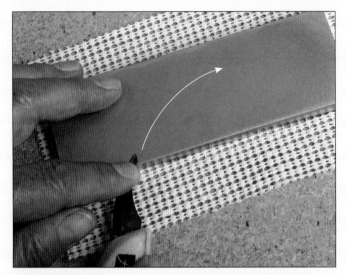

1 Lay the front end of the blade flat on the left end of the sharpening stone, with the cutting edge facing to the left. Hold the knife so you get straight sides from the cutting edge and up the blade about ¼ inch.

2 While holding the handle with your right hand, apply pressure to the blade with your left index finger in the direction of the arrow shown in Step 1. Slide the blade from the left end of the stone to the right end of the stone, following the contour of the blade.

3 Upon reaching the right end of the stone, lift the blade straight up from the stone, lay it again on the left end of the stone, and push the blade across the stone. Repeat four to five times. Turn the blade over and repeat the same process going from the right end of the stone to the left end of the stone. Always keep the cutting edge facing away from the direction you are going. Do four to five sliding strokes across the stone, on each side of the blade, until you've formed a small burr along the entire cutting edge on one side of the blade. Once the burr is formed, go to the next finer stone. Lay the burr side on the stone and repeat the same action until you've removed the abrasions left by the previous stone. Continue going to finer and finer stones until the blade is beginning to polish and the burr flips back and forth with just one sweep across the stone.

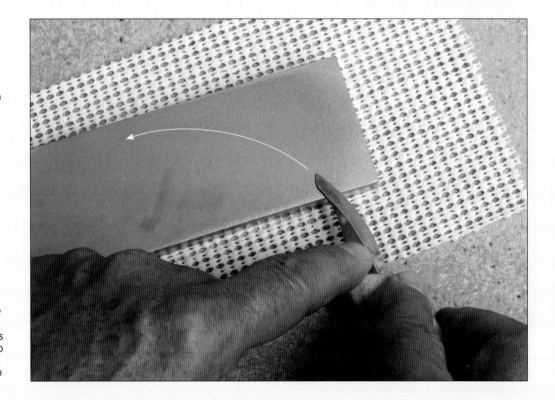

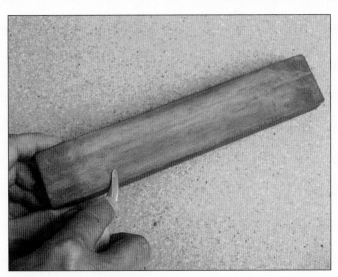

4 Load a strop with honing compound. Lay the knife so the flat surface, from the cutting edge back, is flat on the right end of the strop, with the blade's cutting edge facing to the right, and pull it from the right end to the left end of the strop. As you pull the knife across the strop, rotate the blade to follow the contour of the blade. Keep the knife blade flat as you pull it across the strop. Do this about eight to ten times on one side.

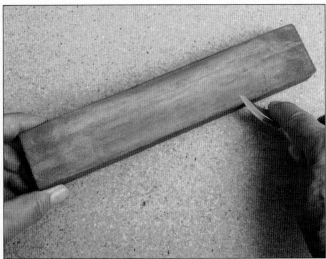

5 Flip the knife over and do the same procedure going from the left end to the right end of the strop. Give the knife a couple of light strops on each side of the blade. Test the knife by cutting across the grain on a piece of soft wood. If it cuts cleanly and leaves a smooth surface where you cut, you're back to carving. If it doesn't cut cleanly, you may need to strop some more or re-evaluate the blade edge (see Troubleshooting on page 110).

SHARPENING CHIP CARVING KNIVES

Normally, a chip carving knife is driven straight into the wood and then pulled straight back out of the wood to complete every cut. Because of this motion, the entire body of the tool supports the cutting edge, so you can apply a tremendous amount of pressure on the edge. To minimize the amount of wood displaced as the chip carving knife is driven into the wood, the blade of a chip carving tool is normally much thinner than that of a regular carving knife and has almost no microbevel. If you're doing conventional chip carving, never twist the blade through the wood.

 Evaluating the Blade

The same criteria used to determine what needed to be done to sharpen a straight-blade knife apply to the chip carving knife (see page 105). Then, make a decision about which grit sharpening stone to start with (see page 110).

 Visualizing the Final Form

❏ The blade should be shaped so it is straight from the cutting edge to the top of the blade.

❏ The blade should be polished like a mirror.

❏ There should be very little microbevel.

Let's Sharpen

If the blade needs major rework, start with a coarse stone to shape it, and then step through the sequence of finer and finer stones until it is properly sharpened. Use the same sawing motion that's used to sharpen a straight-edged carving knife. Once the blade is properly shaped and sharp, many chip carvers use white and black ceramic stones because they stay flat and are fine abrasives. An extrafine diamond stone, an extrafine water stone, or extrafine sandpaper glued to a flat surface also works well.

1 Lay the knife flat on the left end of the black ceramic stone, with the cutting edge facing to the left. Work the blade across the stone in a sawing motion. Keep the blade, from the cutting edge up to the back of the blade, flat on the stone. Continue the left-to-right, right-to-left sawing motion until the blade is polished on both sides.

2 Go to the white ceramic stone and continue the right-to-left and left-to-right sawing motion until the blade looks like a mirror.

3 For a strop, try cardboard from the back of a tablet or the inside of a cereal box because very little microbevel is needed. Load the strop with honing compound far enough so that you can strop the entire blade. Place the cardboard on a surface where the handle of the knife has clearance between it and the benchtop. Lay the blade flat on the strop, with the blade cutting edge facing away from the direction you will go, and pull it from one end to the other, keeping it flat at all times. Repeat this motion about six to eight times on both sides until the blade is highly polished.

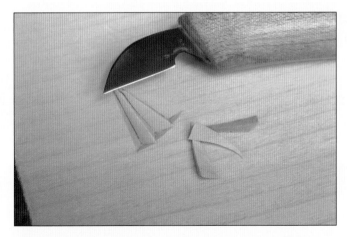

4 Wipe the blade clean with a soft rag, and test the knife by doing some chip carving in soft wood.

SHARPENING GOUGES AND VEINERS

Gouges are one of the most used carving tools. The sharper they are, the more enjoyable carving will be. The keys to getting your gouge properly shaped and sharp are knowing what it should look like to make that optimum cut and then implementing a simple and repeatable process to achieve that end result.

Evaluating the Blade

❶ Gouges and veiners have one of three different shapes along their cutting edge:

- **A. Nose out slightly across the cutting edge.** If you do relief carving, you may want to sharpen a couple of gouges with this shape, where you slope the wings back from the nose of the tool. This shape allows you to cut all the fibers up to a vertical stop cut.
- **B. Flat across the cutting edge with slight rounding at the edge of the wings.** This allows a little latitude before the wings dip under the wood, but it does not cut cleanly in tight corner areas.
- **C. Flat across the cutting edge from wing to wing.** This shape is the most popular because it allows you to get into tight corners. Strive to sharpen most of your tools like this.

❷ A properly sharpened gouge or veiner must be flat from toe to heel, with a cutting angle of about 23 degrees. It should look like *A*. A tool shaped like *B* (rounded from toe to heel) requires you to raise the handle to an uncomfortable angle before the cutting edge enters the wood. If the face of the tool looks like *B*, you need to remove all the metal, shown in red on *C*. Angle *D* is too blunt and requires you to raise the handle of the tool to an uncomfortable level before it enters the wood. It needs to be shaped to look like *A*.

❸ To test if the angle is correct, fold a sheet of paper into the shape of a triangle—you have 45 degrees. Fold it again—you have 22½ degrees. This is the approximate angle you want on all your gouges and veiners.

❹ Set a gouge or veiner on a piece of wood with the paper you folded to 22½ degrees between the wood and the tool. The tool should want to cut into the wood. If you need to raise the handle higher than the paper, the angle on the face of the tool is too blunt and needs to be reshaped to about 23 degrees.

❺ Another way to evaluate the condition of your tool is to check the cutting edge. If yours looks like the tool on the right, the angle on the face of the tool is too blunt, which forces you to raise the handle to an uncomfortable angle before the tool enters the wood.

❻ If the angle from toe to heel looks good, but when you set the tool on the wood, it slides across the surface until you raise the handle, there's a good chance the area from toe to heel is rounded like *B*.

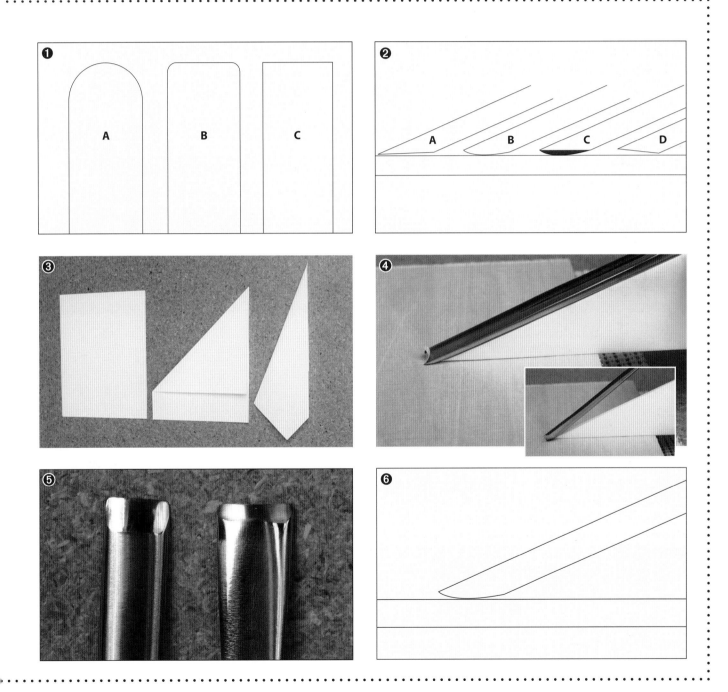

✔️ Visualizing the Final Form

Whatever shape you have along the cutting edge of the blade, your objectives are as follows:

❑ The blade must be flat from toe to heel with a cutting angle of about 23 degrees.

❑ There should be a microbevel on the inside of the blade.

❑ The blade should be polished to look like a mirror.

Quick Ref: Do a Visual Check

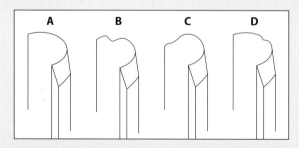

If	Then
Looks okay (A)	Make a test cut
Wavy cutting edge (B)	Major rework
Corner missing (C)	Major rework
Nick (D)	Major rework

Quick Ref: Do a Test Cut

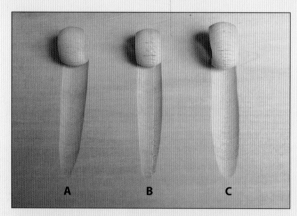

If	Then
Shiny, smooth cut (A)	No action needed
Leaves line(s) (B)	Nick(s) in the blade; major rework (start with the coarse stone)
Dull or slow cut (C)	Minor repair (start with a fine stone)

If you have a tool that is deformed or nicked, the fastest way to correct the problem is to remove metal from the cutting edge until the deformity or the nick is gone; then, start the sharpening process.

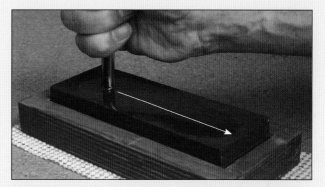

2 Pull the tool toward you to remove the metal from the cutting surface. This is scary the first time you do it, but it is the best and fastest way to remove the deformity. Continue to set the tool at the top end of the stone and pull it to the bottom end until the deformity has disappeared. Holding the tool so the concave surface is toward you removes metal from the cutting edge of the tool and forms a burr on the outside of the tool. It is easier to remove a burr from the outside of the tool than from the inside of the tool. This a simple rule, but one that saves you time in the sharpening process.

1 To remove metal, lay a coarse sharpening stone vertically along the edge of your work surface on nonskid material. Prepare a coarse-grit stone for tools larger than ¼ inch wide or a medium-grit stone for smaller-width tools. Hold the tool vertically, at about a 90-degree angle from the surface of the stone, with the concave side facing toward you.

3 If you want to shape the tool so the wings are back from the toe of the tool, lay the tool on the stone, as shown, with the handle at about a 23-degree angle from the face of the tool. Pull the tool across the surface of the stone until you have it shaped the way you want it. You need to set the tool at the top of the stone and pull it toward you a number of times until it is shaped correctly.

Let's Sharpen

If your tool needs major work, the width of the blade will determine which stone you'll use to start the sharpening sequence. For a tool wider than ¼ inch, start with a coarse stone. If the tool is ¼ inch or smaller, start with a fine stone. Start by placing a coarse stone on nonskid material, and treat it for sharpening (see page 123 if you're sharpening a tool larger than one inch).

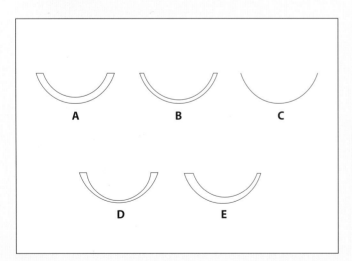

1 Approach the center of the sharpening stone with your gouge as if you were going to carve the stone. This angle should be about 23 degrees. Lock your wrist. As you sharpen, the radius and ulna bones in your arm rotate, but your wrist should remain still. You'll be amazed how well this works to maintain the sharpening angle. Place the first two fingers of your left hand on the inside of the tool to maintain controlled pressure on the tool as you rotate it across the stone.

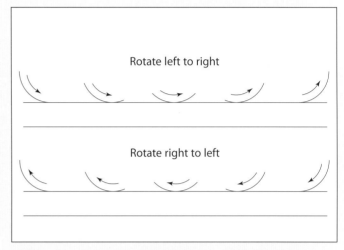

Rotate left to right

Rotate right to left

2 You should maintain the same 23-degree angle from the toe to the heel across the total blade from wing to wing.

A   B   C

D   E

3 After a few passes across the stone, look to see where you're abrading the surface of the blade. If you're abrading more in one area than another, concentrate your effort on the area that needs more attention. As you sharpen a tool, it's important to reduce the metal thickness at the same rate across the total cutting edge of the tool, as shown with *A*, *B*, and *C*. If you don't reduce the metal thickness evenly, you'll have a tendency to deform the tool again as you sharpen, as shown with *D* and *E*.

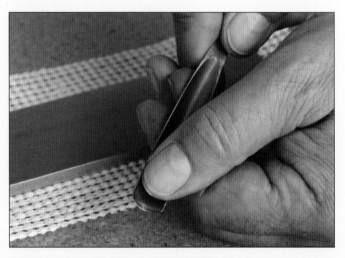

4 Continue to evenly reduce the metal thickness until you have formed a small burr along the total inside cutting edge of the blade. To test to see if you have a burr formed, slide your thumb or a finger from the handle side across the cutting edge of the blade. Never run your thumb or finger into the cutting edge.

5 When you've formed a burr along the cutting edge of the blade, you need to roll the burr to the other side of the cutting edge. You can use a slip stone to accomplish this.

6 Wet/dry sandpaper that is 600 grit also works well. Wrap the sandpaper around a dowel that is the same diameter as the inside of the tool.

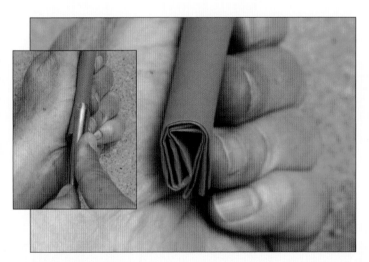

7 Or contour the sandpaper to fit the inside contour of the tool. Keep the blade flat on the surface of the sandpaper (or slip stone) and pull the tool across the abrasive until you can no longer feel the burr.

8 If you feel more comfortable using the sandpaper on a dowel, get dowels to fit the inside of each of your gouges.

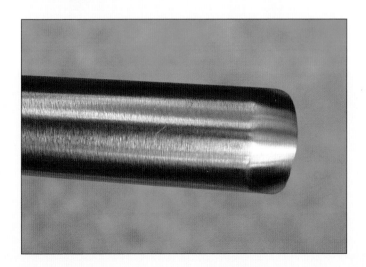

9 You can now start the actual sharpening process by removing the aggressive abrasions, plus begin to make the cutting edge ultrathin so it flows through wood with minimal effort. Prepare a medium-grit stone and do the same process you used with the coarse stone:
- Establish the proper angle of the tool on the sharpening stone (23 degrees).
- Lock your wrist.
- Slide the tool across the surface of the stone, following the contour of the tool.

Continue this until you have once again rolled the burr back to the inside of the blade and removed the major abrasions on the blade surface. (The face of the tool should have the same pattern of abrasion. If you see deep abrasions intermixed with the finer abrasions, stay with this stone until you have all finer abrasions across the face of the tool.)

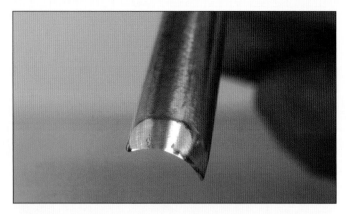

10 Roll the burr from the inside of the tool to the outside of the tool again by using the 600-grit wet/dry sandpaper, as in Steps 5 through 8. Go to your finest-grit stone, or fine sandpaper attached to a flat surface, and do the same procedure as in Steps 1 through 3. Your tool surface, from the toe to the heel, should now begin to look polished, and the burr should flip back and forth with just a couple of passes across the stone and the slip stone.

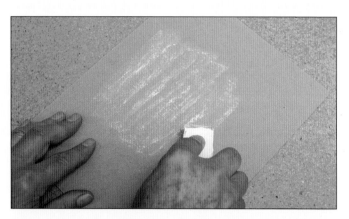

11 Load the cardboard strop with honing compound. Because I want the face area of the blade, from toe to heel, to remain perfectly flat, I use cardboard rather than leather for my strop. The cardboard is flat and firm and strops the blade without changing the outside contour of the tool. It also helps me put a microbevel only on the inside of the tool.

12 Place the tool at the top of the cardboard. Maintaining the proper angle (23 degrees), slide the tool from side to side while rotating it to follow the contour of the tool. Notice the metal that was removed as the tool was moved back and forth across the cardboard strop from the top to the bottom of the strop.

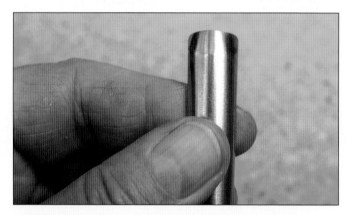

13 Do this process from top to bottom, maintaining the 23-degree angle, until the blade looks like a mirror. By starting at the top of the strop and working the tool to the bottom, you never run the cutting edge of the tool into the abrasive. Each stroke is sharpening the tool.

14 To strop the inside of the gouge or veiner, conform the cardboard to the inside contour of the tool, raise the handle slightly, and pull the tool across the loaded cardboard. This process polishes the inside of the cutting surface and puts a small microbevel on the inside of the tool.

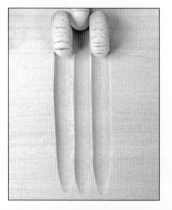

15 Test the tool for sharpness by cutting across the grain on a piece of soft wood, like basswood. The tool should begin to cut immediately when it touches the wood, flow easily through the wood, make a curl of the wood it cuts, and leave a smooth, shiny surface where you cut, with the area between cuts intact.

Troubleshooting

If the wood tears, the tool is not sharp enough and may require more stropping.

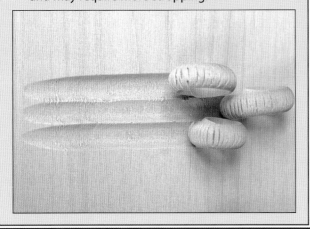

You may have read or heard that you should put one angle on the cutting edge of your chisels, gouges, veiners, and V-tools when you carve soft wood and another angle when you carve hard wood. The theory says that as you drive a tool through wood, soft wood will not put as much stress on your tools as hard wood. I use about a 23-degree angle on the blades of my chisels, gouges, veiners, and V-tools for all woods I carve. Rather than changing angles every time I change woods, I use this angle because it works well for all woods. You will see how I achieve this angle as we sharpen each type of tool.

SHARPENING LARGE- OR SMALL-SIZE TOOLS

When sharpening a gouge greater than 1 inch (25 mm) wide, it is many times easier to sharpen it in small segments as you move the blade across the stone. Move the blade back and forth in small segments as you slowly rotate the tool across its total sweep. By doing this, you have much more control than if you try to move the tool from wing to wing in one sweep.

When sharpening a small tool (less than ¼ inch from wing to wing), *never use a coarse stone*. The less metal there is in a tool, the finer-grit stone you should use—even if the tool needs major repair. A coarse stone removes metal too rapidly, and you can easily deform your small-width tool. The coarsest stone I ever use on my narrow tools is not more than 300 grit. (Remember, the smaller the grit number, the coarser the grit.)

When removing a burr from a very narrow gouge or veiner, such as ⅛ or ¹⁄₁₆ inch wide, fold the 600-grit sandpaper to fit the inside of the tool.

To strop a very narrow gouge or veiner, rub honing compound around the edge of the cardboard strop, and lay the tool over the edge to strop.

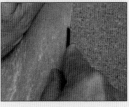

The beauty about using sandpaper and cardboard in sharpening gouges and veiners is that one size fits all. You can conform sandpaper and cardboard to the inside contour of any gouge or veiner. You don't need a number of different slip stones in your sharpening kit. All you need is one sheet of 600-grit sandpaper and a piece of cardboard.

SHARPENING FLAT CHISELS

Flat chisels are not used as often as many of your other tools, but they must be sharp to give you control of any cut you make. The flat chisel most used is a flat skew. Learning how to sharpen a flat chisel is a good precursor to sharpening V-tools.

 Evaluating the Cutting Edge

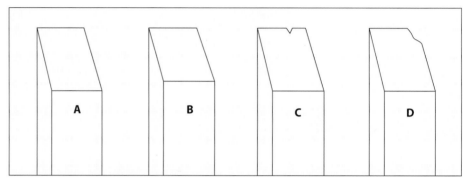

Check the condition of the chisel visually. A lighted magnifying lamp helps you to view the cutting edge.

- The tool should look like *A*.
- If the edge is blunt (*B*), it will not go into wood easily, and you will need to reshape the cutting angle, from the toe to the heel, to about 23 degrees.
- A nick (*C*) looks like a small sparkling diamond. To remove the nick, place the cutting edge vertically on the top side of a stone and pull it toward you until the nick disappears. (Use the same process as you do to shape gouges and veiners, see page 119.) Then, go through the complete sharpening process.
- An uneven edge (*D*) needs major repair. To shape the cutting edge, do the same procedure that is done to remove a nick.

 Visualizing the Final Form

- ❏ The cutting edge should be 90 degrees from the side of the blade.
- ❏ The cutting edge should be straight across from wing to wing.
- ❏ The cutting edge should have a cutting angle from the toe to the heel of about 23 degrees.

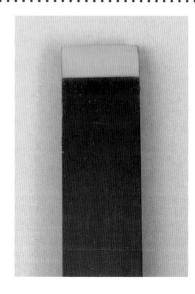

If the tool needs major repair, approach the stone at an angle as if you were going to carve it. (This is normally about a 23-degree angle.) Upon establishing the proper angle on the stone, lock your wrists so you maintain that angle while sharpening.

With your right hand holding the handle and your first two fingers of your left hand controlling pressure on the blade, move the blade across the stone in a figure-eight motion. Doing the figure eight uses the stone's entire surface while sharpening and minimizes the potential of creating a hollowing in your oilstones or water stones.

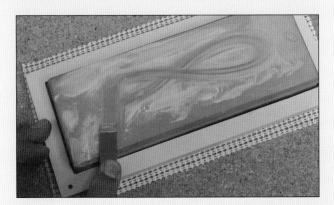

As you slide the tool across the surface of the stone, your wrists on both of your arms should remain locked and your arms should swing like a pendulum. After a few figure-eight strokes, look at the surface you are sharpening to see if you are removing metal evenly across the total surface of the tool.

If you're removing more metal from one side of the cutting edge than the other, move your fingers over the area that needs more metal removed. I check the surface from toe to heel often to make sure I'm removing metal evenly.

Continue the figure-eight sharpening motion until you've formed a burr along the total cutting edge of the blade. Test for a burr by running your thumb or finger from the handle side of the blade across the cutting edge. **Caution:** Never run your thumb or finger into the cutting edge.

When you've formed a small burr along the total cutting edge of the tool, turn the blade over and lay it flat on the stone. Pull the tool toward you until the burr flips back toward the beveled side of the tool. Upon achieving this, go to your next finer stone.

SHARPENING SKEW CHISELS

Use the same criteria to evaluate the skew as you did the flat chisel (see page 124).

To sharpen skew chisels, use the same process you use with the flat chisel (see page 126), but keep the edge of the blade parallel to the top of the stone as you sharpen and on the top of the strop as you strop. I find by keeping the cutting edge parallel to the edge of the stone and the strop, it is easier to keep the proper skew angle across the cutting edge of the tool as you sharpen.

Sharpen a double-bevel skew the same as you do the regular skew, except maintain the angle on both sides of the tool.

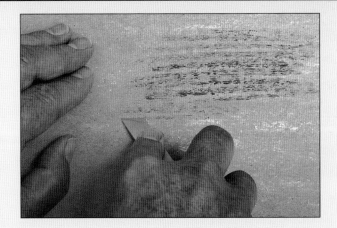

Let's Sharpen

If the tool doesn't need major repair because of a blunt cutting edge, nicks, or an uneven edge, the best test is to cut across grain on a piece of soft wood, like basswood. If it cuts but leaves the fibers torn, start with a medium grit. If it cuts but doesn't leave a smooth surface where you cut, start with a fine stone. Then, go to the extrafine for final preparation before stropping.

1 Lay the face of the tool on the finer stone at the proper angle (about 23 degrees), and do the figure-eight motions again to remove the coarse abrasions made by the coarse stone if you had to do major repair work (see Tool Rescue on page 125) and to make the metal thin at the cutting edge of the blade. This also, once again, rolls the burr over to the outside of the blade.

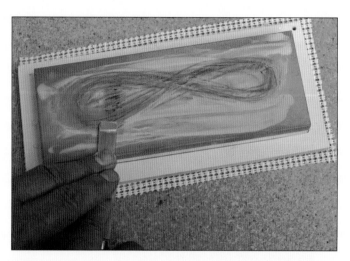

2 Lay the flat side of the blade on the stone and pull it across the stone to flip the burr back. Go to your finest stone and do the same sequence again. The face of the tool should begin to get polished, and the burr should have fallen off or should flip back and forth with just a pass across the stone. Pull the flat side across the stone.

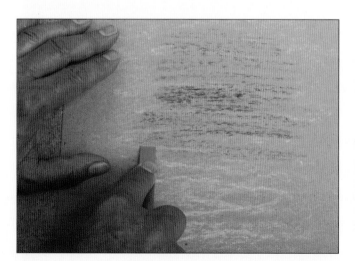

3 Rub some honing compound on a piece of cardboard. Place the face of the tool flat on the strop, and slide the tool from side to side through the honing compound from the top of the strop to the bottom of the strop. This should remove any remnants of a burr and polish the face of the tool so you can read in it. (As you strop, maintain the 23-degree angle on the tool.)

4 Test the tool by cutting across the grain on the edge of a soft wood board, such as basswood. Once properly sharpened, if the tool gets dull from carving, all you should need to do is strop with the honing compound on cardboard. If it gets a nick or a flat spot, shape the cutting edge and go through the entire sharpening process.

SHARPENING V-TOOLS

V-tools are one of the more difficult carving tools to sharpen because of their shape and the various angles you need to deal with when sharpening. You'll find it much easier to sharpen a V-tool if you think of it as being three tools in one: two flat chisels and a small gouge. Each wing is a flat chisel, and the bottom cutting surface is a small gouge.

✔ Evaluating the Cutting Edge

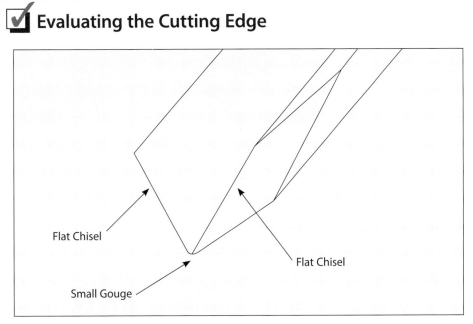

Flat Chisel

Flat Chisel

Small Gouge

To determine if any sharpening is required, evaluate the V-tool physically and visually.

If the tool's cutting edges look good and have the proper cutting angles, test the tool by cutting across the grain on a piece of soft wood, like basswood. Does it:

- Slice through the wood and leave a smooth, shiny surface where you cut? If it does, you're ready to carve.
- Go through the wood, but doesn't leave a smooth, shiny surface where it cut? It needs stropping.
- Leave a little line or lines in the wood? If it leaves a line in the wood, the tool has a nick or nicks in the cutting edge of the blade. Go to your fine stone to remove the nick. Take out any burrs from the inside with your slip stone and then strop.
- Tear the wood at the bottom of the V? Work the little gouge section on your fine stone. Clean up the inside with your slip stone and then strop.

✓ Visualizing the Final Form

When a V-tool is properly sharpened, it has the following characteristics:

❑ Each of the wings is straight from the gouge portion to the top of the wing.

❑ The gouge portion is blended into each wing.

❑ The angle from the toe to the heel on both wings, and the gouge, is about 23 degrees.

❑ The wings and the gouge are polished to look like a mirror.

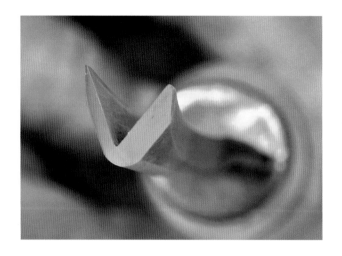

You can sharpen a V-tool with three different shapes on the cutting edge.

Wings at a 90-degree angle from the bottom of the blade. This is the most common way V-tools are sharpened and is the shape most tools have when you buy them.

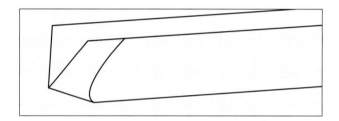

Wings sloping back from the bottom of the tool. If you sharpen like this, the angle should slope back about 23 degrees.

This is a useful angle if you do much relief carving because it allows you to cut flush up to a vertical stop cut. The blade meets square with the face of the vertical stop cut.

A is sharpened with the cutting edge 90 degrees to the bottom of the tool. You can see that when the wings hit the top of the stop cut, the bottom is not near it. The wood will not be cut cleanly up to the stop cut. *B* has the wings back about 23 degrees from the bottom of the tool. This shape allows you to cut flush up to a stop cut.

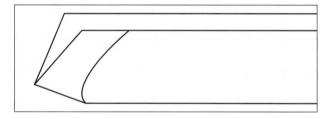

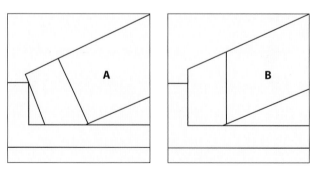

Wings sloping forward from the bottom of the tool. This angle is helpful when making decorative cuts. This contour is used less than the others.

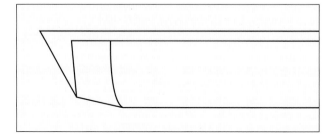

Let's Sharpen

Take your time when sharpening a V-tool. Check the surface you're sharpening often to see if you're abrading it evenly across the entire surface. Sharpen in sequence: flat chisel, flat chisel, small gouge. A V-tool is one of the most difficult tools to sharpen, and the smaller the V-tool, the more difficult it is. Don't rush, and it will be well worth the effort.

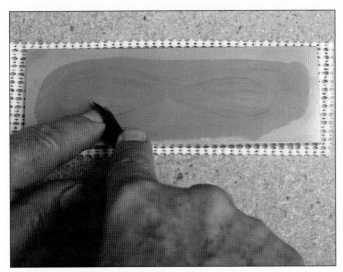

1 If the tool needs sharpening, lay the left wing on a fine-grit sharpening stone at about a 23-degree angle. Holding the handle in your right hand, place the first finger on your left hand inside the wing that is on the stone. Move the tool across the stone with the same figure-eight motion you use to sharpen a flat chisel (see page 126).

2 Check the wing you're sharpening often to make sure you are abrading evenly across the total surface. Sharpen this wing until you have a burr formed along the total cutting edge.

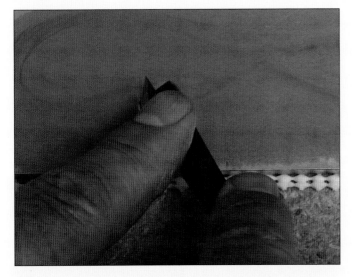

3 When a burr is formed along the total cutting edge, lay the other wing on the stone. Place your fingers on top of the wing that is off the stone. You must be extra careful as you sharpen this wing because you will not have as much control as when you had your finger inside the tool on the wing. Again, check often to see where you're removing metal. You want to remove metal evenly along the total surface of the wing, like on the flat chisel.

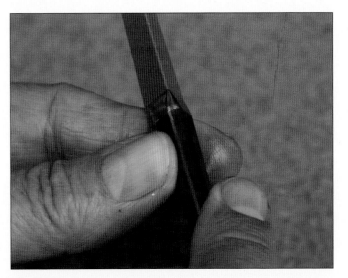

4 When you have a burr along the total cutting edge on both wings, remove it from the inside of your V-tool with a slip stone. If the angle is 60 degrees or greater, I use an India taper triangle slip stone.

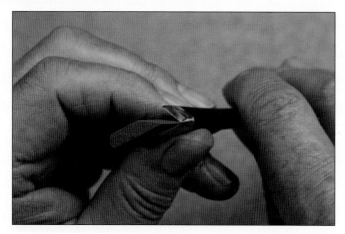

5 If the angle is less than 60 degrees, I use a tight taper shape stone.

6 Lay the tool flat on the slip stone. Apply pressure on one side of the tool and pull it across the slip stone to pull the burr out from the inside of the tool on that wing.

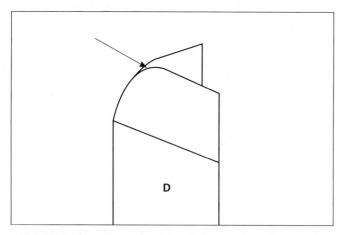

D

7 Do the same on the other wing until you have the burrs pulled from the inside of the tool on both wings. Remember, it's important to keep the tool flat on the slip stone as you remove the burrs. If the tool handle is raised as you pull the tool across the slip stone, you can abrade metal from the gouge portion and end up with your tool looking like a D.

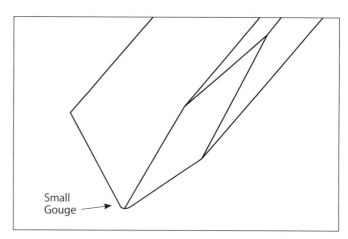

Small Gouge

8 Carefully sharpen the small gouge at the bottom of the V and blend it into the wings. Sharpen this small gouge the same way you do any gouge (see page 120), but carefully blend the gouge into the flat chisel on both sides of the tool.

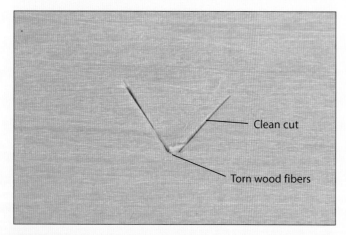

Clean cut

Torn wood fibers

9 I find the best way to see where you may need to focus your sharpening efforts is to place the V-tool vertically on a piece of soft wood and push the cutting edge into the wood. You'll see where it may be tearing the wood and where it is cleanly cutting the wood fibers.

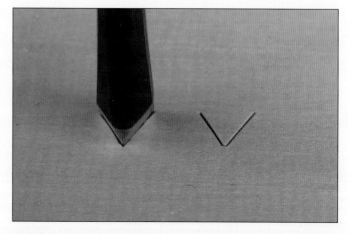

10 Any area where the fibers tear is where you need to concentrate your sharpening efforts. If the tool is sharp along the total cutting edge, it makes a cut like this.

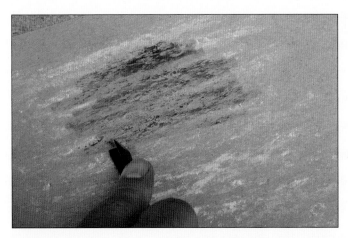

11 When your tool is properly shaped and begins to cut wood easily, go to your strop to put on the ultrasharp edge. I use cardboard for my strop. Load the strop with honing compound and strop each wing the way you strop a flat chisel (see page 126).

12 Strop the bottom of the V as you would a small gouge (see page 122).

13 For the inside of the tool, rub honing compound on the edge of the cardboard. Lay the inside of one of the wings over the edge, raise the handle slightly, and pull the tool through the honing compound.

14 Turn the tool around and do the same with the other wing. By having the honing compound up to the edge of the cardboard, as you strop, it simultaneously strops the insides of the wings and the inside of the small gouge.

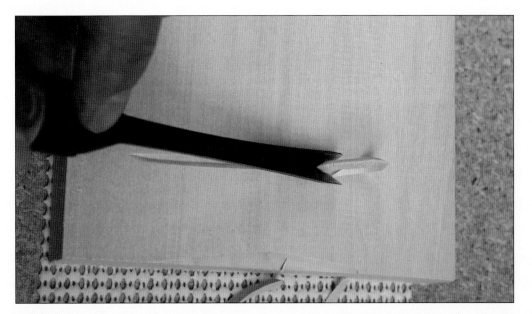

15 Test the tool by cutting across the grain on some soft wood. Also test each wing by dipping the tool from side to side while you cut through the wood. If the tool cuts cleanly, you're ready to carve.

A. The angle is greater than 23 degrees from the toe to the heel. If the tool doesn't cut properly, or you need to raise the handle at a high angle before it begins to cut, the angle from the toe to the heel is incorrect. To correct this problem, reshape each of the wings and the gouge portion so the angle from toe to heel is 23 degrees on each of the wings and the gouge portion. Use a coarse stone to shape the tool, and then go through the complete sharpening process to put on the razor edge.

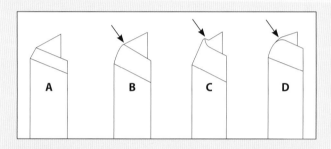

B. The bottom of the small gouge portion has multiple angles. This problem is easy to fix and makes a world of difference for carving. Don't try to reshape the tool and blend the gouge portion with the flat chisels in one operation. This is an area of the tool that can very quickly be deformed. Do this procedure in four steps:

1. Get the proper contour established from toe to heel on the small gouge portion, as shown in the illustration.
2. Blend one side of the small gouge with one flat chisel.
3. Blend the other side of the small gouge with the other flat chisel.
4. Using an India taper triangle or slip stone, remove burrs that may have been formed on the inside of the tool, and then use a cardboard strop.

Use a fine sharpening stone to correct this problem because you want to remove metal very slowly. Remember, approach the sharpening stone as if you are going to carve it. With just a slight side-to-side motion, remove the abrupt angle and form the correct angle from the toe to the heel of the tool.

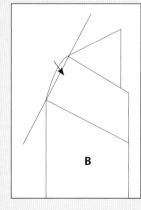

Use light pressure on the tool, just enough to have control of the tool. Make a couple of passes across the stone, and then check that you're beginning to straighten the angle. It is important to check this often because all you want is to straighten the angle from the toe to the heel. If you take off too much metal, you can abrade the small gouge portion and create a problem like *D*. Once you have the proper angle established, blend each side of the small gouge with the flat chisels.

C. The small gouge portion has a protruding point. This normally occurs when you don't remove enough metal from the gouge portion as you sharpen. If the protrusion is not too large, it can be corrected by simply removing metal from the bottom of the gouge portion of the tool. Carefully remove this metal until this area is parallel with each of the wings. Do this slowly and remove burrs from the inside of the V often.

If this procedure doesn't work, place the protrusion vertically on the sharpening stone and pull the tool toward you until the protrusion is gone and the gouge portion is even with each of the wings. Then, contour the gouge portion the same way you do in correcting *B*. Remove any burrs often with a slip stone.

D. The best way to correct this problem is to place the tool vertically on a stone (the same way you remove nicks or straighten a blade, as described on page 119) and remove metal from each of the wings until the tool is properly shaped. As you do this, remove any burrs from inside the tool often. When a burr forms on the cutting edge, the metal rolls over, making the metal at that area look thicker than it actually is.

Once the tool is properly shaped along the cutting edge, follow the sharpening procedure (see Let's Sharpen on page 129). It is not unusual to have one of the wings slope back more than the other on a V-tool. It's aesthetically nicer to have both wings straight with one another, but if this deformity is not too bad, it will not pose a problem for most carving. If it is a problem, follow the instructions for *D*.

SHARPENING MICRO TOOLS

Micro tools have very little metal at the cutting edge and can be ruined quickly if sharpened with a coarse stone. I almost exclusively sharpen my micro tools by just using a cardboard strop loaded with white honing compound. The only time my micro tools see a sharpening stone is if they need to be reshaped, and then the coarsest stone I use is 600 grit.

 ## Evaluating the Cutting Edge

Micro tools are just small versions of any of your other tools. Do the same physical and visual tests as you would on any of your larger tools.

 ## Visualizing the Final Form

- ❏ Flat chisels should be flat from wing to wing.
- ❏ Gouges should have two wings that look the same. One should not be set back from the other.
- ❏ V-tools should have both wings and the little gouge portion on the same plane. The little gouge portion should not be abraded away.

Let's Sharpen

The best way to determine if you need to do any sharpening is to cut across the grain on some soft wood, like basswood. Each tool should flow through the wood and form a little ringlet of wood where you cut. If it doesn't do this, it needs sharpening.

Flat Chisels or Skews

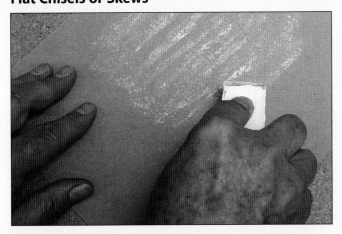

1 Load a portion of the strop from top to bottom with honing compound. I use white honing compound for all my micro tools. That way, as I pull the tool through the compound, I can see a track where metal is being removed. If the track is the full width of the tool, I know the total width of the tool is being sharpened.

2 Lay the face of the tool flat at the top end of the cardboard (with the handle raised about 20 to 23 degrees), and pull the tool through the honing compound. Look for the track of the tool in the honing compound. Check that you're seeing the total width of the tool in the honing compound. If you don't, rotate the tool so the total width is being stropped. Turn the flat tool over and do the other side.

Gouges

1 Load an area of the cardboard with honing compound. Lay the face of the tool on the cardboard and establish the proper cutting angle of the tool on the cardboard strop. Move the gouge back and forth through the honing compound, while rotating the tool in your fingers. This sharpens the outside of the gouge.

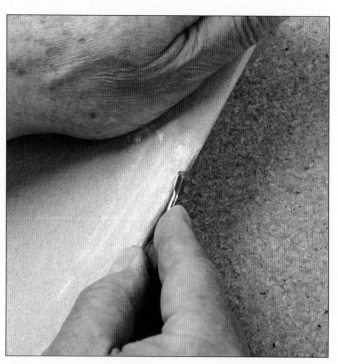

2 To strop the inside of the gouge, load an area of the cardboard with honing compound and fold the cardboard to fit the inside contour of the gouge.

3 For very small micro gouges, rub honing compound around the edge of the cardboard.

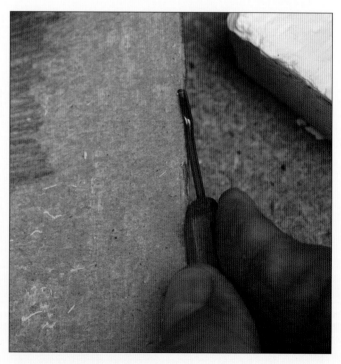

4 Place the inside of the tool over the cardboard and pull it through the honing compound.

V-Tools

 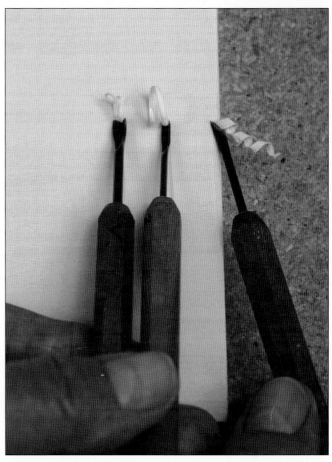

1 Sharpen the outside of each wing as you would a flat chisel (see page 126) and the gouge portion as you would a gouge (see page 120). For the inside, rub honing compound along one edge of the cardboard strop. Lay one of the wings over the edge of the cardboard and pull the inside of the tool through the compound. Lay the inside of the other wing over the cardboard and pull that one through the compound.

2 When your micro tools are sharp, they should flow easily across the grain, making little ringlets of wood as they cut.

CORRECTING MAJOR PROBLEMS

If the cutting edge on any of your micro tools gets damaged, you need to correct the problem by using a sharpening stone. Remember to use only a fine stone, about 600 grit, because coarse stones can ruin a micro tool quickly. If the tool is chipped or has a nick, remove the deformity using the same technique you do for larger tools. Place the cutting edge on the stone at a 90-degree angle from the stone's surface, and pull the tool from the top of the stone to the bottom until the deformity has disappeared; then, shape the face of the cutting edge to the 20- to 23-degree angle. As you're shaping the tool, check often to make sure you're removing metal evenly across the total cutting edge. Once the tool is shaped, remove any burr from the inside of the tool using 600-grit sandpaper; then, use about a 1000-grit stone or sandpaper, and begin to polish the face of the tool. Remove any burrs again and go to your cardboard strop.

Flat Chisels and V-tools

Repairing a deformity in flat chisels or V-tools requires special treatment. Use the same technique as with a gouge, where you set the cutting edge on the stone and pull the tool across the stone until the deformity is removed (see page 119). When you've removed the deformity, you now need to shape these small blades, and that creates the problem. The blades are so narrow on these tools that it is almost impossible to "feel" the shape of the blade on a stone. You can see the blade's track in honing compound, but the tool doesn't leave a track on a sharpening stone.

There are two methods you can use to shape these tools.

> *" If the cutting edge on any of your micro tools gets damaged, you need to correct the problem by using a sharpening stone. "*

Method 1

Flat chisel or skew: Lay the tool on a fine stone, establish the proper 23-degree angle, and then pull and push the tool slowly, and carefully, to remove the waste metal. Keep the cutting edge parallel to the top of the stone.

Check often to see where you're abrading and make sure the abrasions are evenly across the total face of the tool. When the tool is shaped and you've formed a small burr across the total cutting edge, flip the tool over. Lay the tool flat on the stone and pull the tool to flip the burr to the other side of the tool. Go to a 1000-grit stone and do the same push/pull motion. This begins to polish the blade and flip the burr back to the other side. Flip the burr back to the other side and then go to your cardboard strop. Load the strop and pull the tool through the honing compound.

V-tool: A V-tool is two flat chisels and a small gouge. Use the same technique as you do with a flat chisel for both of the wings (see above method used for flat chisel). When you've shaped and formed a burr on one of the wings, use your India taper triangle to pull the burr from the inside to the outside of the tool. Do the same with the other wing. Carefully shape the small gouge and again pull the burr out from the inside of the tool. Go to the extrafine stone and do the same sequence, with the final step on the cardboard strop.

Method 2 (For Flat Surfaces Only)

Hold the tool stationary and slide the stone across the stationary tool. This procedure allows you to see where you're abrading on every stroke across the tool.

Gouges

If a micro tool gouge needs to be shaped, use the same technique used with larger gouges (see page 123), but never use a stone coarser than 600 grit. Once you have the tool shaped, use cardboard to sharpen it.

Using Power Sharpeners

A number of power sharpeners are available to assist you in shaping and sharpening your carving tools. The key word is "assist." Don't think you can place a tool on a power sharpener and it automatically becomes sharp. Like most things we do, there is a learning curve. Learn how to correctly use the power sharpener, because if you don't, it can ruin a tool quickly.

Power sharpeners can assist you in sharpening your carving tools as long as you learn to use them correctly.

The most important step is to know what the tool you're going to sharpen should look like when it's properly sharpened, and then take your time to achieve that end result. Going through the previous sections, learning how to sharpen your tools by hand, and learning what the properly sharpened tools should look and feel like will be useful even if you decide to use a power sharpener.

In addition to sharpening machines, many different types and shapes of wheels and disks are available as attachments for a standard power grinder to strop your tools. These wheels and disks are available in felt, leather, muslin, and cotton. Whatever material they're made of, they are nothing more than binders to hold honing compound to strop your tools. You can also find some that can be attached to your drill or drill press. If you power strop using a converted grinder or drill, be aware that it is capable of rounding the cutting edge of your tools very quickly. Most grinders spin at about 3500 rpm. If you replace the grinding wheel with a stropping wheel, which is just one foot in circumference, the wheel is traveling at a speed of about 58 feet per second. Lay a tool on the strop for only one second, and it is like pulling it across a strop that is 58 feet long.

If the cutting edge gets rounded, no matter how sharp it may be, there will be too much metal mass to efficiently

"Learn how to correctly use the power sharpener, because if you don't, it can ruin a tool quickly."

drive the tool through wood. Remember, a tool is nothing more than a sharp little wedge, and the more metal at the cutting edge of the wedge, the more difficult it is to drive it through wood. When stropping, what you want to achieve is to polish the blade, put on a razor-sharp edge, and develop a microbevel no thicker than a fine hair. If you accomplish the first two and get the microbevel too wide, you've defeated your purpose in stropping.

Whatever type of power sharpening or stropping you may do, use a light touch. Don't ever let your tool get hot enough to lose the temper. If you ever see the metal change color at the cutting edge of the tool, you've lost the temper, and until you remove the metal past the spot that turned color, that area of the tool will not hold a sharp edge. Take your time and don't let the tool get hot.

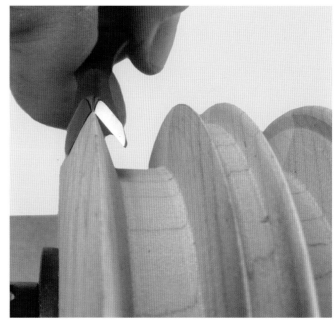

Use a light touch when sharpening or stropping your tools. It's easy to ruin a tool quickly with a power sharpener.

Let's Sharpen

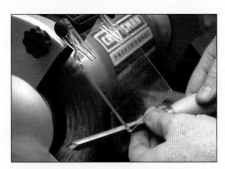

1 With a much-abused tool, the first step is to remove rust and grime using a wire wheel.

2 Square up the edge and remove nicks on a coarse wheel, frequently cooling the tool in water.

3 Wire brushing, buffing, and stropping take place on the part of the wheel that travels away from the tool, not toward it.

4 The tool rest should be very close to the wheel.

5 An edge that is not square to its sides will wander out of control.

6 An out-of-square plane iron will be difficult to adjust and may carve a track in the work.

Photos courtesy *Woodworker's Guide to Sharpening,* by John English, 2008, Fox Chapel Publishing, Inc.

Chapter Seven

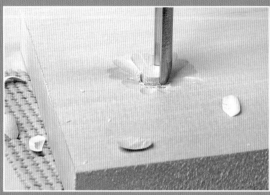

TOOL PRACTICE

Get to know your tools, and they'll become your best friends.

Carving isn't just removing pieces of wood. You also need to know what your tools can and cannot do, and then apply the right tool in the right situation. Sounds complicated, doesn't it? It doesn't have to be. Start by learning the basic cuts for your favorite tools and how to properly work with the grain of the wood. Soon you'll find that no carving is beyond your capability.

Every cut you make should have a specific purpose. If you don't know what you want to accomplish with a specific cut, don't make it until you know what you want to achieve. Take time and learn with each cut you make.

Let's take a look at knives, gouges, V-tools, and chip carving tools individually. We will study the basic cuts, and then I'll present some exercises that will give you a bit of practice. Remember: Keep focused on developing good habits and safe practices as you work your way through this chapter.

Knife Cuts

Most of your hand carving work will likely be done with a carving knife. Master these basic cuts; they are the foundation of any carving project.

Pull Cut and Push Cut

You must learn at least two primary cuts to work proficiently with your carving knife. These cuts, the pull cut and the push cut, will be used time and again as you carve. Before you start, put on a carving glove and thumb guard. Even when wearing protective gear, never put your hands or fingers in a location where they could be cut.

Exercise #1: The Pull Cut

The first cut we'll do is the pull cut, the cut most often made with a carving knife. It is sometimes called a paring cut because the knife is held as if you were paring an apple. **Note:** Use the muscles in your hand to pull the knife through the wood because you'll have more control over the knife, making the cut far safer.

1 Place the knife in your hand with the cutting edge facing your thumb.

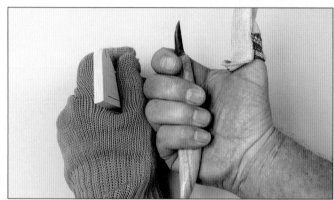

2 Wrap your fingers around the handle.

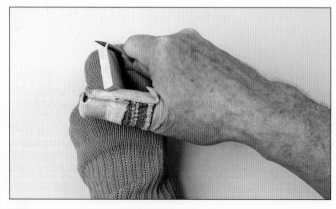

3 Set the blade at the beginning of the place where you want to remove wood. Make sure your thumb is in a safe location near where you want the blade to exit the wood.

4 Pull the knife through the wood with your hand muscles by closing your hand.

Exercise #2: The Push Cut

The other cut you make with a knife is a push cut. Making this cut may feel somewhat uncomfortable at first, but it's a very useful cut that gives a high degree of knife control.

Note: I've removed my glove and thumb guard only so you can better see how my hands are placed on the knife.

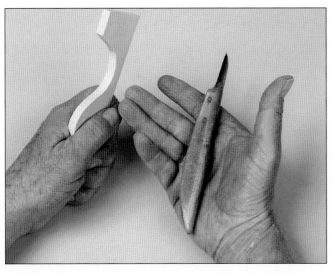

1 Place the knife in your hand with the blade's cutting edge facing away from your thumb.

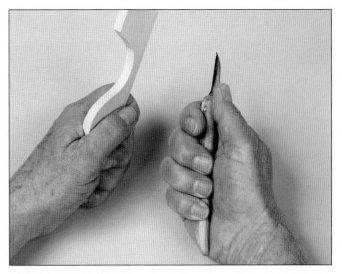

2 Wrap your hand around the handle and place your thumb on the back of the blade.

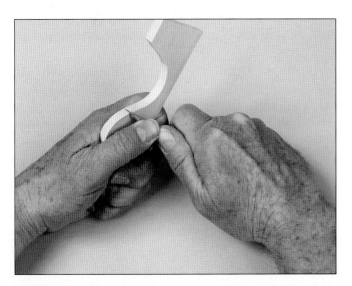

3 Hold the object you're carving in your left hand and place your left-hand thumb next to your right-hand thumb.

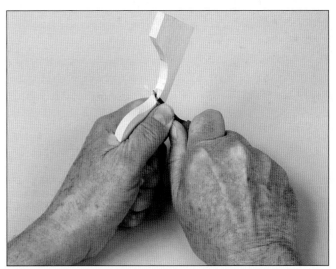

4 Using your left-hand thumb as a fulcrum, push the blade through the wood by pulling back with your right hand and wrist.

Exercise #3: A Lesson on Grain

Whether using a pull cut or a push cut, always cut so your knife blade does not have the opportunity to go between the vessels (the grain) of the wood. Remember, because the blade of a carving tool is shaped like a thin wedge, the wedge tends to go between the vessels. Then, the walls of the vessels tear apart and the wood splits with the grain.

The line on the piece in the photographs that follow shows the direction of the grain. Visualize how the vessels run through this piece of wood and what direction you need to cut so the tool is never given the opportunity to go between vessels. If a carving tool wants to go between the vessels, stop and make the cut from the other direction so you're always cutting across the vessels.

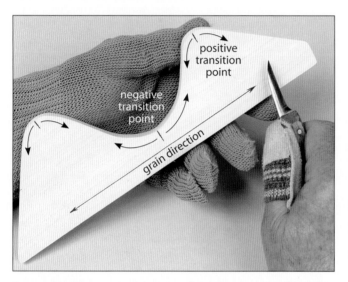

I've cut this piece at an angle across the grain to expose the ends of the vessels.

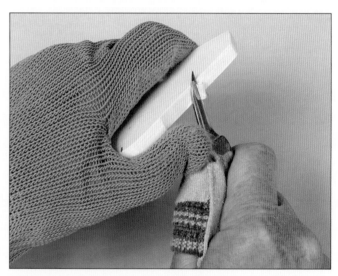

If you always *cut across* the exposed ends of the vessels, you'll get a clean, controlled cut. The result should be a smooth, shiny surface.

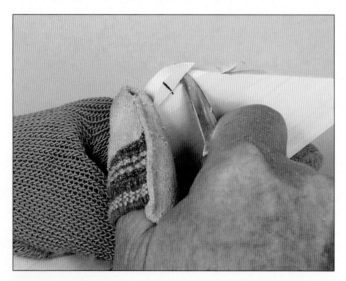

If you *cut into* the exposed ends of the vessels, the knife will attempt to take the path of least resistance and go between the vessels, causing the piece to split or tear. When that happens, you've lost control of the cut.

Tip: *Finding the Grain*

If you can't see the direction of the grain in a piece of wood, lightly pull your knife into the wood to cut it. If your knife wants to go between vessels, you're cutting the wrong direction and need to cut the other direction.

Exercise #4: Negative and Positive Transition Points

There are also what I call "negative and positive transition points" in wood. A transition point is where you need to change the direction you cut so the cutting edge of your tool cannot go between the vessels. You cut toward a negative transition point to get clean cuts; you cut away from a positive transition point to get clean cuts. If you attempt to continue the cut when you reach the negative transition point, you will start cutting into the exposed ends of the vessels and your knife will try to go between them.

Notice how I used a pull cut toward the negative transition point on one side and a push cut toward it from the other side. By using a different cut, I didn't need to turn the piece around to make the second cut.

I've cut this piece to create negative and positive transition points. Every carving will have a number of negative and positive transition points.

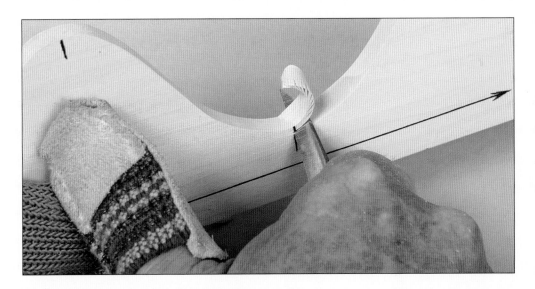

1 Make a clean cut by coming down toward the negative transition point. This will give you a clean, controlled cut across the grain up to the transition point. When you reach the negative transition point from this direction, the knife will attempt to go between the grain. You now need to cut from the other direction to the negative transition point so your knife is never given an opportunity to go between the grain.

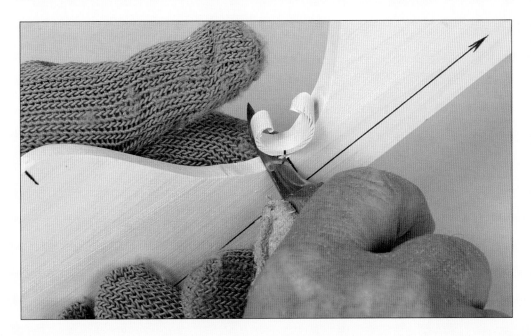

2 At this point, you have reached the negative transition point and need to cut from the other direction so your knife continues to cut across the vessels. Use a push cut to cut from the center of the indentation down toward the bottom of the indentation.

STRENGTH IN SPLITTING

If you want maximum strength in a thin piece of wood, split it with the grain. To make the golf club shaft, I split a piece of wood from a straight-grained scrap piece of wood and then formed it into the shaft. This procedure ensures that all of the vessels are aligned and running parallel to one another, which gives maximum strength to the piece of wood. This method is called a controlled split.

CONTROLLED SPLIT

You'll not use this cut often, but it can be helpful if you want to remove wood quickly or achieve maximum strength in a piece of wood you're going to carve.

You already know that if a wedge-shaped object is given the opportunity to go between the vessels in a piece of wood, the wood will split. You can use this phenomenon to your advantage, if you know which direction the vessels run through the wood.

Do a thin test cut to make sure the piece will split in the direction you want. If it splits properly, you can then do a controlled split to remove large amounts of wood quickly.

Another time you'll use a controlled split is if you want to carve something where you need the strength of long vessels running parallel through a piece. To achieve this,

> *" You'll not use this cut often, but it can be helpful if you want to remove wood quickly or achieve maximum strength in a piece of wood you're going to carve. "*

select a piece of wood that has straight grain. Clamp the piece and split it using an old knife or a gouge with a shallow sweep. Move the tool over slightly more than the thickness of the piece you want the long vessels running through. Split this off. The piece you split off will have long vessels running through the entire piece, giving it maximum strength.

After splitting the wood, remove any fibers that are loose and, using normal controlled cuts, shape the piece into the desired object.

STOP CUT

A stop cut is made when you want to remove wood only up to a certain point. It's a way of controlling a cut. You can make a stop cut with any tool that severs the wood fibers; knives, V-tools, and even saws make excellent stop cuts. The process is the same for any tool. The depth of the stop cut is determined by how much wood you want to remove at that specific area. The more wood you want to remove, the deeper the stop cut needs to be. If you need a deep stop cut, make several passes.

When you cut up to a stop cut, all the wood fibers should be cut so the waste wood falls out. If all the fibers are not cut, don't try to tear out the piece using your carving tool. If you try to tear out the piece, two things will happen:

1. You'll end up with "fuzzies" because the wood fibers were torn rather than cut.
2. You will be prying with your carving tool. Never pry with a carving tool. Prying can damage the cutting edge.

If the waste wood doesn't fall out, make a light cut to sever all the fibers so the waste wood will fall out.

PERFECT STOP CUTS

How a tool is shaped makes a big difference in how the tool cuts up to a stop cut.

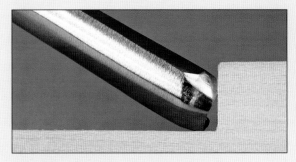

Imperfect: If the cutting edge of the tool is shaped to 90 degrees from the bottom of the tool, it will not cut up to a vertical stop cut, leaving the finished cut looking like figure *A*.

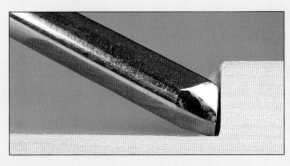

Perfect: If you want the tool to cut flush with the vertical stop cut, the tops of the wings need to be shaped back about 23 degrees from the bottom of the tool. This angle allows the tool to cut flush with the vertical stop cut, like figure *B*.

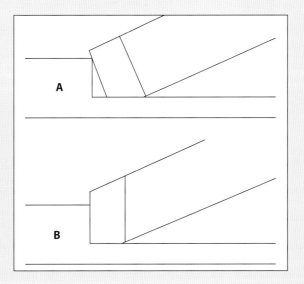

Exercise #5: Making a Stop Cut

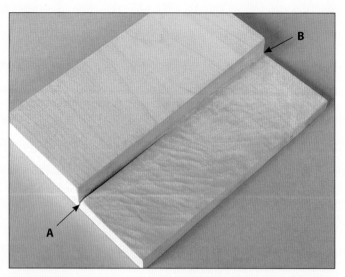

1 Hold the knife the way you hold a pencil. Press down on the knife with your index finger and pull the blade through the wood. To help sink the blade into the wood, add pressure to the blade with the first and second fingers of your left hand.

2 When the stop cut is the proper depth and wood is removed up to it, it should look like *B*. If the stop cut is too deep, it will look like *A*. The stop cut and the wood removed up to it should meet cleanly.

STRONG AND WEAK POINTS

To slice through wood, your carving tools must have almost invisible thin cutting edges that make them ultrasharp. Being thin at the cutting edge makes a knife fragile and vulnerable to breaking if improperly used.

Strong: If you drive a tool straight into and out of the wood, you have the total metal mass behind the blade protecting the cutting edge. With this cutting technique, you can apply a tremendous amount of pressure to the cutting edge without it breaking.

Weak: However, if you pry with the tool, there is nothing protecting the thin, fragile cutting edge, and it can easily be broken.

Prying wood out at the end of a cut is a very easy habit to get into, and it's one of the quickest ways to dull your tools. If you make a cut and the piece doesn't fall out, don't pry it out. Go back and cut all the fibers so the waste piece is free to fall out on its own.

Exercise #6: Keeping Wood from Splitting

When you make a stop cut, remember that your tool is nothing more than a sharp wedge you're driving into the wood, and it's displacing the wood it's going through. If you make a stop cut near the edge of a piece of wood, or near another stop cut, the wood being displaced will take the path of least resistance and probably split. If a split were to occur in a piece you're carving, it could detract from or possibly ruin the carving. Here's an easy way to prevent this from happening.

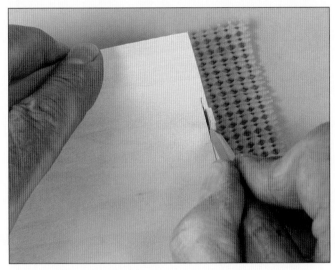

1 Draw a line about ⅛ inch parallel with the edge of a board and make a stop cut with your knife straight into the wood. Because your knife is displacing the wood it's going through, the wood will take the path of least resistance and normally break apart at its weakest point.

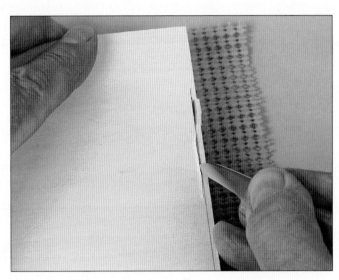

2 If you want to minimize the chance of the wood breaking apart, tilt the handle of the knife over the narrow piece you want to save and make a stop cut. By tilting the handle over the piece you want to save, you've given that area more mass than that in the waste area. The wood will take the path of least resistance and split away into the waste area, leaving the area you want to save intact.

3 Remove the wood from the waste area. Repeat these steps until the stop cut is as deep as you want it.

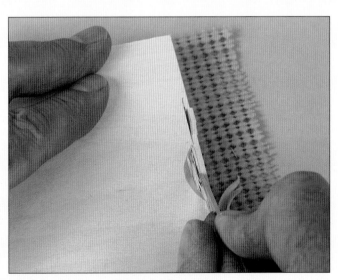

4 Make thin shaving cuts, keeping the knife handle parallel to the edge of the board. Remove sheets of wood that are thinner than the wood you want to save, leaving the piece you want to save intact.

As with a hand tool, holding a power tool correctly is key to making a clean, controlled cut. First, take a look at how the bit is spinning. It should always turn so the wood being removed is coming toward you. This rotation allows you to see the cut as it's being made and gives you good control of the tool.

Second, check your fingers. Depending on the type of cut you're making, either your thumb or little finger should be in contact with the wood at all times. There are two basic grips used for power carving.

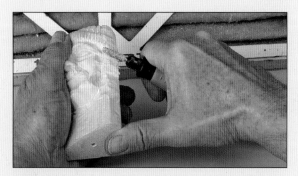

Paring grip: This grip is used when roughing out a carving. Hold the power carver the same way you hold a carving knife when you do a pull cut. Place your thumb in a position on the wood where you pull the cutter toward it, and then pull the tool through the wood by closing your hand. This cut is mostly used to remove large amounts of wood.

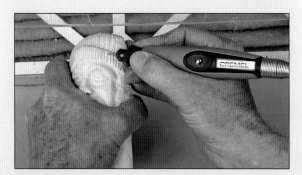

Pencil grip: This grip gives you the most control while carving and allows you to carve as if you were writing with a pencil. Place your thumb and pointer finger on the sides of the tool, and your middle finger under the tool. Rest your little finger on the wood to control the tool as you use a stroking motion to remove wood.

Exercise #7: Making Long Cuts

This simple exercise is an excellent project for developing knife control.

1 Draw a lazy S on the surface of a board. Set the tip of your knife about ¹⁄₁₆ inch from the line, and tilt the handle about 60 degrees away from the line. Sink the tip of the blade into the wood until it is under the lazy S line. Make a pull cut through the wood from one end of the line to the other, keeping the same distance, angle, and depth throughout the cut. When you get to the end of the S, let the knife rise out of the wood.

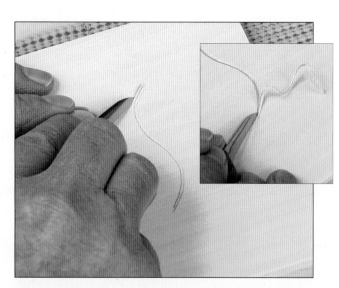

2 Turn the knife over and do the same type of cut about ¹⁄₁₆ inch from the other side of the line. Your goal is to make the piece fall out intact, with the S line through the center of the piece you removed.

Gouge and V-Tool Cuts

Sometimes, using a carving knife may not be the most efficient way to make a cut. At these times, you'll want to turn to your gouges and V-tools.

Palm Tools

There are two ways to hold a palm tool as you carve.

Exercise #1: Holding a Palm Tool

In this first method for holding a palm tool, the handle of the tool lies in the palm of your hand with your pointer finger on the blade pointing toward the cutting edge. Drive the tool through the wood by pushing it with the palm of your hand. You will use this same grip whether you hold the piece you are carving or you place the wood in a vise.

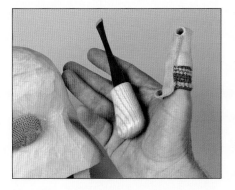

1 Lay the tool in the palm of your hand with the cutting edge facing away from you.

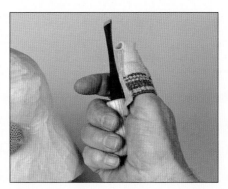

2 Wrap the last three fingers on that hand around the handle.

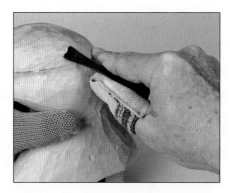

3 Lay your pointer finger on top of the blade and your thumb on the side of the blade.

Exercise #2: Holding a Palm Tool, Variation

In this second method, the palm tool is facing you, and the back-and-forth motion of your wrist removes the wood. These two grips are used like pull cuts and push cuts with a knife. Rather than turning the carving around, you can change grips on the tool to get the blade direction you want.

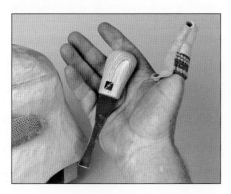

1 Lay the palm tool in your hand with the cutting edge facing toward you.

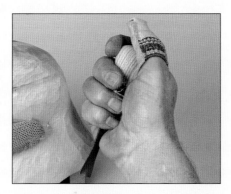

2 Lay your pointer finger across the top of the handle and your thumb on the face side of the handle.

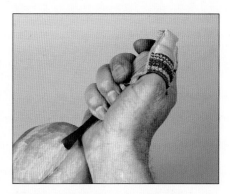

3 Lay the side of your hand pad on the wood, and drive the tool through the wood using your wrist to create a shearing action.

Long-Handled Tools

You can hold a long-handled tool in one of two ways.

Exercise #3: Holding a Long-Handled Tool

The only difference between this grip and how you hold a palm tool is that the handle of the long-handled tool lies across the palm of your hand rather than being in the palm of your hand. If you were to place the end of a long-handled tool in the palm of your hand, you would not have good control because the cutting edge would be too far away from your hand. To have control of the tool, it's important to have your hand near the cutting edge. When you are holding a piece of wood in your hand, place the knuckle of your pointer finger on the wood as you drive the tool through the wood.

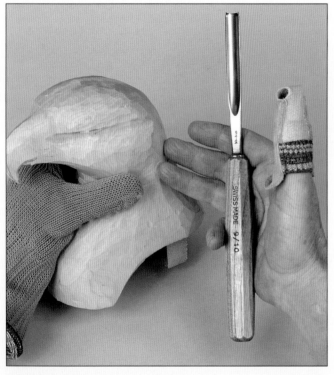

1 Lay the tool in your hand with the cutting edge of the blade facing away from you.

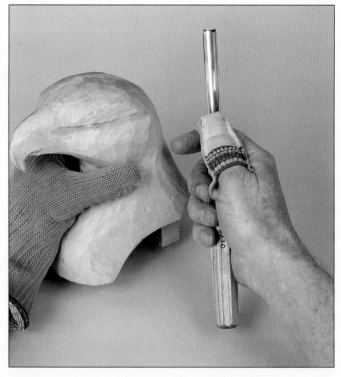

2 Wrap your fingers around the tool as shown, with your thumb on the top of the blade.

Exercise #4: Holding a Long-Handled Tool, Variation

In this alternate method, the cutting edge of the tool faces you, and the motion of your wrist removes the wood.

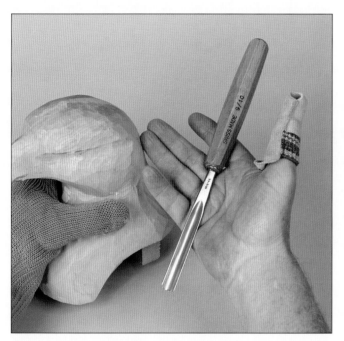

1 Lay the tool in the palm of your hand with the cutting edge facing you.

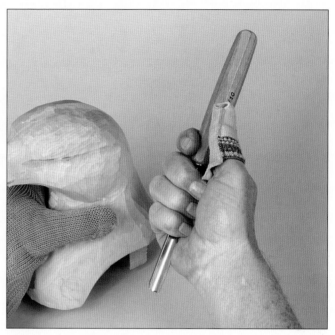

2 Wrap your fingers around the shank of the tool with your thumb pointing up and pressing down on the tool. (Normally, your thumb is on the ferrule.)

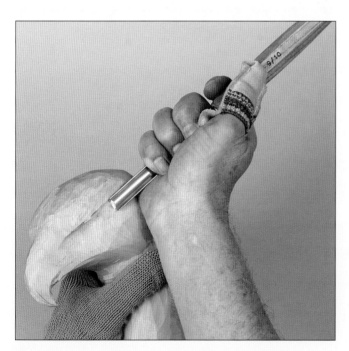

3 Carve by laying the side of your hand on the wood, and remove the waste wood by using wrist motion to push the tool through the wood.

Exercise #5: Holding a Long-Handled Tool, Stationary Piece

If you're right-handed, your right hand is the driver hand and your left hand is the control hand.
If you're left-handed, your left hand is the driver hand and your right hand is the control hand. These
instructions are for right-handed carvers. **Note:** If you're following a line for any distance, the pad of
your left hand will slide across the work surface, or you will reposition the pad about every half-inch.

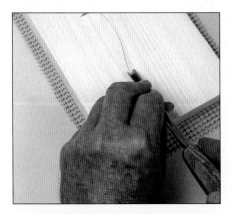

1 Wrap your left hand around the tool near the cutting edge.

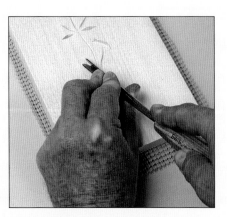

2 You can also place your fingers on the top of the tool with your thumb under the tool.

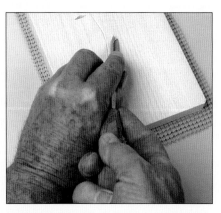

3 Position the tool handle in the palm of your right hand, with your pointer finger facing the cutting edge and your thumb on the side of the handle with the rest of your fingers wrapped around the handle. As you carve, the pad of your left hand rests on the work surface.

Exercise #6: Long-Handled Tool Practice, V-Tool

When carving, practice holding your tools in one hand, and then in the other hand.
If you can become ambidextrous using your gouges, veiners, and V-tools, it will save
you time. If, for example, you're carving on the right side of a carving with your right
hand and want to carve something on the left side, you can simply switch hands
rather than physically moving to the left side.

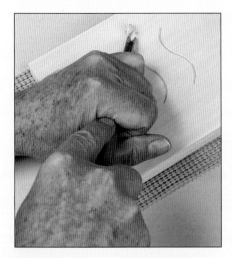

1 Draw a lazy S on a board. With your V-tool, remove the line in one intact piece with the line down the middle of the piece you removed. (It should look similar to the one you did with your knife on page 150.)

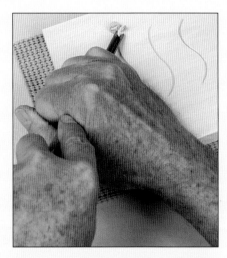

2 Draw another lazy S. If you removed the previous line with your right hand, put the tool in your left hand and remove the line.

Exercise #7: Another Practice Cut

This exercise will show you the difference in how a tool feels cutting across the grain and with the grain.

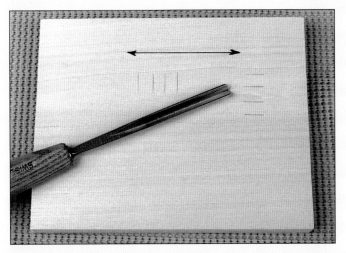

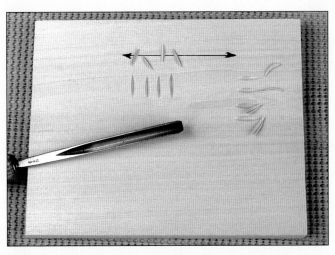

1 Draw four lines, each about ¾ inch long, across the grain and four with the grain. The arrow shows the direction of the grain in this piece of wood.

2 Set your V-tool at the end of one of the across-the-grain lines, and push it into the wood, with the line in the middle of the cut. As you push the tool through the wood, about halfway through the cut, continue to push the tool forward and slowly drop the handle down toward the surface of the board, and push the tool out of the wood. You should remove a sliver of wood the length of the line, with the line in the middle of the sliver. Repeat this for each of the across-the-grain cuts. Now remove the lines running parallel with the grain, just as you did those running across the grain.

I'm sure you noticed that the lines running parallel to the grain were more difficult to remove. When you cut the lines across the grain, you were cutting across the vessels both on the way in and out of the wood. However, when you cut the lines parallel to the grain, you were cutting across the vessels toward a negative transition point as the tool was going into the wood. When you had cut as deep as you wanted and started to push the tool out of the wood, it didn't want to come out easily. You had reached the negative transition point, and as you attempted to push the tool out of the wood, it wanted to take the path of least resistance and run between the vessels. You were then cutting away from the negative transition point. Cutting across the grain, your tool never had the opportunity to go between vessels because it was always cutting across them. When the tool was cutting parallel to the grain, it had the opportunity to go between the vessels because the vessels were parallel to the tool.

Exercise #8: V-Tool Flower

This intriguing project will show you the versatility of the V-tool.

1 Draw five lines, each about ¾ inches long, at the top end of the board. These mark where each of the flower petals will be carved. Make your cut starting in the center of the flower and move toward the outside. Push the tool into the wood, with the line in the middle of the cut.

2 About halfway through the cut, slowly drop the handle toward the surface of the board, and push the tool out to remove a sliver of wood. Repeat this process for each of the lines you have drawn, being extra careful with the line running parallel to the grain.

3 Draw a lazy S for the stem from the middle of the bottom two cuts, down about three inches. Remove the line with your V-tool, as you did with the practice cut earlier (see page 154). Keep the cut shallow.

4 About halfway up the right side of the stem, make the first leaf. Set your V-tool near the stem and begin making a cut by pushing the tool into the wood.

5 As you push the tool into the wood, rotate it clockwise, and as you continue pushing the tool forward, rotate it back to the level position and push it out of the wood. You've made a leaf on the right side of the stem.

6 Do the same procedure on the left side of the stem, but this time rotate the tool counterclockwise.

7 Make a few small in-and-out cuts at the base of the stem to simulate grass. These cuts are similar to the petal cuts in Steps 1 and 2.

8 You've made your first carving. Don't forget to sign and date it.

Exercise #9: Gouge Practice, Circle

In this exercise, you'll carve a circle and round off the surface. Remember that all gouges are a segment of a circle and the circle's radius is determined by the sweep and width of the tool. If you want to carve something round, you can use this gouge characteristic to your advantage.

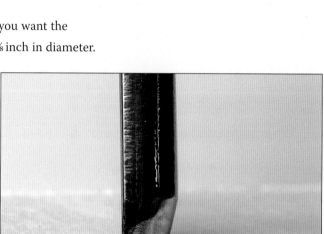

As you work your way through the steps, you'll make stop cuts with the gouge and learn to use the gouge facing up and facing down. See the Flower Relief Carving project on page 224 for an example of a finished work that includes this technique.

To start, select a gouge with a sweep that will make the width you want the circle to be. I will use a ⅜ inch (10 mm) #9, so the circle will be ⅜ inch in diameter.

1 Tilt the handle of the gouge over the piece of wood where you want the circle to be and sink the gouge into the wood to make a stop cut.

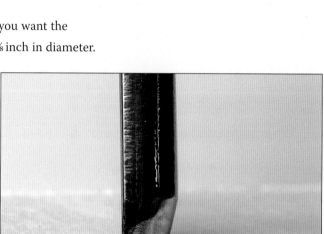

2 Tilt the tool so the front of one wing comes out of the wood to expose about one-third of the cutting edge. Keep the wing out of the wood, and with the rest of the blade remaining in the wood, slide the blade forward about half the radius of the tool and sink the tool back into the wood. Continue this process until you've completed a circle.

3 Remove the wood from around the circle by holding the gouge handle in your right hand and wrapping your left hand around the blade, with the pad of this hand resting on the wood.

4 Carefully push the tool into the wood up to the stop cut; then, move the handle from side to side to cut the wood from around the radius. Do Steps 1 through 4 again until you have removed wood about ¼-inch deep from around the button you've made.

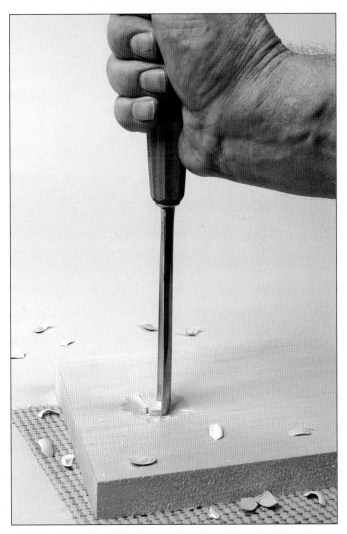

5 Make the sides of the button vertical by setting the gouge vertically at the top edge of the button and sinking it straight into the wood. Do this all around the button.

6 Round the top of the button by turning the gouge over so the concave side is down. Align the gouge in the same direction that the grain runs at one edge of the button. Push the tool to the center of the button, rounding the top.

7 When you reach the center of the button, continue to push forward and slowly raise the handle until it's straight up when you reach the edge of the button. Notice how you've rounded one side of the button.

8 Turn the tool 180 degrees from the first pass and do the same procedure to round the other half of the button.

9 Set the gouge in the wood around the button and clean up any wood fragments so the button and the area around it show clean, crisp cuts without any wood "fuzzies".

Exercise #10: Clean Gouge Cuts

This project is simple, but it's one that will affect every cut you make with your gouges, veiners, and V-tools. To have a clean cut, never allow the wing of a tool to go under the wood. This is a simple rule, but it's one that will always give you controlled cuts.

1 Use your ½ inch (13 mm) #5 gouge to cut across the grain. As you cut, make sure you can always see both wings of the tool so you have a clean cut.

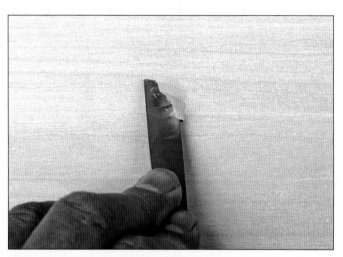

2 Cut across the grain again, but this time rotate your gouge so one wing dips under the wood's surface. Notice how the wood tears where the wing went under the wood.

3 Any time a wing of your tool dips under the wood, you've lost control of the cut, and the wood splits where the wing went under. Notice the difference in the two cuts.

This is a phrase coined by one of the premier relief carvers, William (Bill) Judt. He specializes in relief carvings with religious themes. Four-quadrant carving is based on the same principles as working with negative and positive transition points but describes them from another perspective. It notes what happens in wood when working with gouges, veiners, and V-tools on a flat surface, such as a relief carving.

For example, if you're carving a circle or a curved segment in a carving, one wing of the tool will always be cutting across the wood grain, and the other wing will attempt to go between the wood grain.

Practice four-quadrant carving techniques to help you become familiar with wood grain and quadrant direction so you can make clean cuts on the piece you want to save.

1. Draw a circle and divide it into four quadrants, with the vertical line running parallel to the grain in the wood, and the horizontal line running across the grain (left photo).

2. Label the top of the vertical line with the number *1*, and progress clockwise with *2*, *3*, and *4*. Label the quadrants *A*, *B*, *C*, and *D*. If you want to have clean cuts on the outsides of quadrants *A*, *B*, *C*, and *D*, you must cut in the directions of the outside arrows (left photo).

3. By cutting this direction on each quadrant, the wing on your gouge, which is next to the area you want to save, will always be cutting across the vessels.

4. The other wing will be cutting into the exposed ends of the vessels and will attempt to go between them. Notice how the wood next to *D* is cleanly cut and the channel is torn to the outside. The tool cuts across the vessels next to *D*, but by attempting to go between the vessels on the outside of the channel, it tears those vessels, leaving a ragged edge (right photo).

5. For the inside of the circle, the tool must go in the direction of the inside arrows on each of the four quadrants so the wing next to that segment is always cutting across the grain.

6. To have the outside channel cleanly cut between quadrants *3* and *4*, tilt the gouge and cut along the wall in the direction of the arrow. This cut removes wood across each of the exposed ends of the vessels on the outside, leaving a clean cut on both sides of the channel.

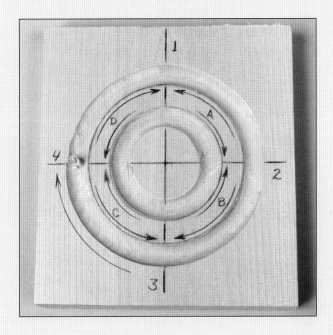

CHIP CARVING CUTS

Chip carving is removing selected chips of wood with a knife. You can use a standard carving knife; however, a chip carving knife is more efficient at removing chips because the blade is thinner and is shaped with a 20-degree angle. This angle makes it ergonomically more efficient to remove the chips.

Chip carving requires only a couple of knives and a piece of wood. It is one of the least expensive forms of carving. Normally, chip carving is done using basswood.

Exercise #1: Chip Carving Practice

The key to mastering chip carving is to cut slowly and precisely, keeping your cuts uniform. Never try to pry a chip loose; all chips should come away clean.

1 Draw two lines ¼ inch apart. Place marks every ¼ inch on the top line. Mark the bottom line every ¼ inch, starting the first mark ⅛ inch over from the top mark. You want a series of equilateral triangles. Draw lines connecting the top marks to the bottom marks. Do the same in the opposite direction.

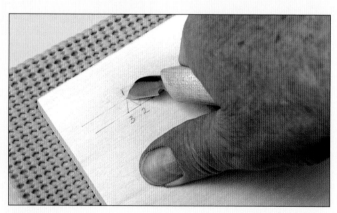

2 Number the first triangle *1*, *2*, and *3*. Hold the knife as shown, with your thumb on the wood surface. Place the tip of the knife at *1*, and tilt the blade to a 65-degree angle.

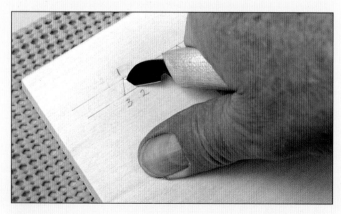

3 Push the blade into the wood up to *2*. The shallowest cut is where the knife entered the wood at *1*, and the deepest cut should be halfway between *1* and *2*. Back the knife out of the cut. Don't pull the blade out of the wood.

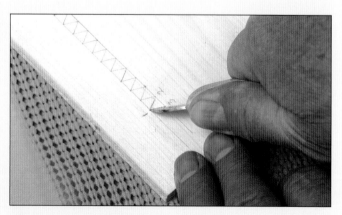

4 Turn the knife over, with your thumb on the back of the handle. Set the knife at *1*, at a 65-degree angle to the wood's surface. Push the blade into the wood toward *3*. The shallowest cut is where the knife entered the wood, and the deepest cut should be halfway between *1* and *3*. This cut should meet the cut you made in Step 2. Back the knife out of the wood.

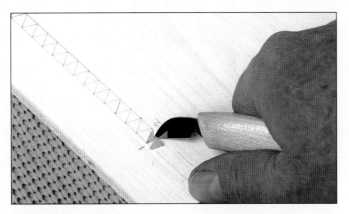

5 Place the tip of the knife at *2*, again tilted away from the line at about 65 degrees. Press the knife into the wood from *2* to *3*. The chip should fall out. Remove the chips across the piece, repeating the same sequence as you did with the numbered triangle.

6 Turn the piece around and repeat the same sequence on this side.

7 Continue this same process across the board, removing chips.

8 When you've removed all of the chips across this direction also, use a toothbrush to clean the carving.

Exercise #2: Stab Knife

The stab knife is also considered a chip carving knife, but you don't remove chips with it. You do just as the name describes—make stab cuts.

1 Hold the knife as shown. Press the knife into the wood, making a straight stab cut.

2 Using this process, you can make interesting designs with a stab knife.

Chapter Eight

GETTING STARTED

The best way to get started . . . is to get started.

Many carvers have an idea bouncing around in their head but have problems getting the idea into a piece of wood. If you find yourself in this situation, there are a number of things you can do to help you get started.

The most important step is to take time to develop a clear mental image of what you want before you start to actually carve.

Preparation will save you time and give you a much better chance of achieving what you really want. It's not unusual for me to spend more time preparing than carving.

In this chapter, we'll take a look at the various items and techniques that will help you to solidify your idea and prepare you to start carving.

DEVELOPING AN IDEA

To develop a mental image of what you want and prepare to put it in wood, you can use almost anything. Clay, plastic or composition objects, sketches, pictures, photos, models, props, and even the Internet are all excellent resources.

I made a full-size clay model prior to carving *Harvest Lunch* so I could take one-to-one measurements.

Professional clay sculpting tools are available, but I still feel the best tools are your hands.

CLAY

Clay is an excellent medium for developing a project. As you create a model in clay, you can add to it, subtract from it, and easily change it until you have a design you like. Once the design is developed, it's easy to use your clay model as a guide to your carving. With it, you can see exactly what you want to transfer to the wood. And if your clay model is dimensionally accurate (full size, half size, etc.), you can take measurements from the model to get an accurate representation of the subject in the wood.

I use extrafirm oil-based clay to make models. Oil-based clay will never harden, so you can use it over and over again. Extrafirm clay also allows you to put more detail in your sculpture than you can with softer clay. Various professional sculpting tools are available, or you can make your own from dowels or wooden craft sticks. A wire loop and secondhand dental tools are also helpful, but the most useful tools are your hands.

If you're going to make a clay model, consider building the model on an armature, or a skeleton of wire, wood, or any material that will support the clay. I recommend plastic-coated aluminum wire for armatures. You can buy aluminum wire in various gauges at

On this armature, I used pipe and couplings to support the wire.

I used an armature like this one to model a dog. The wire was inserted into holes drilled in a board and the clay was built up on the wire.

most hardware stores. I find that 14-gauge wire with a plastic coating makes a good skeleton. Wrapping lighter-gauge wire around the heavier-gauge wire gives a good base for the clay to grip. If your subject has a lot of mass, try wrapping aluminum foil around the armature to save clay.

Before you purchase clay, check the label. Some clay contains sulfur. If the clay you're working with has sulfur in it, never use an uncoated copper wire for the armature. The sulfur will react chemically with the copper wire, and the clay will break away from the wire in a short period of time.

Tip: *Use a Metric Ruler*

If you transfer dimensions from your model to the piece of wood, it is much more efficient to transfer them using a metric ruler. For example, if you want to enlarge your model three times, it is much easier to expand 10 mm to 30 mm than ⅜ inch to ⅝ inches.

DO A TEST CARVE

When you start a carving and you're unsure about a specific element, carve it in a piece of clay or scrap wood. When you have the part as you want it, it's then easy to carve into a piece of wood. It's much better to take the extra time and get it right than to try it in the carving and not end up with what you wanted. The clay or scrap wood can be thrown away, but your carving is forever.

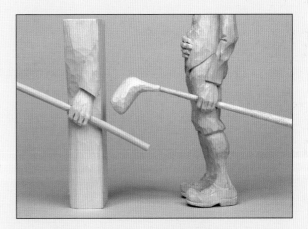

I carved the hand for this golfer in a piece of scrap wood before doing it in the final carving.

Plastic or Composition Objects

Don't limit yourself when looking for models for a carving. Even knickknacks or toys can be useful. When I'm shopping or going to garage sales and see something that has the potential of being a prop for a carving, I pick it up for future reference.

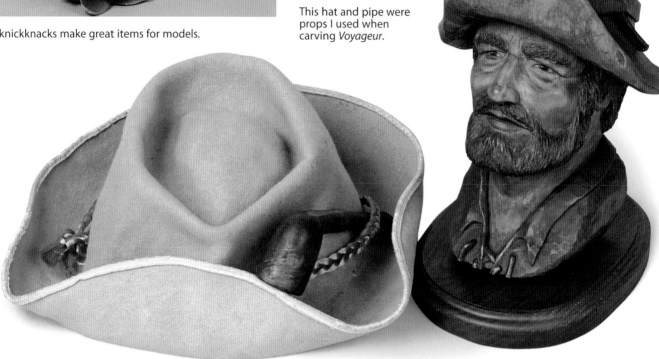

Toys and knickknacks make great items for models.

This hat and pipe were props I used when carving *Voyageur*.

Sketches

You don't have to be an artist to sketch what you have in mind. A sketch should be nothing more than a vehicle to get your thoughts on a piece of paper. Once you get the initial sketch made, you'll be amazed how the ideas begin to flow. Then, you can use pictures from books and magazines, props, models, photos, or anything else to help you refine your idea.

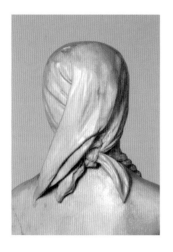

My wife tied a scarf on a mannequin's head to give me a visual for carving the scarf for *Harvest Lunch*. To get an accurate representation of the covered basket my subject's carrying, I laid a cloth over a wicker basket and used that as my prop.

PHOTOS

Photos are an excellent way to develop your model. By taking pictures, you can get exactly what you want. Photos are not only helpful to use as visuals, but they can also be used to take measurements for an accurate reproduction. If you take photos of the same subject from various angles, make sure each photo is taken from the same distance.

INTERNET

The Internet is a powerful resource for finding pictures and information on almost any subject. The Internet was where I found pictures of the wooden bucket my *Harvest Lunch* lady is holding (see top photo on page 166).

SUBJECT LIBRARY

You'll find it helpful to develop a library of various subjects and carving books. I remove pictures from magazines, take photos, and collect brochures, and then put them in a folder labeled with the subject title. I have folders on numerous subjects, such as dogs, cats, deer, male faces, female faces, and so on. Many of these pictures I may never use, but I may use a specific type of eye or nose from one picture and another feature from another picture. My subject library has become an excellent reference source.

If you want to focus on a specific element in a picture, it's helpful to mask out the entire picture except the item you're interested in. For example, if you want to carve a specific eye, you'll see not only the eye but also the nose, the mouth, the hair, and the rest of the face as you study the picture. Covering everything but the eye will keep you focused.

MIRROR

If you're carving a face or a specific pose, a mirror is another helpful tool. You don't have to rely on someone else or attempt to find a picture of what you want. You become your own model.

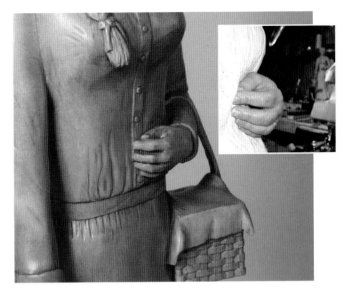

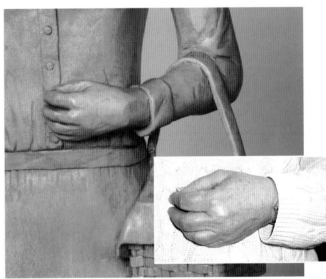

Taking your own photographs or using other photos for reference can help you to create a more lifelike carving.

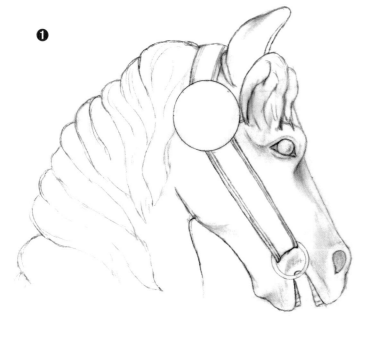

❶

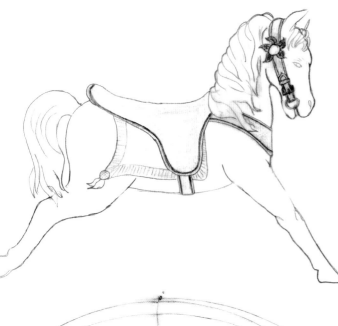

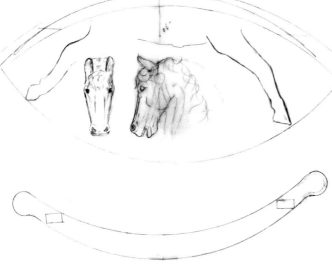

PUTTING IT ALL TOGETHER

Often, you'll need to combine techniques to completely flesh out an idea for a carving. I used a number of elements to create a carved rocking horse.

❶ I made some drawings of what I wanted my rocking horse to look like.

❷ I then did the head in clay.

❸ Next, I made a pattern of how each section of the horse would be cut and glued. As you can see, I drew arrows showing how the grain runs through the legs to give them maximum strength. (Patterns for this project appear in the Appendix on pages 262–266.)

❷

❸

WORKING WITH PATTERNS

Patterns are probably the carver's most useful tools for laying out a carving. Once you develop your initial idea, there are a number of ways that you can create a pattern. You can also use provided patterns, such as the ones found in the project section of this book, beginning on page 199.

MATERIALS

For the projects in this book, we'll use three different materials for patterns: regular paper, cardboard or cardstock, and tracing, carbon, or graphite paper. Which one you choose to use will depend upon the type of carving and your personal preference.

Regular paper is probably the easiest material to find and use. You'll use this paper when you are tracing a pattern or using a pattern for reference.

Cardboard or cardstock is ideal for making templates, which will be used over and over again. Like regular paper, you'll use cardboard or cardstock to trace simple shapes onto the wood.

Tracing, carbon, or graphite paper is great for making complex patterns that can't simply be traced around or for copying detailed parts of a pattern.

Regular paper.

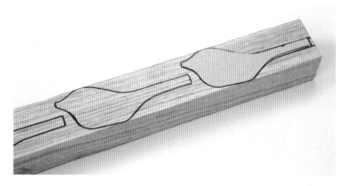

Cardstock.

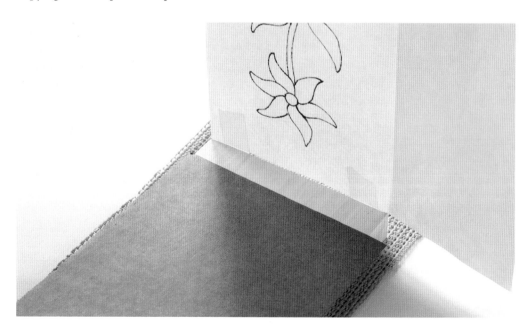

Carbon paper.

A template makes it easy to transfer the same pattern many times.

Chip carvers often use marking instruments and measurements to create geometric patterns and have no reference pattern at all.

TRANSFERRING PATTERNS

Each pattern material also has its own method of transfer and its own purpose. We'll take a look at the most common techniques used in this book.

Paper patterns are often glued with temporary glue and taped down on the wood for sawing out blanks with a band saw, a scroll saw, or a coping saw. Photocopiers or your computer make it easy to enlarge or reduce the patterns to the size you need. Simple patterns can also be cut out in paper or cardstock and traced onto the wood. Then, they can be sawn out or used for reference.

Drawing patterns freehand is another common method of transfer. This technique allows you to modify sections as you go, if needed, using the pattern as a guide. Often, freehand drawing is supplemented with rulers, compasses, and other measuring devices. Measurement marks, reference lines, and centerlines can sometimes be more helpful than drawing the complete pattern on the wood.

Tracing a pattern onto the wood using tracing, carbon, or graphite paper is easiest for complex patterns in which you need all of the lines. If possible, tape the pattern and the tracing paper to the carving so the pattern stays in place but can be lifted up to check your progress.

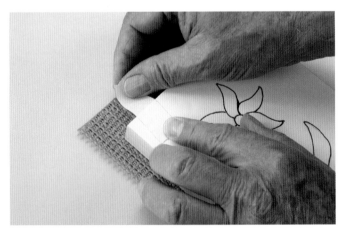

When the carving surface allows for it, you can tape the pattern and graphite paper to the wood for easy transfer.

CHOOSING AND PREPARING WOOD FOR CARVING

Select your wood based on the criteria described in Chapter 3, "Wood for Carving," on page 23). You can also purchase prepared blanks or roughouts. Blanks are cutouts made by removing the major amounts of waste wood from around the object you want to carve. Having much of the waste wood removed gives you a predetermined shape to start a carving and will save you time in creating the project. You can buy blanks of all sorts from most woodcarving catalogs, or you can make your own. A roughout also has the majority of the waste wood removed, but it normally has much more wood removed than a blank. For many roughouts, all you need to do is clean up the piece by removing the cutter marks, and then put in the details. Roughouts are made by a machine that cuts out shapes by using an existing carving as the model.

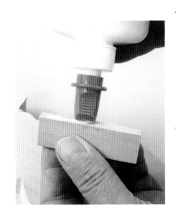

▲ It's sometimes helpful to draw grain direction arrows on the wood, so you have a quick reference for which direction you need to carve.

WOOD GRAIN AND GLUING

The direction of the grain running through a piece of wood has a major impact on the wood's strength. Taking grain into consideration is an important issue in creating a successful carving. You'll want most of the pieces you're going to carve to have straight grain. Lay out the parts that need the most strength in the area of straightest grain. It is also important to consider wood grain in the aesthetics of your carving. Lay out your carving so the wood grain enhances the carving. If needed, use glue to add wood for specific parts, to make the entire wood piece the correct size for your carving, or to add strength.

◄ Part of preparing to carve can involve assembling extra wood, such as the pieces needed here for a snowman's hat. When gluing, rubber bands make great clamps for small pieces.

REMOVING WASTE WOOD

Once you have chosen wood and determined the best layout for your pattern, you'll want to transfer the pattern and possibly remove waste wood with a band saw, a scroll saw, or a coping saw. If you're using a band saw, keep the blade guard no more than ¼ inch from the top of the wood. Whatever type of saw you're using, never put your fingers in harm's way.

MOUNTING THE CARVING IN A VISE

As the final step in preparing for carving, mount the wood in a vise whenever possible. Remember, this is also a great way to keep your hands safe because you won't have to hold the carving in one hand as you carve.

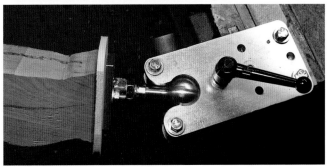

To mount a carving on a vise, drill a hole in the body of the carving and insert a lag bolt using a vise grip pliers. Mount the blank with a wood buffer between it and the vise mounting plate to protect your tools from being driven into the metal plate.

To show how grain direction influences how you lay out a carving, I conducted an experiment. I cut ¼-inch-wide pieces from a piece of ¼-inch-thick board. The arrow on each piece shows the direction of the wood grain. The pieces from the top of the board are composed of short vessels lying next to one another. The pieces from the side of the board have all the vessels running the full length of each piece. (Remember that vessels form the grain in the wood.)

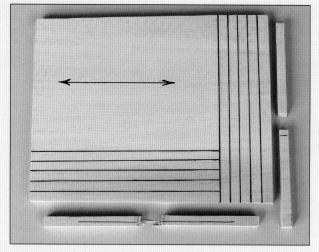

Keep in mind that the way long and short vessels run through the wood affects the strength of the piece of wood.

A simple test proves that the direction of the vessels has a profound impact on the wood's strength.

The three pieces with short vessels running through them were my first test group; the three pieces with long vessels were my second test group. I placed a metal bar across the test piece of wood and attached a hanger to the metal bar and to a container. I added sand to the container until the test piece broke.

The sand used to break each test piece was weighed, and an average for each group was calculated to see how much weight it took to break each piece of wood. The short-vessel pieces averaged only 2 pounds and 13 ounces before they broke. The long-vessel pieces averaged 30 pounds and 11 ounces before they broke.

From my results, we can deduce the following: On the pieces with short vessels, the fibers that make up the vessel walls are very short (meaning the grain is running up and down), so they split apart from one another under very little stress. The pieces with long vessels have the grain running the full length of the piece, so each of

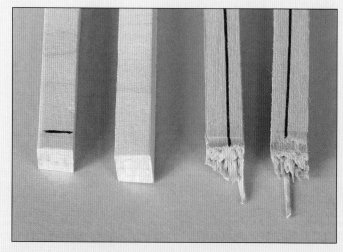

As you can see, the pieces with short vessels split apart under very little stress. The pieces with long vessels broke under much more stress.

the fibers that make up the vessel walls had to physically tear before the piece broke. This physical structure is what makes these long-vessel pieces very strong.

Through this experiment, you can see how important it is to lay out a project so the wood grain runs the length of the most fragile area to give it maximum strength.

Not all carvings will work out so nicely. For example, in this carving of a dog, the wood grain runs parallel through the head, body, tail, and the top part of the raised leg, leaving the area below the knee (where the short vessels run) as one of the most fragile parts of the dog. To move this fragile part away from the normal viewing area, I turned the head of the dog so it looks away from that side. The leg that is up is to the back of the carving and is less likely to get bumped.

Carvings can be laid out so the wood grain enhances the carving. Notice how the grain lines match the natural flow of the face. The thin feather was carved separately by using a controlled split to align all the fibers for strength.

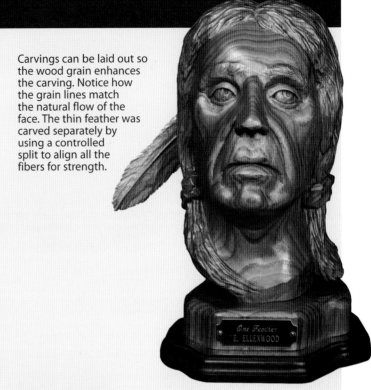

The most fragile part of this carved dog is the tail. To give it strength, I laid out the carving so the grain ran parallel through the tail.

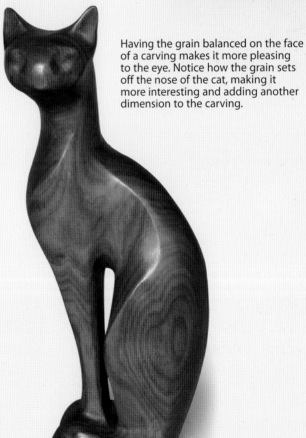

Having the grain balanced on the face of a carving makes it more pleasing to the eye. Notice how the grain sets off the nose of the cat, making it more interesting and adding another dimension to the carving.

The raised leg posed another fragile area.

Chapter Nine

Painting & Finishing

If you ask one hundred carvers how they finish a carving, you'll get about one hundred different answers.

Painting and finishing a carving is an art in and of itself, and these processes incorporate an almost unlimited number of mediums and techniques. The first step in painting and finishing is to decide what you want as an end result. There are three general choices:

- No finish, where you see the natural wood without anything on it
- Some finish, where you see the natural beauty of the wood, like butternut, catalpa, walnut, cherry, and mahogany, enhanced
- Paint, where you see some or no wood grain and mostly color

If you choose to go with no finish, your carving will be bare, with no protection from the oils and grime on hands or from the natural collection of dust, all of which can make the carving look dirty over time. While bare wood is a valid choice, we'll spend most of this chapter looking at the two other options: some finish and paint.

ENHANCING THE WOOD GRAIN

If you want a protective coating on your carving, one through which you can see the wood grain, there are two basic types of finishes you can use: surface finishes and penetrating finishes.

Surface finishes consist of:

■ Varnish
■ Water-based varnish
■ Shellac
■ Lacquer
■ Paste wax

SURFACE FINISHES

Surface finishes are made with resins, natural or synthetic, and only slightly penetrate the wood. Because of their composition, all surface finishes, except water-based varnish, will add a golden tint to the wood.

Surface finishes offer protection from wear and tear and don't mask the wood grain.

Tip: Preparing the Carving for Finish

Make sure your carving is ready for finishing. If the carving has "fuzzies" or the cuts are not clean, don't try to cover your mistakes with paint. Also, remove any pencil lines. If you use an eraser, use one that doesn't have color in it. If an eraser has color, it can get on your carving.

Varnish

. . . .

Use over: bare wood, painted wood, stained wood

Use under: wax

Do not use: if skinned over or thick in can, with other brands of varnish, over a waxed surface

. . . .

The base ingredient in most varnish is oil, such as boiled linseed oil or mineral oil, with tough, durable synthetic resins, such as alkyd, phenolic, or urethane, added.

Natural varnish has no pigment added, so it is transparent, as opposed to paints or wood stains, and is available in gloss, satin, and flat finishes. Gloss varnish is the natural varnish and will leave a shiny finish on the surface of your carving. It does not need to be stirred before use. Satin and flat finishes have flattening agents that reduce surface glare. Whether the finish is satin or flat depends on the amount of flattening agent added—flat finishes have more flattening agents, making them less shiny. The flattening agent is heavier than the varnish, so it will settle and appear as a white residue in the bottom of the can. This agent must be completely mixed and kept in suspension to achieve the satin or flat finish.

Varnish is available in liquid, brushable form or in spray cans. If you prefer not to brush on your finish, spray is a convenient way of applying a topcoat over stain or paint. Follow the manufacturer's directions on the spray can. Most important, don't spray too much at a time. Hold the spray can about 12 inches from the carving and apply just enough to coat it without actually seeing any on the surface. Allow at least two hours between coats and apply three to five coats. Remember, after each coat, clean the spray nozzle by turning the can upside down and spraying until no varnish comes out.

To apply liquid

1. Thin the varnish slightly, if desired, using the manufacturer's recommended thinner. The thinned varnish will penetrate slightly more and stay workable longer than thick varnish.
2. Liberally spread varnish over the carving by brushing.
3. Allow it to slightly penetrate into the carving for about five minutes.
4. Wipe off the excess varnish with a rag.
5. To remove all the varnish from any crevices, use a dry, soft-bristle brush, wiping the brush off on an old terry cloth towel as you go.
6. Take your time removing the excess varnish. If it is allowed to build up on the surface, the carving will look as if it's been coated with plastic.
7. Allow the carving to dry for 24 hours.
8. Repeat the sequence each day for three days.

To apply spray

1. Apply at least three light coats.
2. Each time you spray, turn the carving so you spray it from another direction to fully cover the carving.

VARNISH PROS AND CONS

Pros
- One of the most durable finishes
- Heat, water, and chemical resistant
- Long lasting
- Available in gloss, satin, or flat finishes
- Gives a slightly golden tint that enhances some woods

Cons
- Slow drying
- Petroleum based
- Gives off an odor until dry
- Requires solvent for cleanup
- Gives a golden tint to wood

This butternut carving was finished using satin-finish varnish.

Water-Based Varnish Pros and Cons

Pros

- Durable
- Water and scuff resistant
- Easily cleaned up with water
- Environmentally friendly
- Has an absolutely clear finish
- Does not have much odor
- Fast drying

Cons

- Must be applied in thin coats
- Needs to be in an environment where the temperature is over 73 degrees Fahrenheit when applied
- Fast drying
- Should not be thinned

Water-Based Varnish

Use over: any dry surface

Use under: wax

Do not use: with other brands of varnish, with water

Made of microscopic beads of acrylic and polyurethane resins dispersed in water, this varnish is milky white in solution but will dry absolutely clear. Water-based varnish will also not change the color of the base it's covering. Never add additional water to water-based varnish; it has a fragile formula that can be disturbed by thinning it with more water. If the directions on the can say "clean brushes with water," you can rest assured that you're working with a water-based varnish.

To apply

1. Use a synthetic brush (poly or nylon) with split ends.
2. Because water-based varnish dries fast, apply it in thin coats. Remove any puddles of varnish immediately.
3. Don't apply another coat until the base coat is entirely dry, or you may drag some of the semidried finish. You'll usually need three coats.

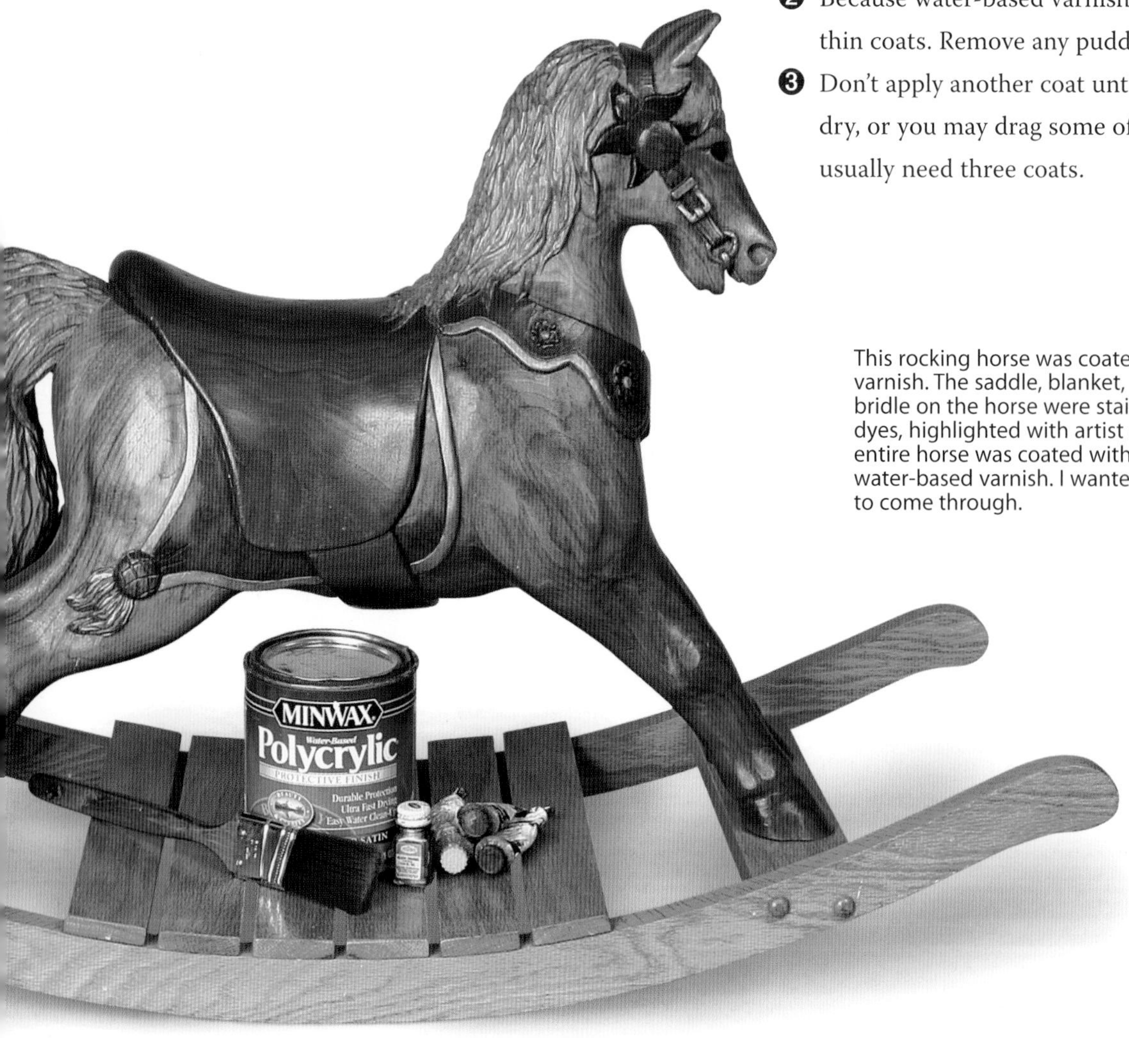

This rocking horse was coated using water-based varnish. The saddle, blanket, breast collar, and bridle on the horse were stained using aniline dyes, highlighted with artist oils, and then the entire horse was coated with three thin coats of water-based varnish. I wanted the natural colors to come through.

Shellac

Use over: bare wood, painted surfaces, non-alcohol-based stain, varnish

Use under: any finish that does not contain alcohol

Do not use: if wood is damp, on a humid day

Shellac is a natural resin secreted by the lac bug. This insect attaches itself to certain trees, primarily in India and Southeast Asia, and deposits the resin on twigs and branches to form a protective cocoon for the developing lac bug larva. Lac bug resin is scraped from the twigs and branches, melted, strained to remove foreign material, and then formed into thin sheets and broken into flakes. Shellac is available premixed or in flake form. The flakes should be stored in a cool, dry place until needed. If you buy premixed shellac, check the date of manufacture on the can. If it's more than six months old, don't use it.

Because shellac has a short shelf life after being mixed, it's best to purchase the flakes and dissolve them yourself in denatured alcohol or shellac thinner. Mix it well, and then strain it through a paint strainer before using. A concentrate of shellac in its dissolved solution is called a cut. I recommend buying dewaxed shellac. If the natural wax in shellac has not been removed, it may create adhesion problems when other finishes, such as varnish, are applied over it.

A ½ cut is ½ ounces of dry shellac to 8 fluid ounces of alcohol. A number 1 cut is 1 ounce of dry shellac to 8 ounces of alcohol. A number 2 cut is 2 ounces of dry shellac to 8 fluid ounces of alcohol, and so on up to a number 4 cut. A ½ cut is an excellent sealer as an undercoat for staining or painting. Apply it liberally and let it soak into the wood. A finish coat will normally be a 2 or 3 cut.

Shellac is available in colors from yellow to garnet. You can also buy white shellac, which is obtained by bleaching orange shellac. Shellac can be colored and used as a stain by adding alcohol-based stain or aniline dye. When applied, it colors the wood and seals the wood at the same time. (Always test the stain on a piece of scrap wood before applying it to your carving.) Fresh-mixed shellac is easy to use, dries fast, and leaves a nice finish on the wood, but because of the effort required to prepare it, it's not used by many carvers.

A natural resin, shellac forms a shiny, hard coating on woodcarvings.

SHELLAC PROS AND CONS

Pros
- Easy to apply
- Adds warm luster to wood
- Can be used as a base to minimize end-grain absorption of paint
- Fast drying
- Derived from renewable material

Cons
- Should not be applied in humid weather
- Has a short shelf life when mixed
- Has a weak resistance to heat, water, solvents, and chemicals
- Only available in gloss sheen (sheen could be flattened with steel wool or a flattening agent)

To apply

1. Apply with a brush. Work quickly because the alcohol evaporates fast.
2. Allow about two hours between coats. Normally, you will apply three coats.
3. If you're applying it as a sealer coat, a ½ cut is recommended. Apply one coat liberally and let dry.

LACQUER PROS AND CONS

Pros

- Easy to spray to coat a carving
- Fast drying
- Excellent for a clear coating
- Provides a good base to seal end grain for staining
- Provides a durable finish

Cons

- Highly flammable in spray form
- Air polluting in solvent form
- Must be applied in a well-ventilated area

Laquer is a fast-drying clear coating.

Lacquer

Use over: bare wood, shellac, water stain

Use under: wax, stain (if lacquer is used as a sealer)

Do not use: with varnish or oil-based stain, in cold temperatures with high humidity

Lacquer is a clear coating that dries by solvent evaporation. Originally, lacquer was a derivative of the lac bug. Today, most lacquers are made from nitrocellulose, which consists of cellulose fibers from cotton and wood treated with nitric and sulfuric acids and a plasticizer resin.

Lacquer dries fast and is normally applied as a spray. Brush-on lacquers are available, but if you're putting a lacquer finish on your carvings, I recommend you spray it on. Because it dries fast, lacquer is difficult to control when brushed on. Lacquer in spray cans is available at any hardware or paint store.

Lacquer is easy to use and gives a nice, fast-drying coat. It also works great as a base to seal end grain before staining. **Caution:** The solvents used to make lacquer are toxic and very volatile, so only use it in a well-ventilated area away from any open flame.

To apply

1. Spray a thin coat over the entire carving.
2. For best results, apply a number of thin coats and allow each coat to dry about 20 minutes before adding the next.
3. Rotate the carving each time you put on a coat so you spray the carving from a different direction each time. If the carving is small, a handle with a screw attached works great for holding the carving while spraying it. You may also use a glove to protect your hand from getting sprayed.

Paste Wax

Use over: bare wood, any other finish

Use under: nothing

Do not use: under varnish

Wax is one of the older finishing compounds known. It is inexpensive and easy to apply, but it does require more elbow grease than most other finishes. Though it is normally used over an existing finish, such as varnish, shellac, lacquer, or oil, paste wax can also be used on its own as a finish.

Paste wax starts as a solid and is made into a paste by being dissolved in a solvent of mineral spirits and/or toluene. Most commercial paste waxes are much the same, whatever brand they may be.

If you want to give your carving some color as you're applying wax, look for a wax that has color added. Whatever type of wax you use, apply it in thin coats using a brush or a rag, and don't wait too long to remove the excess, or the solvent will evaporate and the wax will again turn into a solid. If you do have buildup, apply more wax and it will dissolve the previous coat, allowing you to easily remove any buildup.

Paste wax is rubbed on a carving to give it a dust-proof, fingerprint-proof finish.

To apply

❶ Rub the brush or rag on the wax to collect some of the polish.

❷ Apply a light coat over the total carving, getting into the crevices.

❸ Reload the brush as necessary.

❹ Allow the wax to set for about five minutes.

❺ Buff the carving with a dry brush to bring out the sheen of the polish. Again, get into all of the crevices.

❻ Buff the surface with a soft, lint-free rag to deepen the shine on the high areas of your carving.

❼ For more shine, apply another coat.

PASTE WAX PROS AND CONS

Pros
- Easy to apply
- Can produce a satin to bright sheen
- Keeps natural color of wood
- If colored, can be used like a stain
- Protects from dust and grime

Cons
- Dries soft
- Least protective of all finishes
- Least durable of all finishes

Linseed oil penetrates the wood of your carving and leaves it with a beautiful soft gloss.

LINSEED OIL PROS AND CONS

Pros
■ Easy to apply
■ Can be mixed with varnish for a more durable finish
■ Provides a good medium to mix with artist oils to thin them or to make your own stain
■ Gives nice color to wood
■ Transparent, so it shows the wood grain

Cons
■ Has an odor
■ Not very durable
■ Not water resistant
■ Not UV resistant
■ Slow drying
■ Will continue to yellow
■ Can cause rags to spontaneously combust, so rags need proper disposal

PENETRATING FINISHES

Penetrating oil finishes go on easier than surface finishes and are absorbed into the wood. They penetrate and harden the wood while allowing the natural grain color and texture of the wood to show through. These finishes become part of the wood rather than building on the surface of the wood. Unfortunately, penetrating finishes don't have the durability of surface finishes.

Linseed Oil

Use over: bare wood

Use under: linseed oil stain, varnish, paste wax

Do not use: if thick in can

Linseed oil is a derivative of flaxseed and is available as raw and boiled oil. All of the linseed-based oils must penetrate the surface of the wood to dry. It's important that you wipe any excess off the surface, or the residue will get gummy and never dry properly.

For best results, use only fresh linseed oil because after a container is opened, it can become thick and gummy over time. Don't use it in such a state because it will never dry properly.

■ Raw linseed oil is not recommended because it can take well over a week to cure. It has a natural golden color that will change the color of the wood slightly and continue to darken over time.

■ Boiled linseed oil has chemicals added, called dryers, to accelerate curing and is the recommended linseed oil to use. It also has a natural golden color that will change the color of the wood slightly and continue to darken over time.

To apply

❶ Saturate the wood with the oil and keep it wet for about 15 minutes.

❷ Wipe off the excess with a clean, lint-free cloth.

❸ Dry brush to get any residue out of the crevices.

❹ Apply additional coats every 24 hours. Usually, three coats are enough. Make sure you don't have buildup on the surface of the wood. It must penetrate the wood to dry properly.

Tung Oil

Use over: bare wood, stain, shellac

Use under: oil-based stain, oil-based paint, paste wax

Do not use: with varnish or thinner, with water-based varnish

Extracted from the nut of the tung tree, which was originally grown only in the Orient but is now cultivated in South America and the Gulf States in the United States, pure tung oil penetrates deeply into the wood, providing a tough, flexible, and highly water-resistant coating. It is the most durable of all natural oils. Tung oil cures by oxidation to a soft matte finish. It will never give a shiny gloss finish, no matter how many coats you add.

Most tung oil sold is not pure but has additives, normally a varnish. If the container says "contains pure tung oil," there is a good chance that tung oil is only an additive. When you apply that type of product to the wood, you may end up with a gloss finish. To be sure you get pure tung oil, look for a container that says "100 percent pure." Pure tung oil has a slightly paler color than linseed oil and will not darken as it ages.

Artist oil paints can be mixed with tung oil to make your own stains. For a more durable finish, mix tung oil with varnish. Apply straight tung oil first for deep penetration; then, apply two to three coats of a 50:50 mixture of tung oil and varnish.

To apply

❶ Saturate the wood with the oil and keep it wet for about 15 minutes.

❷ Wipe off the excess with a clean, lint-free cloth.

❸ Dry brush to get any residue out of the crevices.

❹ Apply additional coats every 24 hours. Usually, three coats are enough to create a low sheen.

TUNG OIL PROS AND CONS

Pros
- Enhances the natural color of the wood
- Easy to use
- Cures to a hard, flexible finish
- Water resistant
- Will not darken with age
- Has a long shelf life
- Is FDA approved for food contact (pure tung oil)

Cons
- Cures slowly
- Requires several coats

Tung oil gives a beautiful matte finish.

SAFETY

Care must be taken to properly dispose of rags or paper towels that have wet varnish, paint, or oil on them, because they have the potential of spontaneously combusting. Spontaneous combustion occurs when cloth or paper towels are coated with varnish, paint, or oil and are put in a loose pile. When the drying oils in varnish, paint, or linseed oil are exposed to oxygen, it creates the chemical reaction of oxidation, which creates heat. A cloth or paper towel with a thin layer of combustible material on it exposes a large area to oxygen and generates more heat. If the rags or paper towels are stacked and the heat cannot escape, the internal heat continues to rise until it ignites the rags.

When using rags or paper towels with any varnish, paint, or oil that contains drying oils or is petroleum based, never leave the rags in a pile. Either hang them individually, lay them flat where there is good airflow to allow the sheets to dry, or better yet, soak them in water. I have a gallon can, painted red, about half full of water. Any potentially dangerous rags or paper towels are put in the can and when fully saturated, I wring them out and hang them outside to dry. Once the cloths and paper towels are dry, they are totally inert and can be disposed of without any concern of them spontaneously combusting.

Also remember, if you're working with media that have fumes, make sure you have good airflow taking the fumes away from you.

Danish Oil

Use over: bare wood, stained wood

Use under: paste wax, varnish

Danish oil is a commercial finish made by blending a small amount of varnish in curing oil, such as tung or linseed, and thinning it with mineral spirits. Because Danish oil gives the protection of varnish and the easy application of straight oil, it is a popular finish.

To apply

1. Saturate the wood with the oil and keep it wet for about 10 minutes.
2. Wipe off the excess with a clean, lint-free cloth.
3. Dry brush to get any residue out of the crevices.
4. Apply additional coats every 12 hours. Normally, two to three coats are sufficient.

This stylized butternut cat was finished with three coats of Danish oil applied over a three-day period. After the last coat was applied, it was allowed to dry for one week and then coated with a paste wax and buffed to highlight the lines of the carving.

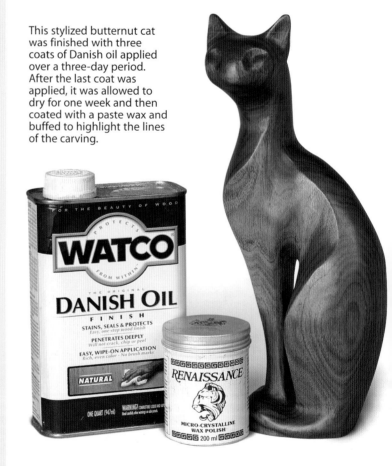

COLORING THE WOOD

Carvers add color to their projects through two main products: stain and paint. Within each category, there are products and methods that allow you to see more or less wood grain. Let's take a look at each of the categories.

STAINS

A stain will not protect wood; it only colors the wood by either collecting in the pores of the wood or actually staining the surface of the wood. To protect the wood, you need to apply a final finish of some kind. Two basic types of colorant are used to make stain: pigment and dye.

Prestain Wood Conditioner

Use over: bare wood

Use under: stain

Do not use: with stains that aren't compatible

Carvings are very susceptible to unevenness in stain absorption because many cuts expose end grain, the open ends of the vessels. These vessel ends absorb more stain than the vessel walls, creating a blotchy appearance. Conditioners can include linseed oil, tung oil, shellac, water, or commercial prestain conditioners. Any of the prestain conditioners will penetrate deeply into the wood and seal the open ends of the vessels to promote a more uniform acceptance of stain, giving a more even color appearance to the wood. Test the effectiveness of the wood conditioner by applying it on a piece of scrap wood with cuts similar to those in your carving. Then, apply the finish you plan to use on your carving.

To apply

❶ Liberally apply the prestain wood conditioner with a soft brush or cloth and allow the conditioner to absorb into the wood.

❷ Wait 15 minutes to 2 hours before applying the stain. From my experience, it is better to stain closer to the 15-minute time than to wait 2 hours.

> **Stains include:**
> - Prestain wood conditioner
> - Pigment stain
> - Dye stain
> - Aniline dye
> - Gel stain
> - Shoe polish

PRESTAIN WOOD CONDITIONER PROS AND CONS

Pros
- Helps eliminate blotchiness in soft woods

Cons
- Creates another step in the finishing process

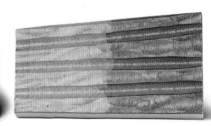

Basswood often gets blotchy when stained without conditioner.

PIGMENT STAIN PROS AND CONS

Pros
- Available premixed at any paint store
- Allows wood grain to show through

Cons
- Prone to blotching or mottling

To apply

1. Apply the stain with a soft brush or a lint-free cloth.
2. Remove excess stain with a lint-free rag or a dry brush.
3. The harder you rub, the more stain you will remove.

DYE STAIN PROS AND CONS

Pros
- Available in powder or liquid
- Available in many colors

Cons
- Masks wood grain
- Can be darker in some areas than in others
- Water-based dye stains will raise wood grain

To apply

1. Wet the wood with the base solvent before applying the stain.
2. Apply the stain in light coats using a brush.

Pigment Stain

Use over: bare wood, wood sealed with conditioner
Use under: paste wax, varnish
Do not use: with incompatible conditioners and topcoats

Pigment stains are made from finely ground pigments. These pigments don't dissolve; they stain wood as the pigment collects in the pores and scratches of the wood. Pigments are normally opaque, so they add a semi-opaque color to the wood and highlight the wood grain.

Always test a stain on a scrap piece of wood with cuts similar to your carving before using it on your carving to see if you need to apply a prestain conditioner. In soft woods, like basswood, if the vessels aren't sealed, more pigment will be trapped in the open ends of the vessels than in the walls of the vessels, creating a mottled look on the carving. Mottling can ruin a carving.

Dye Stain

Use over: bare wood, shellac, sanding sealer, mediums compatible with liquid the stain is mixed with
Use under: paste wax, varnish, any oil
Do not use with: mediums other than recommended on container, on damp wood

A dye stain penetrates everywhere and soaks into the wood. It will color all of the wood, so in some woods, it will mask the grain. This may be okay for some woods, but if you want the grain to be prominent, test the stain on a scrap piece of the same type of wood before putting it on your carving to see if you like the result.

Dye stains are available in ready-to-use form. They are also available in liquid or powder, which you mix with a solvent. The solvent medium can be alcohol, oil, or water based. Dye stains can also be added to 100 percent oil products, such as tung oil or boiled linseed oil. Prewetting the wood with the base solvent, shellac, or sanding sealer is useful before applying the stain.

Gel Stain

Use over: bare wood, conditioned wood

Use under: paste wax, oil finishes, varnish, shellac

Gel stain is a dye incorporated into a thick carrier about the consistency of mayonnaise. The stain will not be absorbed into the wood like a liquid stain, so you normally won't have as much blotching as you would with thin liquid stain. Also, because of its thick consistency, gel stain won't run when applied the way thin liquid stain does. Again, test it on similar wood, and if there is any blotching, use a prestain wood conditioner. The carrier for gel stains is normally petroleum based, so any rags must be disposed of properly. The fumes can also be toxic. Use this product in a well-ventilated area.

To apply

❶ Apply the stain with a brush or lint-free cloth.

❷ Leave it on the surface a couple of minutes, and then remove it with a lint-free cloth or a dry brush.

Shoe Polish

Use over: bare wood, wood sealer, paint

Use under: paste wax, shellac, varnish

Shoe polish is stain in a wax binder and will not be absorbed into the wood; instead, it tints the surface fibers. You are limited by colors, but it can be an effective stain.

To apply

❶ Apply the shoe polish with a soft brush or soft cloth. A brush works best because it will get into deep crevices, allowing a more even application.

❷ Remove the excess from crevices immediately after applying.

❸ Allow the polish to dry for about 10 minutes.

❹ Buff with a soft brush and a soft rag.

❺ If one coat doesn't give you the depth of color you want, apply another coat and do Steps 1 through 4 again.

❻ To achieve a very high shine, apply a few drops of water and buff with a soft cloth.

GEL STAIN PROS AND CONS

Pros
- Easy to use
- Less blotchy than liquid stain
- Does not penetrate very much

Cons
- Stain pigment is opaque
- Difficult to get out of crevices

Shoe polish is a viable option for finishing carvings, but it is available in only a small range of common earth tones and white.

SHOE POLISH PROS AND CONS

Pros
- Easy to apply
- Readily available

Cons
- Limited colors
- Not durable

189

PAINTS

If you decide to paint your carvings, you can choose from acrylic paint, oil paint, and oil pencils. Each type of paint offers a wide variety of colors and options for how much the medium will cover the wood.

Whatever type of paint you use to finish your carving, when the paint is dry, it's always good practice to put a protective coating on it. However, be aware that some paints and spray finishes will make the paint underneath wrinkle. Before you apply any protective coating, test it on a piece of scrap wood.

> **Paints include:**
> ■ Acrylic paint
> ■ Artist oil paint
> ■ Oil pencils

When you want color on your carving, choose from acrylic paint, oil paint, or oil pencils.

COLOR TERMINOLOGY

Hue is the property of a color that distinguishes it from other colors.

Shade is a darkened version of a color created by adding black or a small amount of the color's complement.

Tones are created when one color is added to another. A tone is any step as the color passes from a light shade to a dark shade, or vice versa.

Tints are lighter shades of a color that are created by adding white.

Value distinguishes a light color from a dark color. It refers to the lightness or darkness of a color. You change the value of a color by adding white or black. Adding white will give a color a higher value, often referred to as "tinting up" the color. Adding black will give the color a lower value, referred to as "shading down" the color.

Black and **white** are considered neutral because they don't make a new color when mixed with another color; they simply change the value of the color.

White is the absence of all color, but adding white to any color will make a lighter tint. White has strong pigment, so it will not be opaque but will look milky if added to a color, even if thinned.

Black is made from mixing equal amounts of the three primary colors, red, yellow, and blue. Adding black to any color will make it a darker shade.

Brown is made by mixing a color with its complementary color.

Colors can be further classified:

■ **Transparent.** Light can travel through. Colored cellophane is a good example, where you can vividly see an object behind it even if you're looking through the color.

■ **Translucent.** Some light can travel through. This is like looking through a frosted glass where you see the outline of an object but not any detail.

■ **Opaque.** Light cannot travel through. The natural color of the object on which it is applied is obscured.

COLOR THEORY

When you start working with colors, you don't have to be an expert at color mixing, but it does help to know some of the terminology used and how you can mix various colors to achieve the desired results you're looking for. Let's take a look at why some colors work better with others and how they affect your carving.

When you see a rainbow, you're seeing every color in the spectrum, and if you examine each color carefully, you will see that the colors fall into a specific pattern. Sir Isaac Newton recognized this pattern and was the first person to develop a circular diagram of how colors are arranged sequentially. The arrangement he developed is called a color wheel. You will see some variations from one color wheel to another, but the color pattern will always remain the same.

All colors are derived from only three primary colors: red, yellow, and blue. There are no colors you can mix to create any of these colors; however, you can create all other colors with combinations of these three primary colors. The colors created from mixing primary colors are called secondary colors, which are created by mixing equal amounts of the adjacent two primary colors, and tertiary colors, which are created by mixing equal amounts of one primary color with an adjacent secondary color. Secondary colors are orange, violet, and green. An example of a tertiary color is red-orange.

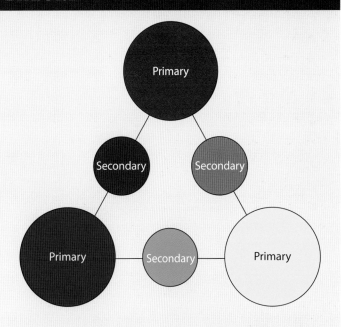

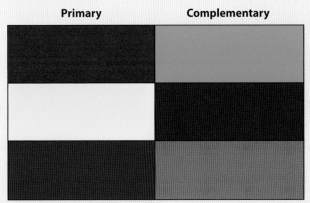

Complementary colors are those colors directly opposite one another on the color wheel. They complement each other because they share no common colors. For example, red is a primary color, and its complementary color, green, is made from yellow and blue.

Complementary colors make both colors look brighter when they are placed next to one another. However, you can make any color less bright by mixing it with a small amount of its complementary color. If you mix any of the complementary colors together in equal amounts, they will make a neutral brown.

Understanding how colors work together is extremely important when you are choosing colors for and applying them to your carving. A beautiful carving can be enhanced by color or ruined by it if color is applied without regard to the color wheel.

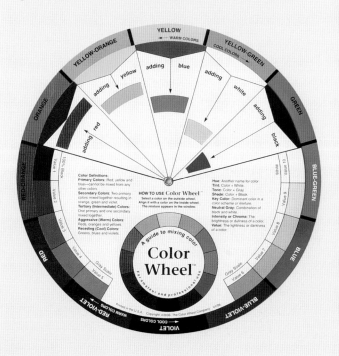

ACRYLIC PAINT PROS AND CONS

Pros
- Easy to use
- Fast drying
- Vast array of colors
- Easy cleanup
- No solvent smell

Cons
- Opaque
- Fast drying time makes blending difficult
- Will ruin brushes if it dries in them

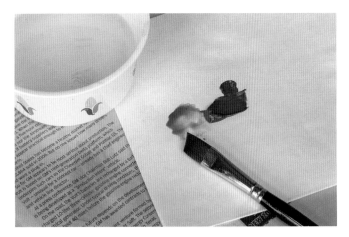

A wash coat of acrylic paint should be thin enough that you can see color yet be able to read through it if you paint a coat of it on a piece of newspaper. If you only want to give a hint of color to a carving, this type of wash will do that.

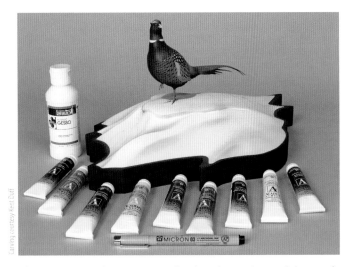

This carving was done using acrylics, but done using wash layers of paint to achieve the beautiful color depth you see. The lines on the breast of the pheasant were done using a micro line marker.

Acrylic Paint

Use over: bare wood, wood primed with gesso

Use under: paste wax, shellac, varnish

Acrylics are opaque water-based paints made from pigment mixed with acrylic resin and an emulsion. Acrylics can be applied in a variety of ways, from straight from the tube to in a thin wash. You have a lot of latitude in how thick or thin to apply acrylics.

If you want to see the wood grain through acrylic paint, thin the paint with water. It will make the acrylics semi-opaque, but they will never be transparent.

You can also use washes to build up colors on top of one another, giving depth to the painted carving. If you do this, make sure the previous wash is completely dry before applying another one over it, or they will blend together and you'll lose the depth illusion.

You can speed up the drying process by blowing warm air from a hair dryer across a painted carving. Under normal conditions, you won't need a hair dryer to dry the paint because acrylics are water-based and the water evaporates rapidly, causing the paint to dry fast.

When you start painting using acrylics, don't put too much paint on your palette, or it may dry out before you can use it. Once acrylics dry, they are water resistant and can't be reconstituted, so if you want to blend the colors on the item you're painting, you must work fast. There are retarders that can be added to acrylics to slow the drying process somewhat, but don't add too much, or the paint will never dry properly.

To slow the drying process of paint on your palette, place a dampened paper towel between the paint and the pallet. (Artist supply stores sell stay-wet palettes, but they are not necessary unless you're doing a major project.) You can also

Practice

If you're going to use paint, practice on some scrap wood before actually painting the carving. Play with the medium to learn its characteristics, and when you do paint, don't rush. If you take your time, you'll be far happier with the results.

This carving was painted with acrylics. When the acrylics were dry, it was coated with satin-finish polyurethane varnish and allowed to dry. To give the carving an antiqued look, it was then coated with burnt umber artist oil thinned to a wash, left to set for about five minutes, and then wiped with a soft cloth and dry brushed to remove any puddling. It was allowed to dry again and then coated with flat polyurethane varnish. When this last flat-finish coat was completely dry, it was buffed with a soft cloth to give highlights.

spray a fine mist of water on your paint from time to time to slow the drying process.

Acrylics are available in nearly every color imaginable. Or you can buy some red, yellow, blue, and white and mix your own colors. They are relatively inexpensive and easy to use.

Because acrylics are water based, brush cleanup is easy, requiring only water; however, don't allow the paint to dry in your brushes. If it dries, aggressive solvents, which may ruin your brushes, will be required to clean the dried paint from the brush.

To apply

❶ Prepare the surface to be painted.

❷ Determine how thick or thin you want the paint consistency (thin with water).

❸ Apply colors with a good-quality brush.

❹ If you want to create depth, allow the color to dry before applying the next color over it.

❺ Don't rush.

❻ Seal with a light coat of clear spray finish.

A CARVER'S COLOR PALETTE

If you choose to use acrylics or oil-based paints to finish your carvings and don't want to mix your own, include the following colors in your collection for a good selection.

Primary colors: Red, yellow, blue
Secondary colors: Green, orange
Earth colors: Yellow ochre, raw umber, burnt umber, raw sienna, burnt sienna, Vandyke brown
Neutral colors: White, black

■ Raw umber is a cool brown made of blue-green and red. When mixed with white, it produces a cool, neutral gray.

■ Burnt umber is a warm brown composed of red, red-orange, and green. When mixed with white, it produces a warm beige.

■ Raw sienna is composed of yellow, red, and blue-green. Extended with white, raw sienna yields a warm cream color.

■ Burnt sienna is composed of red, red-orange, and blue. White added to burnt sienna will produce a light brick color and with more white, a reddish pink.

■ Extended with white, Vandyke brown will produce a purplish beige.

■ Red and black with a little yellow make brown.

■ Gray added to red will make russet.

■ Gray added to blue will make olive.

■ Light tints of all colors are made by adding white.

■ Dark shades of all colors are made by adding brown or black.

To apply

1. Apply straight from the tube, or thin with paint thinner or one of the oils.
2. Blend as you paint.
3. Let dry before applying a finish coat.

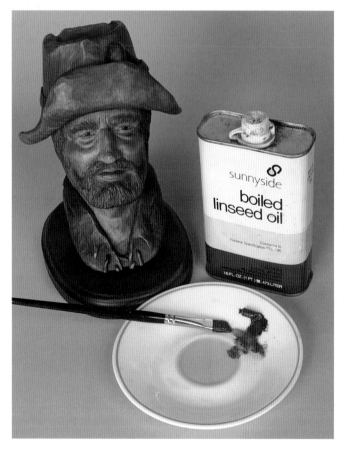

This carving was finished using linseed oil as a base to seal the grain of the wood and then painted with a linseed oil/artist oil mixture. This process must be completed in one sitting so the linseed oil remains in a liquid state to blend with the artist oil. The carving was saturated with boiled linseed oil, wiped off, and dry brushed to remove excess oil.

Artist Oil Paint

Use over: bare wood, wood primed with gesso, sealed wood, linseed oil, tung oil, dry acrylic

Use under: paste wax, shellac, varnish, oil, lacquer

Artist oil paint is a combination of finely ground pigment, which gives the paint color, and binders, which give the paint its consistency and working properties. The most commonly used binders are the oils from linseed, poppy seed, or safflower.

Artist oils are more transparent than acrylics. They dry slowly by oxidation, which allows you to easily blend colors on the object as you're painting it. Depending on how thick artist oils are applied, they will feel dry to the touch in a day to two weeks.

You can paint directly on your carvings with oil paints right from the tube, or they can be thinned. Turpentine, mineral spirits, white spirits, or any of the oils can be used to thin artist oils. If you thin the paint, be aware there's a good chance it will bleed through the wood if the exposed vessels aren't sealed. Bleeding is when the paint migrates through the wood because it was absorbed by the vessels around a painted area. This can cause paint to flow where you don't want it.

If you want to minimize the bleeding problem and have the wood grain show through, I like a process where you use linseed oil as a base to seal the grain of the wood and then paint with a linseed oil/artist oil mixture. Using this process, the artist oil becomes a stain.

To clean brushes that were used with oil-based artist paints, use a solvent. When the brushes are fairly clean, rub the bristles in a container that has brush conditioner or human hair shampoo in it. Rinse and then dry your brushes with the hair or bristles hanging lower than the handle. When they are dry, store the brushes in a protective container. Take care to dispose of any rags properly; many of the mediums used to thin paint and clean brushes are prone to spontaneous combustion.

Oil Pencils

Use over: bare wood, sealed wood, gesso
Use under: water-based varnish, spray varnish, wax, spray acrylic

Oil pencils are a quick, clean way to put color on your carving. They are similar to colored pencils, but the lead is softer and is an oil base. Most oil pencils are semi-opaque, so the wood grain will show through somewhat. You can also blend the paint and move it into tight places using a small brush or a toothpick and paint thinner. Artist oils, acrylic paints, or water-based stains of the same base color will fill any places the pencils won't reach.

To fix colors so they won't smudge, brush on water-based clear varnish, or spray a couple of light coats of varnish or acrylic on the carving. Never brush petroleum-based fixatives on the carving because the brushing action will smear the colors.

To apply

❶ Prepare the surface.
❷ Apply the same as you would using colored pencils on paper.
❸ Colors can be blended as you apply.
❹ In areas where the pencil won't reach, blend colors using paint thinner or other paints of the same color.
❺ Fix the colors with a light spray of clear varnish.

OIL PENCILS PROS AND CONS

Pros
- ■ Easy to use
- ■ Easy to blend colors
- ■ Semi-opaque
- ■ Not messy
- ■ Pinpoint precision for adding color

Cons
- ■ Lead can break
- ■ Semi-opaque

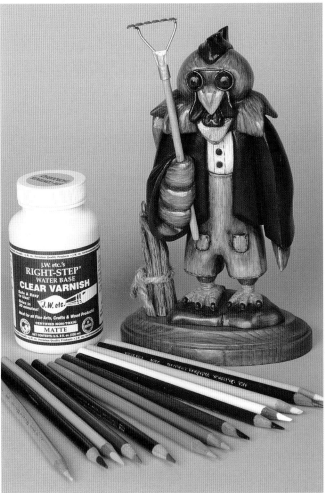

Oil pencils are available in as many as 60 colors, or you can blend them together on your carving to make your own colors.

PAINTING AND FINISHING SUPPLIES

Whatever medium you use to finish a carving, here are a few accessory items that may be helpful.

Palettes give you an easy-to-use surface for mixing paint.

■ **Krylon matte finish:** This is an excellent permanent nonglare spray coating to seal your carving after painting. It dries quickly, is easy to use, and provides a clear, durable, nonyellowing protection.

■ **Gesso:** This primer base coating can be applied to wood before painting. It looks like paint but is thinner than paint and dries harder. Gesso gives gripping action (called "tooth") so the paint will stick better. It should be applied thin so you get the gripping action without a buildup on the surface of the wood. Gesso will make the surface opaque so the wood grain will not show through. Applying gesso is not a necessity; however, most carvers who do detailed painting on their carvings will use a gesso base coat.

■ **Work surface cover:** Put a covering over your work area so you don't ruin it if paints or stains get on it. You can use freezer paper, brown wrapping paper, or a section from a cardboard box. Don't use newspaper because the ink can come off and ruin your carving.

■ **Palette:** This term is the fancy name for the surface on which you place and mix paints prior to applying them to the object you're painting. Commercial palettes are available, but everyday objects also work well, like plastic lids from ice cream containers and butter containers, freezer paper, wax paper, Styrofoam plates, saucers, a piece of glass, and anything that will keep paint on the surface.

■ **Palette knife:** If you do any paint mixing, a palette knife is a very helpful tool. They are available in either metal or plastic.

■ **Brushes:** Brushes are available in many styles and types of hair or bristles, such as synthetics, ox, hog, squirrel, camel, sable, badger, horse, and others. Whatever type you're going to use, buy good brushes for painting your carving. Good brushes will retain their shape and allow you to control the paint application. Cheap brushes tend to lose bristles and leave brush marks in the paint.

- **Rice:** Pour some uncooked rice into a small container to hold your brushes while you paint.
- **Container with thinner and foam:** Cutting a piece of foam to fit the bottom of a small container works great for cleaning your brushes. The foam has some gripping action to gently wipe the paints from your brush as you move the brush back and forth through the thinner.
- **Brush carrier:** One of the better carriers is made of metal. The springs keep the brushes separated while storing or carrying them.
- **Miscellaneous small containers:** You'll need some to mix stains, to hold water or paint thinner, and to clean brushes.
- **Latex-type gloves:** These are great to keep your hands clean when doing any staining or wiping paint on or off a project. If you have latex allergies, use gloves made of neoprene, nitrile, butyl, or vitron.
- **Rags:** Old T-shirts and cloth diapers are great for wiping off stain or paint and for general cleaning up. Make sure the rags you use are lint free. Lint left behind in paint or stain can make a mess of your carving.
- **Paper towels:** Paper towels are great for cleaning brushes and for all-around cleaning up.
- **Felt-tip markers:** Various colors of felt-tip markers can be helpful to do touch-ups on a carving. You can also use fine felt-tip markers for making eyes and other details on a carving.
- **Color board:** Make one-inch squares on a board of the type of wood you normally paint. In the top row of squares, write the color names. In the second row of squares, apply a color straight from the tube. In the third squares, add one part black. In the fourth squares, add one part white. In the fifth squares, thin with one part water. This is a good way to learn how adding white, black, or water will affect a specific color on your commonly used wood.

Rice in the bottom of a bottle will keep your brushes standing upright.

A jar with thinner and foam is a great setup for cleaning brushes.

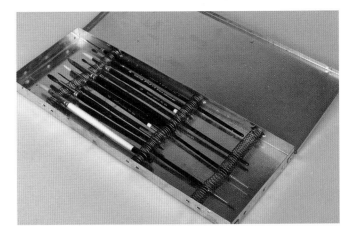

This excellent carrier for brushes is made of metal.

Chapter Ten

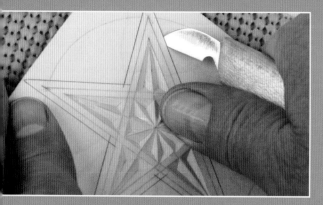  

STEP-BY-STEP PROJECTS

Take your time and you'll find carving well worth your effort.

All carvings, no matter how simple or complex, have one thing in common: They're all done just one chip at a time. In this chapter, you will learn how to correctly remove those chips to create your work of art.

Each project is designed to teach you how to work with the wood grain and use your tools to develop the necessary skills required to guide you through your carving journey. As you complete each project, keep in mind that each cut you make should have a specific purpose. Don't ever make a cut until you know what you want to accomplish with it. Take time and learn with each cut you make.

STYLIZED BIRD

Carving stylistically forces you to look at the shape of the object you are carving, not the details like eyes and fur and color. By starting with a simple stylized project, you can begin to train your eye to see the basic shapes in every carving. You will learn to focus on the pose and posture of your subject as well.

Project objectives:

- Lay out a project
- Use a carving knife
- Do pull cuts and push cuts
- Work with positive and negative transition points
- Work with the wood grain

MATERIALS AND TOOLS

Materials
- Butternut blank (1½" x 1½" x 5" long)
- Pattern

Tools
- Band saw, scroll saw, or coping saw
- Carving knife
- Sandpaper (220, 320, 400, and 600 grit)
- Pencil
- Carving glove and thumb guard
- Narrow base (to find balance point)
- Eye screw
- Scribe or sharp nail

Finishing Supplies
- Satin-finish polyurethane varnish
- Foam brush or bristle brush
- Soft cloth or rag
- Pencil or fine tip felt-tip marker

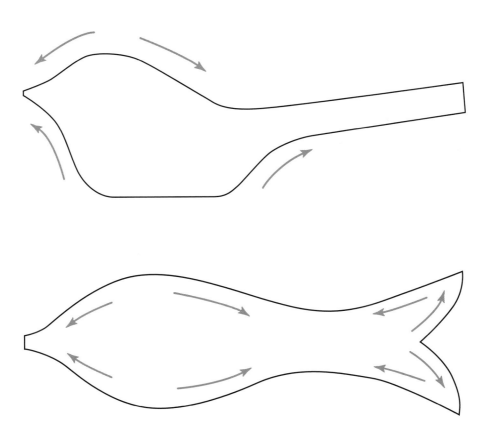

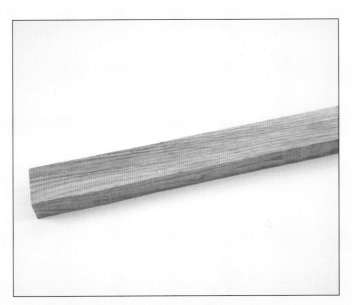

1 **Select the wood.** I chose a piece of butternut. Because the tail of this bird is very thin, choose wood with straight grain running through the thin area to give it added strength.

2 **Transfer the pattern.** Draw the pattern on the wood with the long wood fibers running parallel to the tail.

3 Cut out the side view.
Use a band saw, a scroll saw, or a coping saw to cut out the blank. Remember to keep your fingers clear of the blade no matter what type of saw you're using.

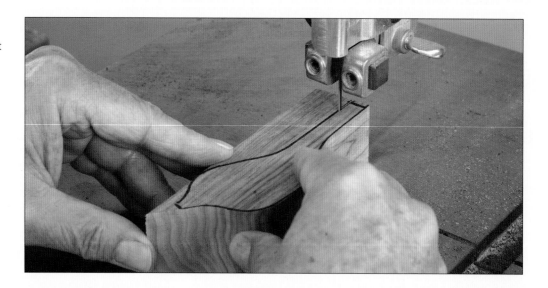

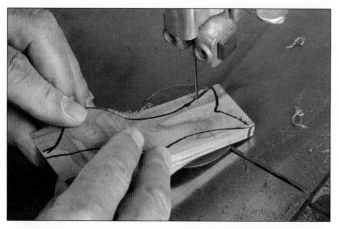

4 Lay out the top view. Lay the tail flat on the band saw table. The top-view cut is started with the tail lying flat on the band saw table so it has a firm base. Finish the cut.

5 Remove the waste wood. When the cut gets to the body of the bird, raise the tail off the table and, while holding the blank by the tail, pull the blank to cut off the waste wood on both sides.

6 Cut the tail. With the tail again flat on the table, cut the waste wood from the middle end of the tail.

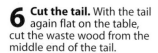

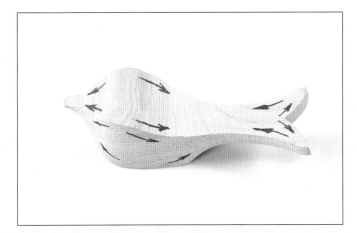

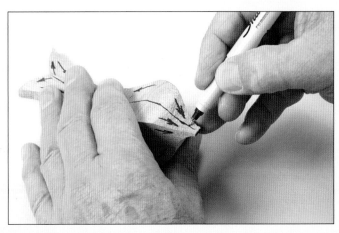

7 Draw arrows to show cutting direction. If you always cut in the direction of the arrows, you'll always be cutting across the grain so your knife will never be given an opportunity to go between the vessels.

8 Draw a centerline on the top of the bird from the beak to the center of the tail. Continue the line on the bottom.

9 Round the head. Put on a carving glove and thumb guard. Using a controlled split, do a pull cut with a carving knife and remove the wood to round both sides of the head. Keep the centerline to give you a reference so the head will be balanced on both sides.

Tip: *Keeping Your Carving Balanced*

Any time you carve something symmetrical, a centerline helps to keep the carving balanced. With a centerline, you always have a reference so you can carve equal amounts of wood from both sides of the line.

10 Mark the positive transition point. Draw a line from side to side across the top of the head showing the positive transition point at this area of the carving. Always cut away from a positive transition point.

11 Shape the head. Use push cuts done with the carving knife to shape the head into the beak. Be cautious that you don't cut off the beak.

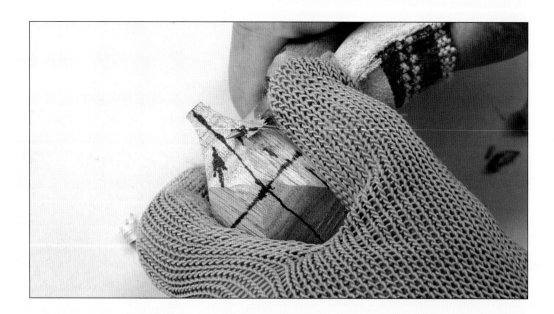

12 Shape the body. Use pull cuts to shape the body.

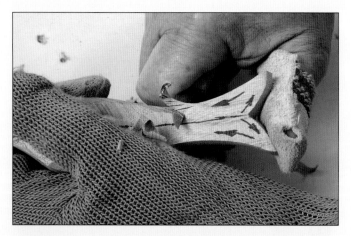

13 Don't cut too far toward the tail. When you feel your knife wants to go between the vessels, don't cut any farther because you've reached a negative transition point.

Mistakes Happen

Carving the tail requires extra caution because of a negative transition point at which you must change the direction of carving. If you don't change direction at this point, the knife will go between the vessels, splitting off the tail. In the bottom left photo, you can see how the knife is taking the path of least resistance and separating the vessels from one another. To stop the piece from breaking off completely, stop the cut as soon as you feel your knife going between the vessels.

If you haven't lost the piece in a pile of chips, you can reattach it with white, yellow, or cyanoacrylate glue specially made for gluing wood. Apply glue to one surface. Carefully align the two pieces and hold or clamp them until they're set. It's very important to get them perfectly aligned, or the glue joint will show. Allow the glue to fully cure before you resume carving.

14 **Mark the negative transition point.** I've drawn in a line showing the negative transition point in this area of the tail. Always cut toward a negative transition point. When you reach a negative transition point, you must cut toward it from both directions.

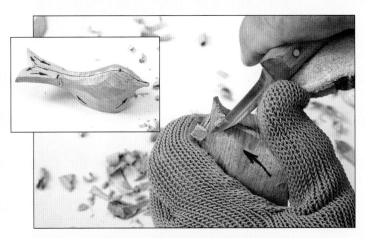

15 **Shape the bottom of the bird's body.** Shape the bottom from the breast to the beak on both sides of the bird using the carving knife. Be careful so you don't cut off the beak. The bird should now look like the inset photo.

16 **Check the contours.** View the carving from the front to check the contours.

17 **Shape the beak.** Carefully shape the bottom of the beak. Remove the centerline and contour both sides around the neck and bottom of the beak.

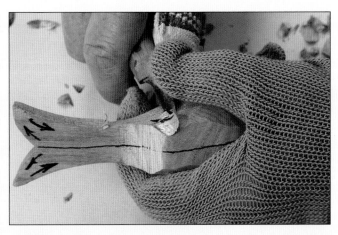

18 **Shape the bottom of the bird.** Using a push cut, shape the bottom of the bird up to the negative transition point on the bottom of the tail. Do this on both sides.

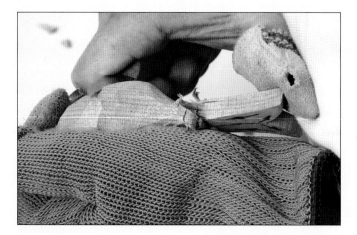

19 **Remove the centerline.** Shape the bottom of the body. When it is shaped properly, cut off the centerline.

20 **Shape the top of the tail.** To shape the top of the tail, use a pull cut and start at the end of the tail. Cut in the direction of the arrows.

21 **Use short cuts as you near the negative transition point.** Using short pull cuts and push cuts, remove the wood from both sides of the negative transition point and up to it.

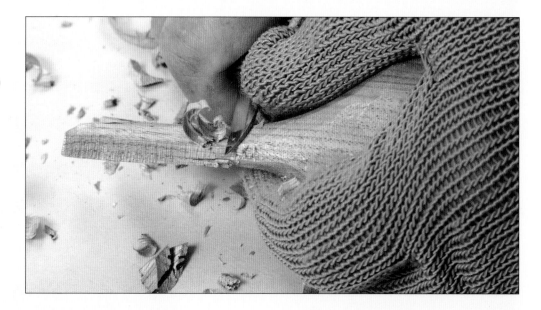

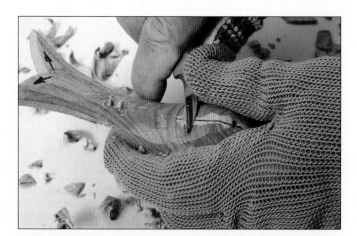

22 **Shape the body.** Shape the top of the body and remove the centerline.

23 **Shape the bottom of the tail.** Repeat Steps 20 and 21, remembering to make shorter cuts as you reach the transition point.

24 **Shape the center of the tail.** Place the tip of your knife at the center of the tail and carefully remove the wood from this area of the tail out to the tip of the tail.

25 **Remove the wood from the tail.** Take extra care so you don't break the tips of the tail. With a pull cut, remove the wood from the other side of the tail. Again, be extra careful so you don't break off the ends of the tail.

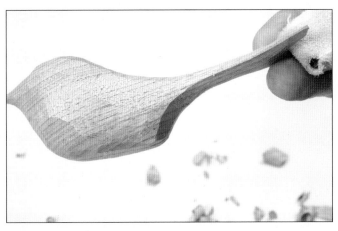

26 **Thin the tail.** Thin along the edges of the tail section. Your bird should now look like this.

27 **Remove any large facets from the surface of the bird.** With small cuts, smooth the surface of the bird.

Tip: *Keep Your Tools Sharp*

Have you checked your tools lately? Remember to keep an eye on how your tools are performing throughout the carving process. If they seem dull, take the time to sharpen them.

Before you start any carving, test your tools to make sure they're sharp. When you pick up a tool to make a specific cut, you want it to cut as it should.

28 **Find the balance point.** If you want to hang the bird, like a Christmas tree ornament, find the balance point by balancing the carving on a narrow base. Mark the center of the balance point and insert the eye screw.

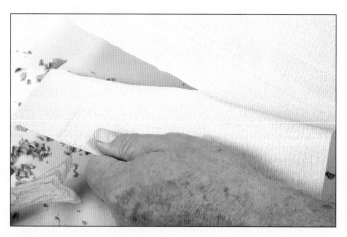

29 **Flatten the bottom.** If you want the bird to sit on a tabletop or shelf, flatten the bottom by removing the extra wood with the carving knife.

30 **Sand the surface.** You can leave knife cuts showing on your project, or you can sand the surface. If you choose to sand, start with a coarse grit, such as 220, to remove all the facets left from the knife cuts. Tear a full sheet of sandpaper in fourths and fold it so it's easy to hold.

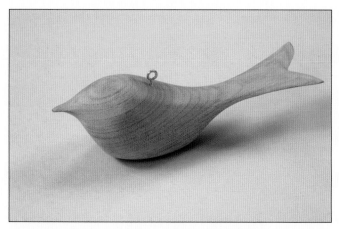

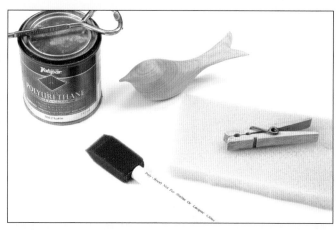

31 **Step through the sequence of sandpaper.** When all of the facets are removed, step through a sequence of sandpaper grits, such as 320 to 400 to 600, to get a smooth surface. The 220-grit sandpaper cuts fast but leaves scratches that need to be removed. The surface should be shiny, smooth, and free of any wood dust before varnishing.

32 **Put on a finish.** I'll use satin-finish polyurethane varnish on the bird.

MAKE A SIMPLE BRUSH

To make a simple brush for small jobs, start by cutting a small section from a dense piece of foam. Trim both edges from one end of the foam. Use a clip clothespin as a handle. (This works great for small jobs, and when you're done putting on the finish, simply open the clothespin and drop the foam into a container.)

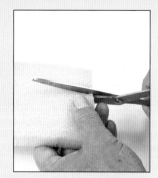

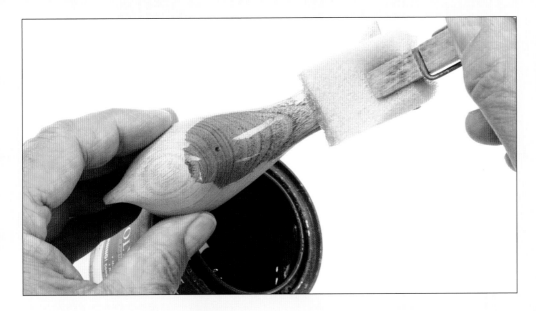

33 **Apply varnish.** Thin the varnish a little and liberally apply it to the bird. You can apply varnish with a cloth, a bristle brush, or a foam brush.

34 **Allow the varnish to penetrate.** Cover the entire surface and let the varnish set for about five minutes to allow it to penetrate into the wood. (Varnish is a superficial finish, so it won't penetrate very deep into the wood, but it will seal the wood.)

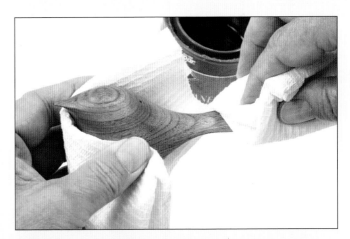

35 **Remove the surface varnish.** Wipe the surface varnish from the carving. The only varnish left is what has penetrated into the wood. There will be no varnish buildup on the surface to make your carving look like plastic.

36 **Sign your finished piece.** You start with a blank, such as the one in the back, and end up with a carving, such as the one in the front. Write your name and date on the bottom of the carving and enjoy your work of art.

SNOWMAN

This snowman is an in-the-round carving that is fun and very popular. It can be a stand-alone carving, or it can be hung on the wall or on your Christmas tree.

As you carve his hat, give it some character. It's old, so make it look old. The body should be painted white, but the other colors are optional. You can paint the hat, gloves, and boxes any color you want.

Project objectives:

- ■ Lay out a project
- ■ Cut out the blank
- ■ Add wood for his hat brim by gluing it on the blank
- ■ Make stop cuts
- ■ Use a gouge
- ■ Work with the wood grain
- ■ Paint a carving

MATERIALS AND TOOLS

Materials
- ■ Basswood board (3¼" x 8½" x ⅞" to 1" thick)
- ■ Two pieces from board for hat
- ■ Piece of wood for nose
- ■ Copy of pattern

Tools
- ■ Band saw, scroll saw, or coping saw
- ■ Carving knife
- ■ ½" (13 mm) #5 gouge
- ■ V-tool
- ■ Saw, any fine tooth
- ■ ³⁄₁₆" drill bit
- ■ Drill
- ■ Micro tools (optional)
- ■ Carving glove and thumb guard
- ■ Pen or pencil

- ■ Toothbrush
- ■ Wood glue
- ■ Clamp or rubber bands
- ■ Carbon or graphite tracing paper (optional)
- ■ ¾"-thick piece of board (for work surface)
- ■ Nonskid material (2 sheets)

Finishing Supplies
- ■ Acrylic paints:
  - • White
  - • Red (optional)
  - • Green (optional)
  - • Black (optional)
  - • Yellow (optional)
- ■ Brushes: ⅜" or ½" flat, ¼" tapered (optional), script/liner
- ■ Fine tip felt-tip marker

Pattern appears at 80% of actual size.

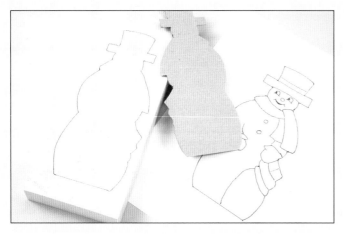

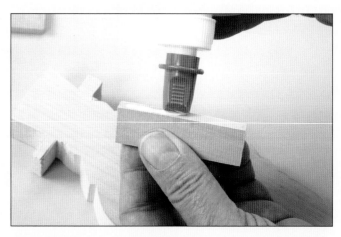

1 **Copy the pattern.** Make a copy from the book to trace or to make a template. Use a band saw, a scroll saw, or a coping saw to cut out the blank. Also cut two 2¼" long x ⅜" wide x ¼" thick pieces from one end of the board, which will be added to form the brim of his hat.

2 **Put glue on the hat brim.** Spread glue on one surface of the brim pieces.

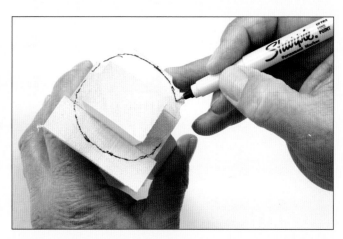

3 **Attach the pieces to the hat brim.** Using a clamp or rubber bands attach the pieces to the brim of his hat and allow the glue to dry for at least four hours.

4 **Sketch the outline of the hat brim.** Use a pen or pencil to draw the outline of the hat brim. Make it any size or shape that looks good to you.

5 **Draw on the pattern.** Using the pattern from the book, transfer it to the blank. You can trace the pattern onto the wood using carbon or graphite paper, but it's good practice to do it freehand.

6 Shape the hat brim. Put on your carving glove and a thumb guard. Using pull cuts, cut the outline of the hat brim with a carving knife.

7 Draw in the top of the hat. Again, you can use carbon or graphite paper, but I draw it freehand.

8 Shape the hat. Make a stop cut up to the point where you will remove wood to round his hat. Do this on all four corners. You can use your knife to make the stop cuts, but I like using a fine-tooth saw to make them.

9 Round the hat. Do controlled splits with the carving knife to round his hat.

10 Clean up the area. Use your knife to clean up the area where the brim and dome of the hat meet.

11 Shape the top of the hat. This is an old hat, so make it look that way by cutting the top unevenly. Give it some character.

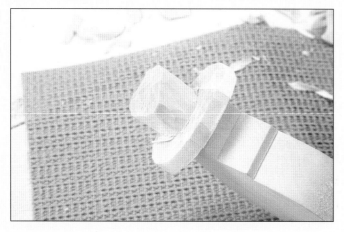

12 **Change the work surface.** Place a ¾"-thick piece of board between two sheets of nonskid material. The brim of his hat will lay over the edge of the board.

13 **Make body stop cuts.** Using the picture of the finished snowman, make stop cuts at all the areas where you need to round to. I find a saw works great for doing this.

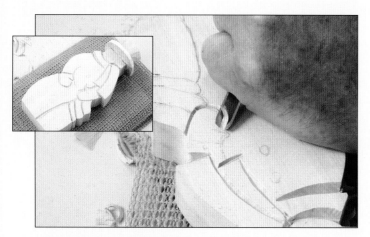

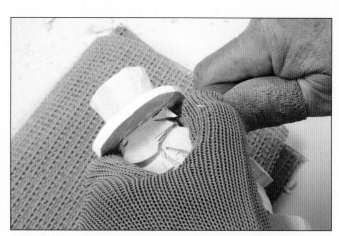

14 **Remove the lines drawn on the body.** Using a V-tool, remove all the lines you drew on the body. This step creates stop cuts that define each element of the carving. The snowman now has all vertical cuts made for the stop cuts and all the lines carved, as shown in the inset photo.

15 **Round the head.** Shape the top part of the head under his hat.

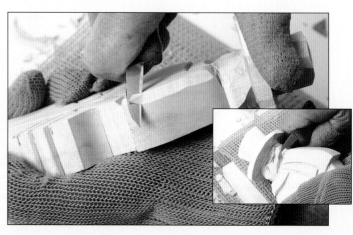

16 **Shape the bottom of the hat brim.** Use your ½" #5 gouge to shape the bottom of the hat brim.

17 **Round the scarf.** Think of how a scarf hangs around someone's shoulders. Blend the scarf up to his face with the knife.

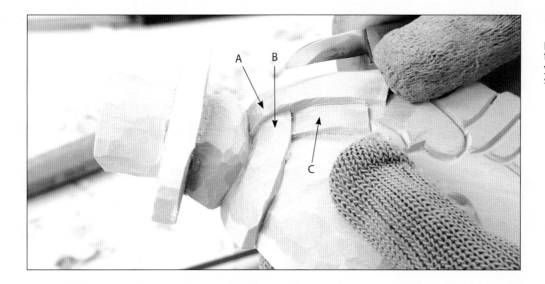

18 **Study the shape of the scarf.** Look at the picture and see how the scarf folds over itself. If it will help you see this, physically tie a scarf around something.

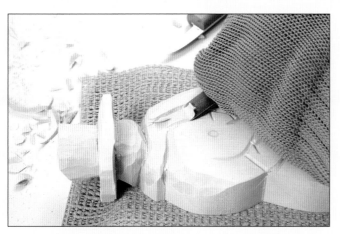

19 **Shape the scarf** in three distinct steps. First, shape the highest level of the scarf (*A*) using a V-tool or knife to outline and the ½" #5 gouge to remove the waste wood. Any time you carve something with various levels, focus on the top level first.

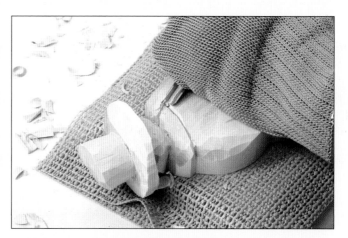

20 **Redraw the *B* segment of the scarf,** which you carved away in Step 19, and remove the wood so it looks as if this part of the scarf comes from under *A*.

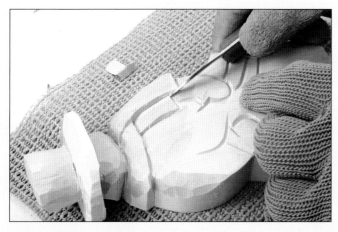

21 **Draw and carve the lowest level** of the scarf (*C*) so it looks as if it comes from under *B*.

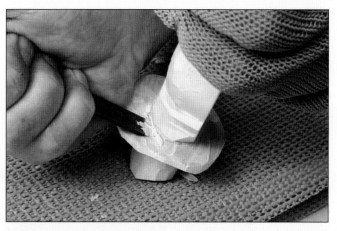

22 **Blend the hat and head.** Round his head under the hat so it looks as if the hat sets on the snowball head.

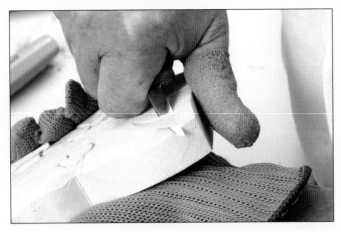

23 **Round the body.** Round his body and take off the wood from around his gloves and up to the bag. The gloves and bag should protrude off his body.

24 **Shape the bag.** You want it to look like it has folds.

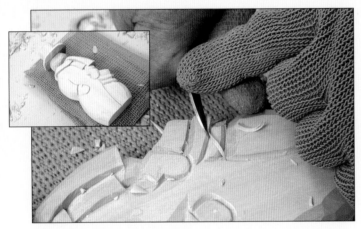

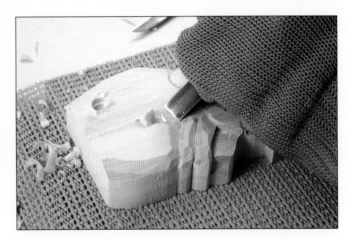

25 **Round the folds.** Your knife works great for this. Give the bag some contour and character. Your carving should now look like the one in the inset photo.

26 **Round the body next to the bag using the gouge.** Make it look like the bag is in front of the body.

27 **Make the buttons using micro tools.** If you have micro tools, make the buttons with them. Use the same technique used to make the center of the flower in the Flower Relief Carving (see page 226), but in a miniature version. Remove the wood so the buttons protrude off the body.

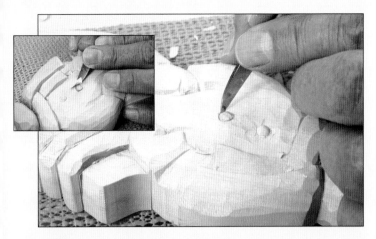

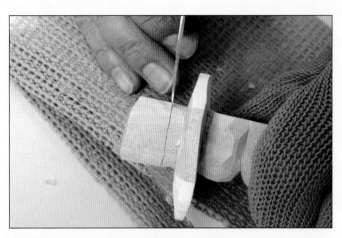

28 Make the buttons with your knife. If you don't have micro tools, use your knife to make the buttons by cutting around the small circles. Then, remove the wood around the buttons so they stand off the body.

29 Make a stop cut for the hatband. Make a stop cut with your knife all around the hat to the width you want the band.

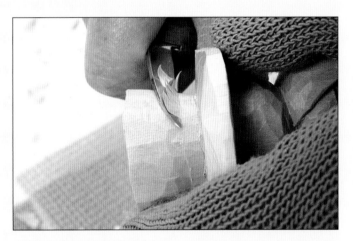

30 Refine the hatband. Remove the wood so the band stands off the hat.

31 Blend the band into the brim of the hat. Use the knife to contour wood from the portion of the hat above the hatband down to the hatband, and all around the hat.

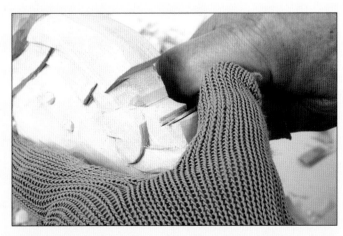

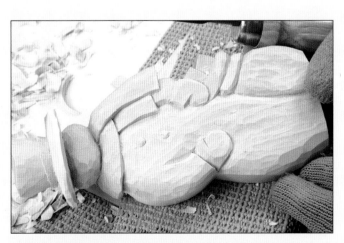

32 Shape the boxes. Use your knife to make it look as if there are two individual boxes protruding from the bag.

33 Make sure the front of your snowman now has the following features: hat shaped, face rounded, scarf folded over itself, bag and packages defined, gloves shaped, buttons defined, body rounded and showing gouge cuts over the entire carving.

34 **Lay out the back.** Turn the snowman over and draw the pattern on his back.

35 **Draw the side contour.** Use the side pattern to see how much wood should be removed from the back near his scarf and to form the back of the bag.

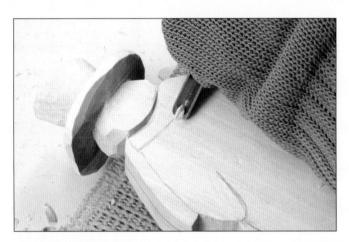

36 **Define the scarf.** Use your V-tool to make stop cuts around the scarf.

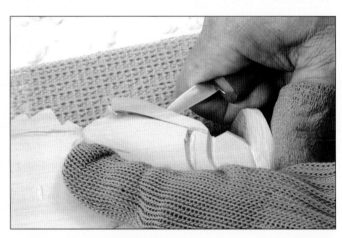

37 **Form the scarf.** Make a stop cut along the line you drew on his back. Turn him and cut into the side line you drew in order to remove the piece of wood from behind his scarf.

38 **Continue removing wood** until you've eliminated the wood between the line on his back and the line on his side.

39 **Define the bag.** Make stop cuts with your knife to remove the wood from the back of his bag.

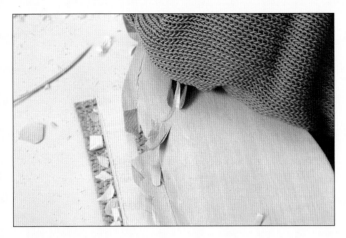

40 Define the arms. Use the V-tool to define the backs of his arms.

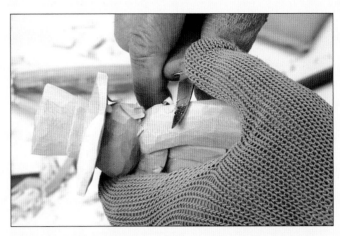

41 Round the head and scarf. Round the back of his head, and then round his scarf to make it flow around the back of his head.

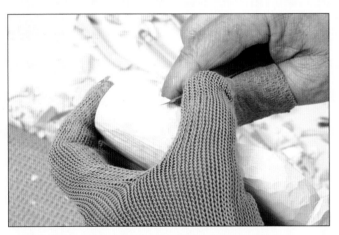

42 Contour the body. Round his body on the sides.

43 Relieve wood from around the scarf so it sets off his body.

44 Carve the surface. Using your ½" #5 gouge, make gouge-cut facets all over the carving. You should see only gouge cuts, not flat spots.

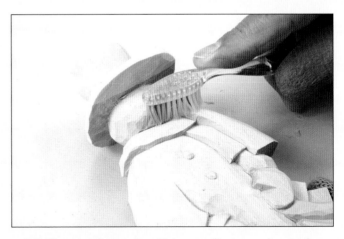

45 Clean up the carving. Make sure all cuts are clean and remove any loose chips. A good tool to remove any loose chips is a toothbrush. If any chips still hang on the carving, cut all the fibers so the chips fall out.

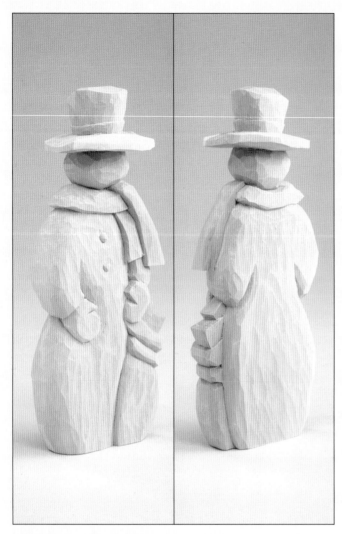

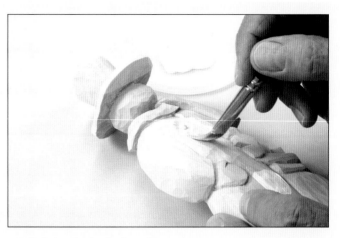

47 Paint the body. Put white paint on your palette and paint the body white. I'm using a flat ⅜"-wide brush. Wash the white paint from the brush.

46 Prepare for painting. Your carving should now look like this.

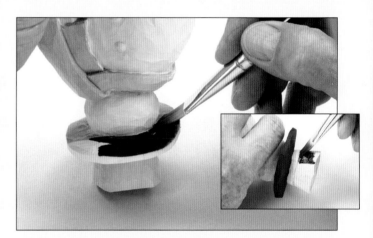

48 Paint the hat. Apply a dab of black on your palette. Start by painting the bottom of the hatband. Be cautious not to get any black on the white you've just painted.

49 Paint the top of the hat, but don't paint the hatband; that will be red. Remember to wash your brush thoroughly before you move on to the next color.

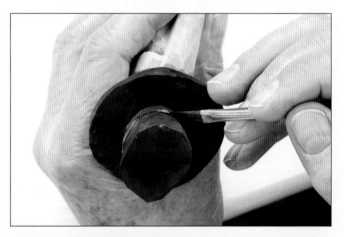

50 Paint the hatband and scarf. A tapered brush is helpful when painting up to another color.

Tip: *Painting Up to an Existing Color*

To paint up to an existing color with another color, remove the paint from the side of the brush that will be adjacent to the existing paint by wiping it on a paper towel. You end up with paint on only one side of the brush, which will minimize the possibility of getting new paint on the existing paint.

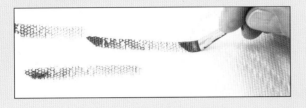

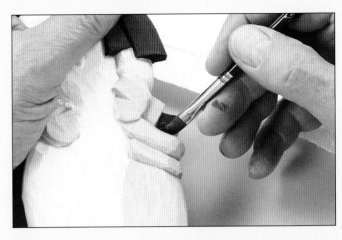

51 **Paint one of the boxes in the bag.** I chose red, but you can use any color you like.

52 **Paint the gloves green.** Clean the brush. Tone down some green by adding a little black. Paint his gloves.

53 **Paint the bag brown.** Thin the paint slightly. Use a soft-bristle brush about ¼" wide to apply the paint. Be cautious that you don't get paint on his white body or on the packages.

54 **Paint the other box.** I used yellow.

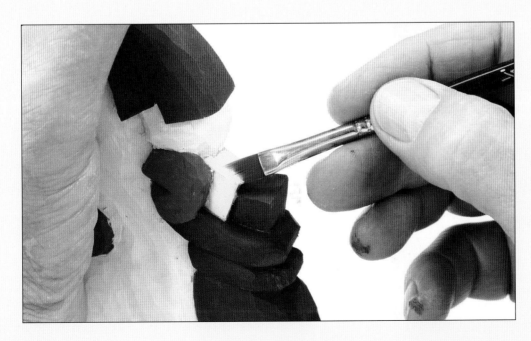

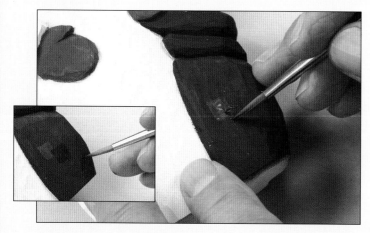

55 **Add patches to the bag.** To add another dimension to the bag, paint a couple of patches and add stitches to them.

56 **Paint the buttons black.** Mix water with some black paint to the consistency of ink. Then, use a long-bristle liner brush to apply the paint.

57 **Paint a pattern on the scarf.** The liner brush works great for painting lines over a distance and holds the paint like a pen. Do a crosshatch pattern.

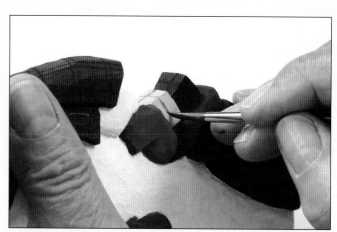

58 **Paint ribbons on the packages.** I used green.

59 **Make the eyes and mouth.** A fine tip felt-tip marker works great for this step.

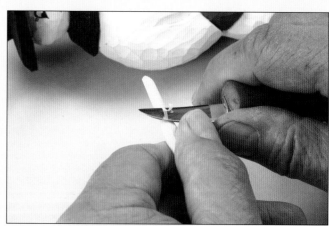

60 **Drill for the nose.** Drill a hole for his nose and trim a piece of wood to fit the hole.

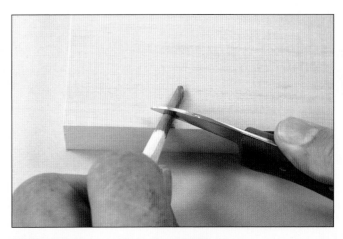

61 **Make orange paint.** Mix red and yellow to make orange for a carrot nose.

62 **Make the nose.** Paint the piece for his nose and cut it to length.

63 **Glue the nose.** Add a drop of wood glue in the hole for his nose and insert the nose.

64 **Add snow to the surface of the carving.** Spread a thin coat of white paint on a palette. Use a toothbrush and dip just the tips of the bristles in the paint. Pull your finger across the brush to spray a fine mist of paint across the carving, creating a snow pattern.

65 **Make your own designs.** When I was finished, I felt the snowman needed a companion, so I carved him a snow lady. The next step is to carve a snow child to make it a "snow family." Your assignment is to design and carve what you think the snow child should look like, and send me pictures of your snow family.

FLOWER RELIEF CARVING

Relief carving is removing wood from around the object you're carving to create shadows so it looks as though it's standing off the surface of the surrounding wood. Black-and-white photos use varying shades from black to white to create a picture. In relief carving, you're using shadows to create the picture. Rendering a three-dimensional object in a collapsed form like this takes practice and skill. The subjects are endless. This flower may look simple, but depending on the amount of surface detail you give it and the amount of undercutting and shadows you create, the end result may be astoundingly complex.

Project objectives:

- Lay out a pattern
- Work with hand tools
- Do stop cuts and undercuts

MATERIALS AND TOOLS

Materials
- Basswood board (5" x 7" x ¾")
- Copy of pattern

Tools
- Carving knife
- V-tool
- ⅜" (10 mm) #9 gouge
- ½" (13 mm) #5 gouge
- ½" (13 mm) #3 gouge
- Flat skew (optional)
- Dental tool (optional)
- Hand grinder (optional)
- Carbon or graphite tracing paper
- Pencil
- Hammer
- Nail
- Sandpaper (320 grit)
- Toothbrush
- Tape
- Lighted magnifying glass
- 3M pad

Finishing Supplies
- Varnish, linseed oil, or paint (optional)

1 **Set up your workstation.** It can be any flat surface. If you carve on a kitchen or dining room table, make sure you have a protective surface under the piece you're carving. The protective piece should be larger than the piece you're carving and be set on some nonskid material or a terry cloth towel so the surface of the table doesn't get scratched.

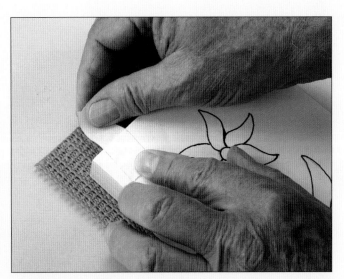

2 **Attach the pattern.** Make a copy of the flower pattern. Center the pattern on the board. Tape the top edge of the pattern to the board.

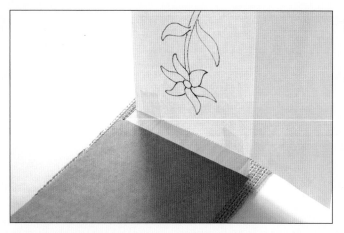

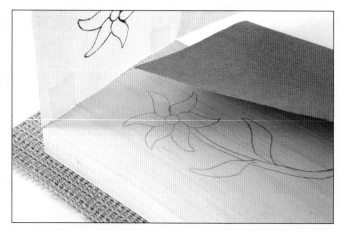

3 Insert tracing paper. Place carbon or graphite tracing paper between the copy and the board.

4 Trace the pattern onto the board. Check to make sure you've copied the entire flower on the board; then, remove the pattern and the tracing paper.

5 Make the center button of the flower using a ⅜" #9 gouge. Place the tool's cutting edge on the circle. Tilt the handle over the piece you're going to carve and sink the tool into the wood. Lift about one-third of the front edge of the tool out of the wood.

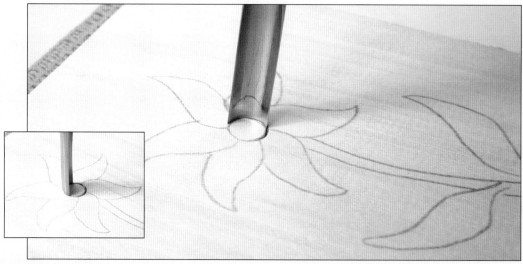

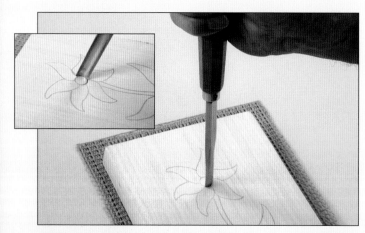

6 Continue cutting the center. Slide the tool forward in the cut and sink the tool back into the wood. Continue this process until you've cut a complete circle.

7 Remove the wood from around the center of the flower. Start about ¾" from the circle stop cut and push the gouge up to the stop cut. Rock the tool from side to side so you remove wood up to the stop cut. Do this all around the stop cut.

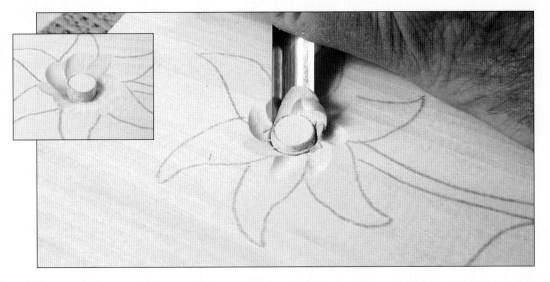

8 **Make the stop cut deeper and remove more wood.** Do Steps 5 and 6 once again around the button until you've cut into the wood about ⅜" deep all around the center of the flower. Again, remove the wood from around the center of the flower.

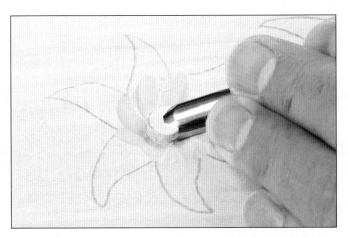

9 **Round the button.** With the concave side down, place the gouge at the bottom edge of the center. Push it through the wood, rounding the surface of the piece. When you reach the center of the button, begin to slowly raise the handle while you continue pushing the gouge through the wood.

10 **Finish one side.** You should end with the handle straight up at the edge of the button. You now have one side of the button rounded.

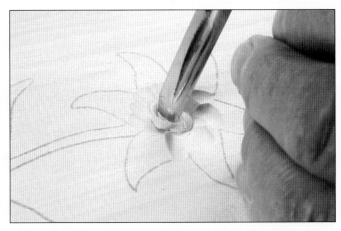

11 **Round the other side.** Turn the piece around and round off the other side of the button.

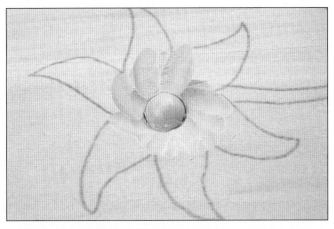

12 **Check your work.** It should look like this. Before you move on to the next step, redraw the petal segments.

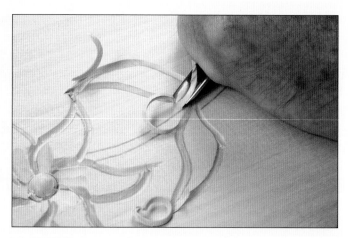

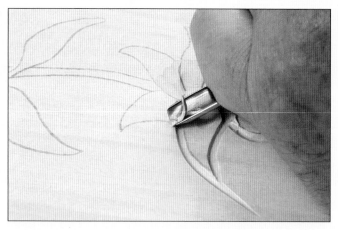

13 **Remove the wood from around the flower.** Use your V-tool to remove wood around the flower, starting with the petals. Remember, always cut away from the piece you want to save and toward the waste area.

14 **Continue around the entire flower.** Keep the same depth of cut so the entire flower will be the same distance above the background.

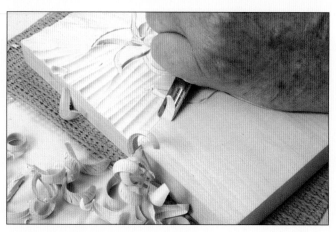

15 **Remove the background wood.** Use your ⅜" #9 gouge to remove wood all around the flower background.

16 **Make stop cuts with your knife.** When you've completed roughing out the background, use the carving knife and make stop cuts following the pencil lines.

17 **Remove more background.** Use your ⅜" #9 gouge and remove wood up to the stop cuts.

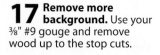

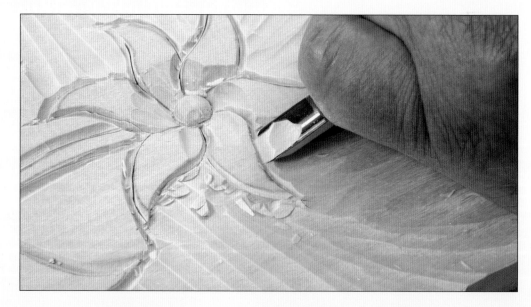

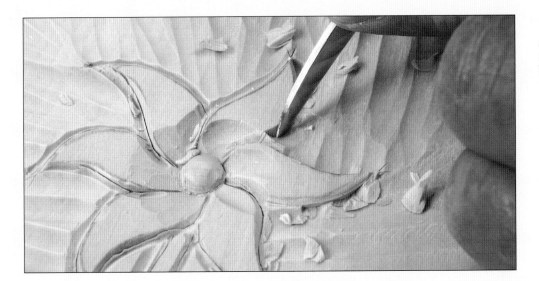

18 Clean out tight areas with your knife. In areas that your gouge can't reach, make stop cuts with your knife.

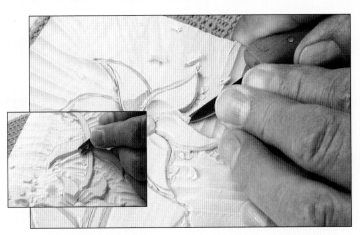

19 Continue cleaning up the background. Tilt the knife so the blade is parallel to the wood surface, and slice the wood from between the petal and the leaves. It's areas like this where a flat skew is helpful. You can also use the V-tool to clean around the flower. Remove wood from between the leaves and flower.

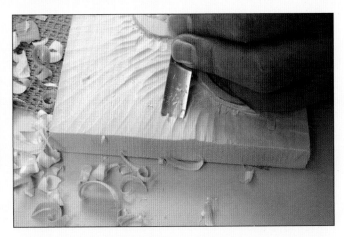

20 Flatten the background. Use a ½" #5 gouge and flatten the background all around the flower. To get a clean cut, you must always see both edges of the gouge.

21 Contour each petal. Now use your ½" #5 gouge to make one edge of each petal look as if it is lying behind the petal next to it. Refer to the pattern and the completed carving photo for reference. Overlapping the petals gives more life to the carving.

22 Shape each petal. With your ⅜" #9 gouge, shape each petal by cutting from the tip of the petal to the button. Let it flow to give each petal some character. Look at a real flower to see what petals look like.

23 **Remove the wood from the stem** so it looks as if it's coming from behind the petals.

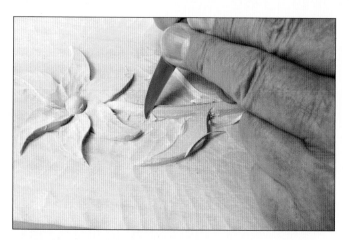

24 **Shape the stem with the carving knife.** How the grain runs through the stem will determine which direction you need to cut. Turn the board if you need to cut the other way.

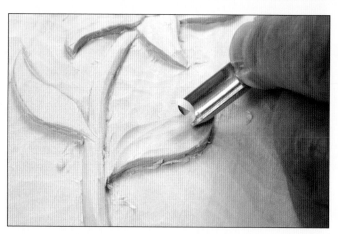

25 **Shape the leaves.** Give each leaf some contour to make them look real with the ⅜" #9 gouge. Look at the leaves of real flowers for reference. Cut from the tip of the leaf toward the stem. Give them some movement because leaves don't lie flat.

CREATING MORE SHADOWS

To create more shadows and make the petals and leaves look as if they are off the surface of the background, remove some wood from under their edges (undercut). However, make sure you have all superficial carving completed before you undercut. Once you remove wood from under any area of your carving, you can't change the surface because there will be no wood under it to support changes.

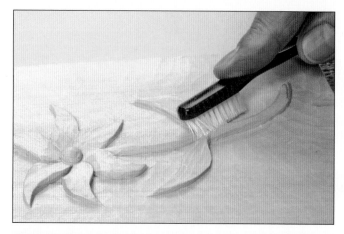

26 **Clean up the loose chips with a toothbrush.** The bristles are stiff enough to remove loose chips, yet not so stiff as to scratch your carving.

27 **Smooth the petals.** Use a ½" #3 gouge to clean up the petals so they have a smooth surface. Notice how I'm holding the tool. Get down near the cutting edge so you have good control of the tool, and do small slicing cuts.

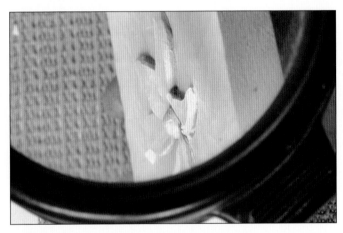

28 **Check your work.** A lighted magnifying glass helps you see details as you clean up your carving.

29 **Undercut the petals.** Cut at an angle under the petal with the knife. Then, cut flush with the surface of the background to release the chip. If the chip doesn't fall out, don't pull on it. Make the cut again to sever all the wood fibers so the piece will fall out.

30 **Check the result.** Notice how the top petal is off the surface.

31 **Remove hanging "fuzzies".** A dental tool works great to remove hanging pieces from the undercuts. You can also use folded 320-grit sandpaper.

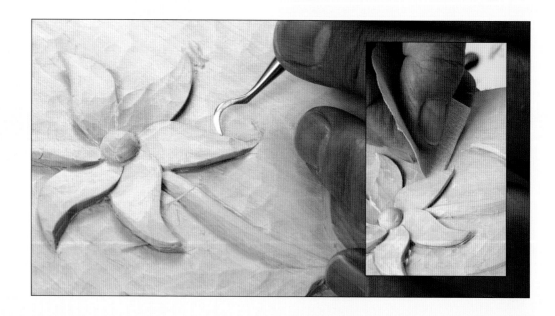

UNDERCUTTING PETALS

You can undercut any petal that has long wood fibers running lengthwise through it. However, if the tips of the petals are located where short fibers run through them, don't undercut the tips of those petals because they will easily break. If you number the petal with the gouge under it as 1 and count clockwise, you can undercut the ends of number 1 and number 4 because they have the fibers running the full length of them. If you undercut the ends of petals 2, 3, 5, and 6, which have very short fibers running through them, they could break at the tip. These petals can still be undercut on the sides. I normally flow the tips of the petals toward the surface of the base.

32 **Shape the stem end.** Using the knife, cut the stem so you expose the end of it. A simple cut like this adds another dimension to the carving.

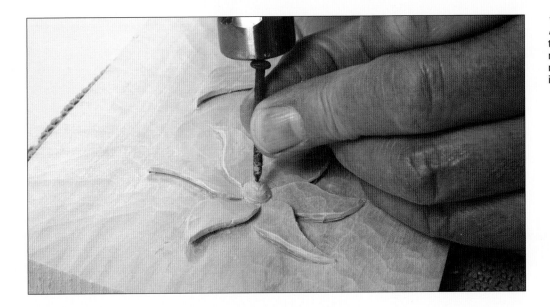

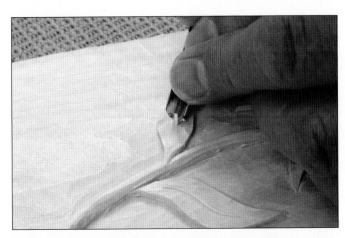

33 **Add texture to the button.** To add some texture to the button in the middle of the flower, use a nail and hammer. Lightly tap in the dimples.

34 **Add veins to the leaves.** Using the V-tool, add a vein down the center of each leaf.

35 **Clean the carving.** A 3M pad works great to clean up the background and undercuts. You can do this by hand or attach a section of pad to a hand grinder for quick removal. To use a hand grinder, cut a piece of pad about 1½" square and attach it to a mandrel. Put a small washer on both sides of the pad to give more gripping area in the mandrel. You don't need to cut the pad round; it will round as you use it.

36 **Decide whether or not to use finish.** You can leave the carving unfinished, as shown here, or you can finish it with varnish, linseed oil, or paint.

STYLIZED CAT

This stylized cat has a bit more wood and a bit more complexity than the bird we carved earlier (see page 200). Like the bird, the cat carving has smooth, flowing lines that are enhanced by the beauty of the wood grain. Carving the cat will also help you to focus on form above detail.

MATERIALS AND TOOLS

Materials
- Butternut, walnut, or cherry. (The finished carving is 12" high x 5½" wide x 3½" thick, but the block you start with should be at least 12" high x 6½" wide x 4½" thick.)
- Copy of pattern (front and side views)

Tools
- Band saw
- Carving knife
- ⅜" (10 mm) #9 gouge
- ½" (13 mm) #5 gouge
- Vise
- Drill
- ⁵⁄₁₆" drill bit
- Lag bolt
- Vise-grip pliers
- Wood block for vise buffer
- Pencil
- Carbon or graphite tracing paper
- Masking tape

Finishing Supplies
- Various grits of sandpaper (120 grit through 600 grit)
- Satin-finish varnish, boiled linseed oil, or tung oil
- Brush
- Old brush and cloth
- Fine tip felt-tip marker

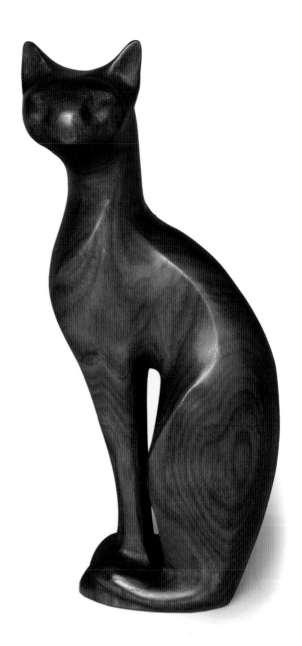

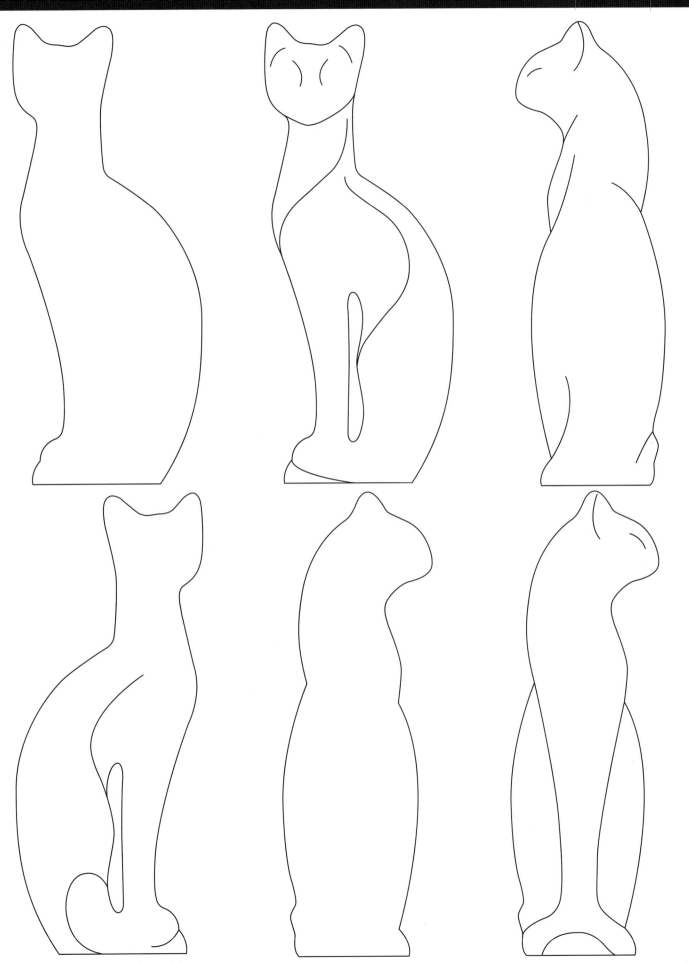

Pattern appears at 40% of actual size.

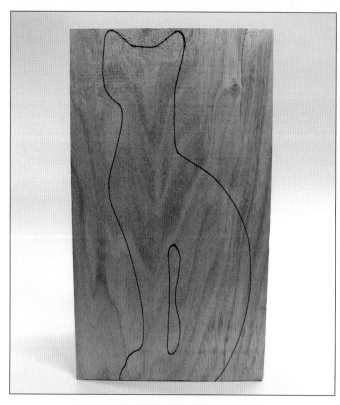

1 **Make copies of the front- and side-view patterns.** You can make them any size you want the carving to be, but it is important to make both of the views the same size. Trace a copy of the front view on the block of wood.

2 **Leave some wood on both sides of the carving.** You will use this when you cut the side view.

Tip: *Grain Considerations*

Lay the pattern on the wood so the wood grain lies symmetrically across the face. If you can do this, it will aesthetically enhance the carving. It is not always possible, but if you are going to put a clear finish on your carving, you should always attempt to use the wood grain to aesthetically enhance the carving.

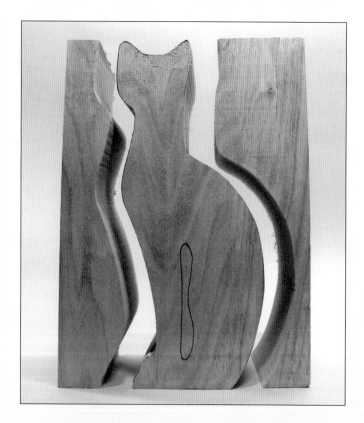

3 **Cut the front profile.** Use a band saw to cut out the front profile.

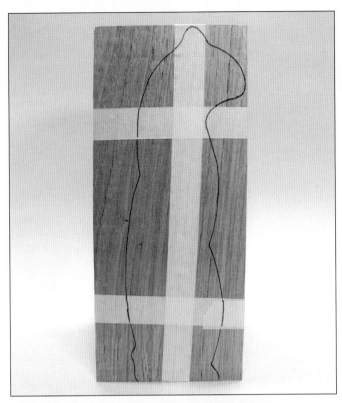

4 **Attach the waste wood back to the blank with tape and trace the side-view pattern.** Masking tape works great to hold the waste wood in position, giving you a flat surface on which to accurately draw the side pattern and cut this side of the blank.

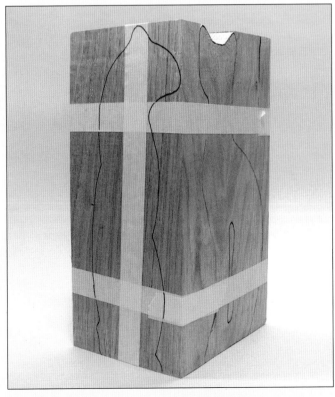

5 **Cut out the side view** of the blank with the band saw.

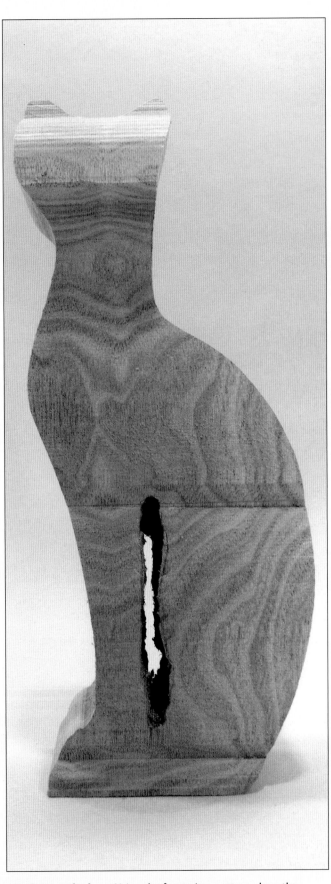

6 **Cut out the legs.** Using the front-view pattern, draw the area between the legs and the body, and drill out this area.

7 **Check your blank.** An angled view from one side shows how the cut-out blank, with the drilled-out area, should look.

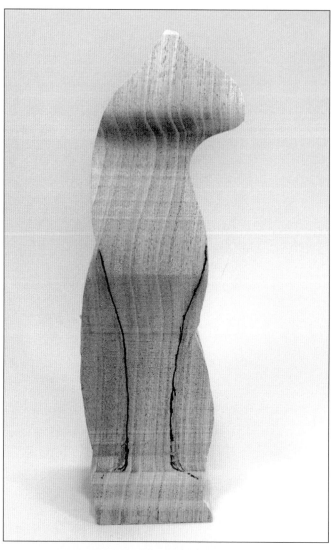

8 **Draw lines establishing the front legs.** Wood will be removed from both sides of the legs.

9 **Mount the carving on a vise.** Drill a hole in the body of the carving and insert a lag bolt using vise-grip pliers. Make sure the hole is in the body area and not in the drilled-out area between the front legs and the body.

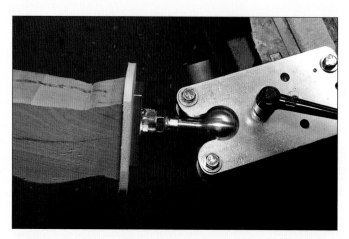

10 **Use a wood buffer.** Mount the blank with a wood buffer between it and the vise mounting plate. The wooden buffer must be larger than the vise mounting plate so it will protect your tools from being driven into the metal mounting plate.

11 Draw a centerline, and use the photos of the finished project and the patterns as a guide to carving your cat.

12 When the carving is complete, sand it. If you want your stylized carving to have a smooth surface, without gouges and cuts showing, sand it with about 120-grit sandpaper to remove the facets and continue with finer and finer sandpaper, down to about 600 grit.

Sign the piece with your name and date so years from now people will know when this piece of art was created and who created it. Remove all wood dust, put on the clear finish of your choice, and enjoy.

ACANTHUS

Acanthus carving is an elaborate type of carving based on the acanthus leaf. Its flowing style conveys a sense of movement and is primarily composed of concave and convex cuts. The concave cuts are normally done on the inside of curved areas, with the convex cuts done on the outside of the curved areas. All acanthus carvings will challenge you with a number of negative and positive transition points. The finished designs can be applied to the surface of wooden items, or they can be incorporated directly into furniture, boxes, moldings, picture frames, and more.

Project objectives:

- Lay out a project
- See how gluing a small or an elaborate carving to a larger piece of scrap wood will give you more control of the project as you carve it
- Recognize negative and positive transition points
- Use a gouge to make cuts with the concave sweep facing up or facing down

MATERIALS AND TOOLS

Materials
- Butternut (5" x 2" x ¼")
- Copy of pattern
- Scrap piece of wood (approximately 7" x 5" x ¾")

Tools
- Band saw, scroll saw, or coping saw
- ⅜" (10 mm) #9 gouge
- ½" (13 mm) #5 gouge
- V-tool
- ⅝" (16 mm) or ¾" (19 mm) #5 gouge (if available)
- Flat chisel
- Pencil
- Carbon or graphite tracing paper (optional)
- Piece of cardboard, like that from the back of a tablet
- Glue or double-sided tape
- Clamp or nonskid material
- 3M pad or toothbrush
- Sandpaper (220 and 320 grit)

Finishing Supplies
- Varnish or oil
- Soft-bristle brush

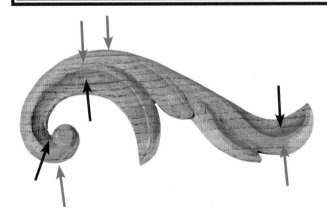

——▶ = positive transition point

——▶ = negative transition point

Frame pattern appears at 80% of actual size.

1 **Make a copy of the book pattern.** Draw or trace the outline of the pattern on the piece of wood you'll carve.

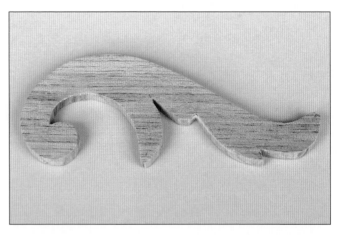

2 **Cut the blank.** Use a band saw, a scroll saw, or a coping saw to cut out the blank.

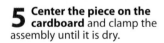

3 **Mount the blank to cardboard.** This small detailed carving needs to be attached to a larger board to make it easier to carve. Cut a piece of cardboard slightly larger than the carving and glue it to a rectangular piece of scrap wood. **Note:** Double-sided tape also works well.

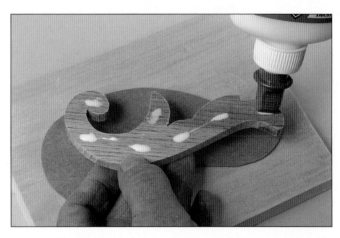

4 **Glue the blank.** Apply a small amount of glue on the back of the piece.

5 **Center the piece on the cardboard** and clamp the assembly until it is dry.

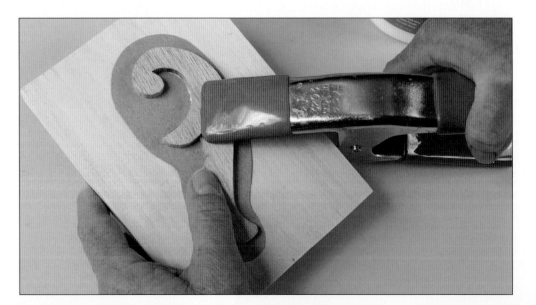

6 **Draw the pattern.** When the glue has dried, remove the clamp and draw the pattern on the blank.

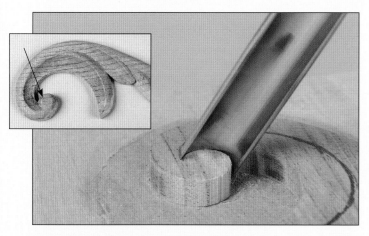

7 **Make a stop cut.** Use a ⅜" #9 gouge to make a stop cut at the button scroll by tilting the handle of your gouge so the right wing of the tool goes into the wood and the left wing remains out of the wood. Check the photo of the finished carving to see what you want to achieve.

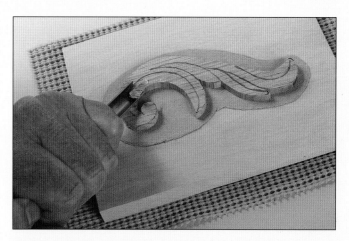

8 **Remove the wood to the negative transition point.** Start from near the stop cut you just made and remove the wood up to the negative transition point at this part of the carving. Check the illustrations, which point out the transition points and the directions of your cuts.

9 **Cut from the other direction.** When you reach the transition point, you now need to cut from the other direction to this negative transition point.

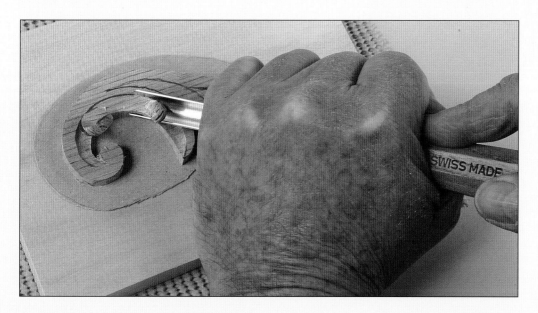

10 **Remove the waste wood.** The piece should fall out. If it doesn't, make short cuts from both directions to sever all the vessels.

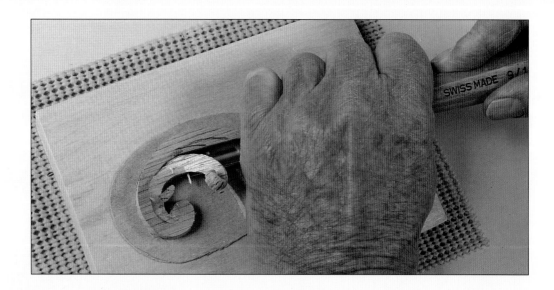

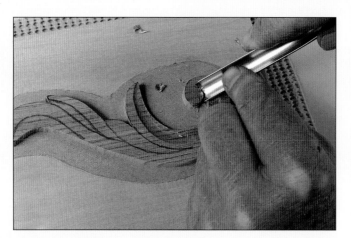

11 **Clean the button area.** Rotate the carving and go back to the button area. Clean the wood up to it.

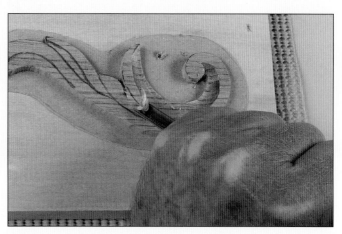

12 **Use a V-tool to make a stop cut in this area.** (The pencil line should be in the middle of the cut.)

13 **Define the stop cut.** Raise the handle of a ½" #5 gouge vertically and define the stop cut along this area.

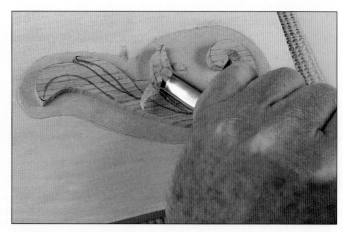

14 **Round the convex surface** of the scroll up to the bottom of the stop cut with your ½" #5 gouge. Make sure the wing of the tool doesn't dip under the wood at the bottom of the stop cut. If it does dip, the wood will tear.

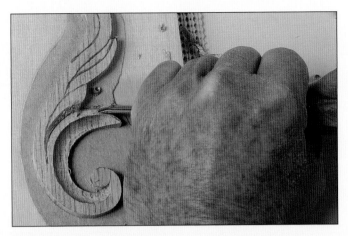

15 Turn your gouge over and round this area. Check the arrow direction.

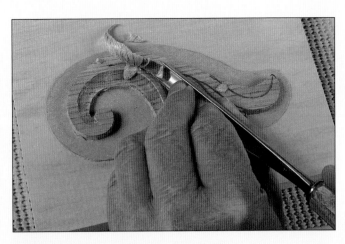

16 Remove the second concave scroll area with the concave side of your ⅜" #9 gouge facing up. Be cautious that the wing of your gouge doesn't dip under the wood, but only up to the bottom of the stop cut.

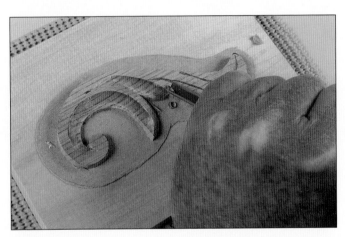

17 Use your V-tool to define this area behind the concave cut. Make sure your tools are sharp so they make clean cuts when defining areas like this.

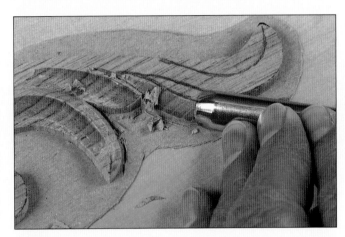

18 Turn your ⅜" #9 gouge over so the concave side is down, and round this area down to the base. Be cautious that the wing doesn't cut beyond the stop cut and into the adjacent convex area. Always be aware of where the wings of your tools are.

19 Use your V-tool to make a stop cut. Then, use the V-tool to define the area.

20 Turn the piece around and make a concave cut with your ⅜" #9 gouge. Again, don't allow the wing of the tool to dip under the wood.

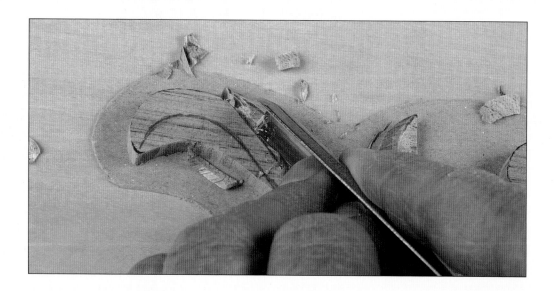

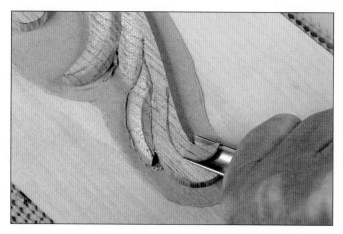

21 Make a concave cut up to the negative transition point from this direction.

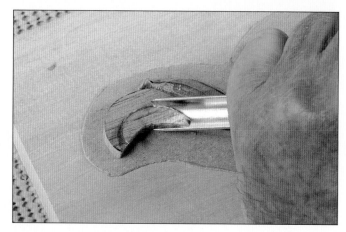

22 Turn the piece around and cut from the other direction to remove the piece.

23 Turn the piece around again and do a convex cut from the positive transition point toward the center of the carving.

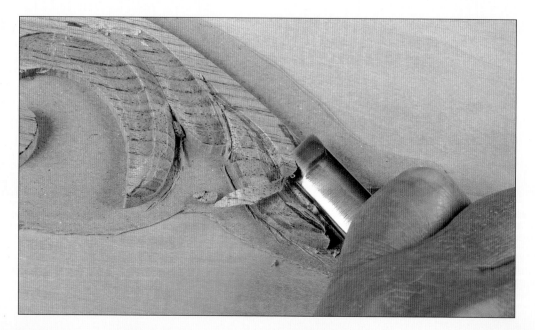

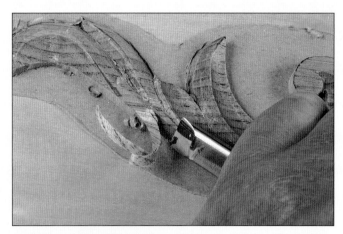

24 Turn the piece around and do the convex cut toward the end of the carving.

25 Round this portion of the carving from the top positive transition point.

26 Turn the piece around and, again from the top positive transition point, round the carving in the other direction. A ⅝" or ¾" #5 gouge would be helpful. When doing acanthus carving, it is helpful to have tools that will cut the proper concave or convex radius with one cut.

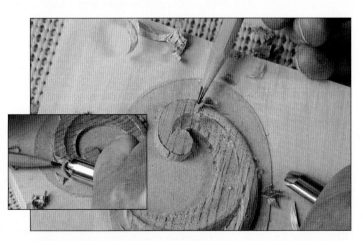

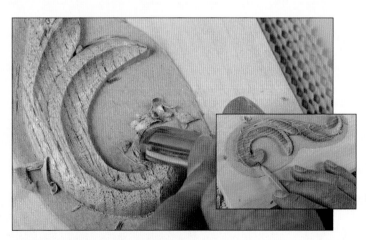

27 Cut from the other direction. When you reach this point, cut from the other direction so your tool is never given an opportunity to go between the vessels.

28 Round the edges of the button. Use the ⅜" #9 gouge to round the button edges. Here is another transition point where you'll need to be careful.

29 **Shave any rough areas.** If you have a rough area at any of the negative transition points, you can remove it by placing a gouge at the top of the cut and shaving off the area.

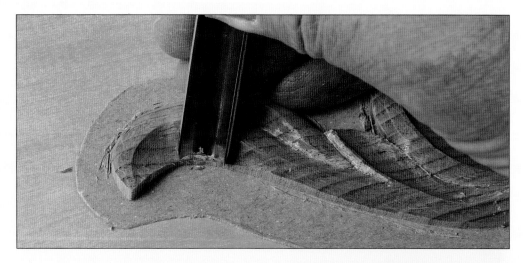

30 **Sand and clean the carving.** A 3M-type pad is helpful to smooth the surface and clean the carving. You can also use a toothbrush to clean your carving.

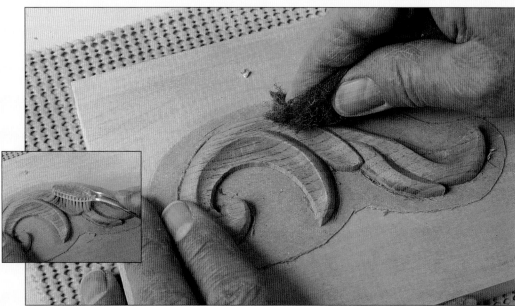

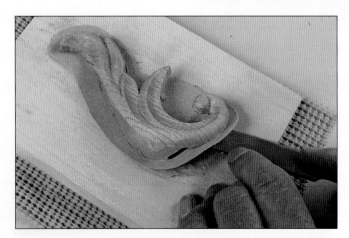

31 **Carefully peel the carving from the base** using a flat chisel. Slide the chisel between the cardboard and the base in the direction of the long grain, and pry off the carving. Be careful so you don't break off any fragile areas.

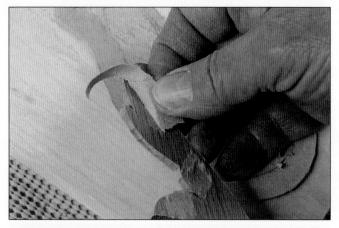

32 **Peel off any loose cardboard.** A light sanding with coarse sandpaper will also remove any remaining cardboard.

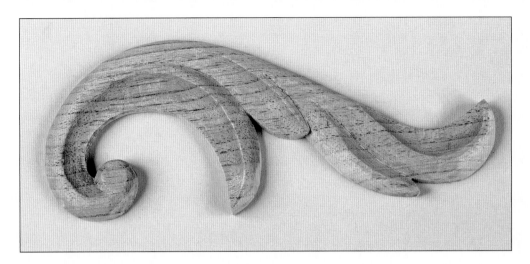

33 Apply the finished piece to a surface. This could be a decorative addition to items, such as a jewelry box, a serving tray, a chair, or anything else where this type of carving would enhance the object.

34 Add a mirror image. By adding a mirror image of the carving you just did, you can create a beautiful decorative acanthus carving like this.

35 Use your creativity. Think of unique ways to use your decorative appliqué, such as on a piece of furniture or across the top of a picture frame.

CHIP CARVED STAR

Chip carving is a decorative form of carving that takes some practice but results in many applications. Chip carving has decorated homes, jewelry boxes, ornaments, and other objects for centuries. It is a popular form of carving, primarily because it requires few tools and the techniques are basic. We will lay out a five-point star ornament and then carve it using just one knife.

Project objectives:

- Lay out a chip carving design
- Use your chip carving knife to get clean, crisp cuts
- Remove a chip with just three cuts
- See the variety of carvings you can make with one basic pattern

MATERIALS AND TOOLS

Materials
- Basswood (3½" x 3½" x ¼")

Tools
- Standard chip carving knife
- Compass
- Protractor
- Straightedge
- Nonskid material
- Thin lead pencil (0.5 mm)
- Lighted magnifying lamp
- Toothbrush
- White eraser
- Eye screw (optional)

Finishing Supplies
- Clear varnish (optional) or an oil

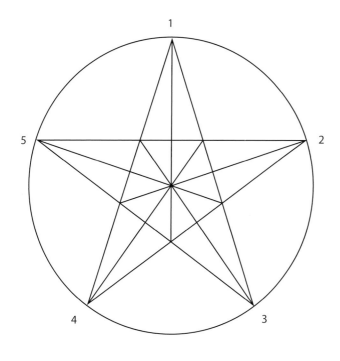

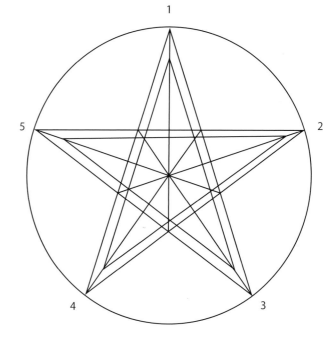

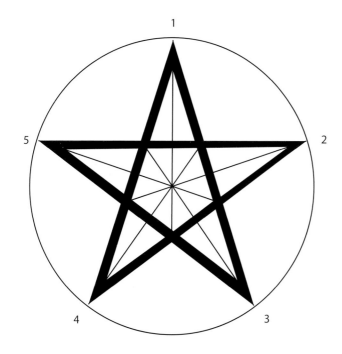

1 **Set your compass.** Adjust it to 1½".

2 **Find the center** of the 3½" piece and draw a 3" circle.

3 **Mark every 72 degrees around the circle** using a protractor and a straightedge. To make a five-point star, each point will be 72 degrees from the next. (A circle is 360 degrees; divide it by 5, and it equals 72 degrees.)

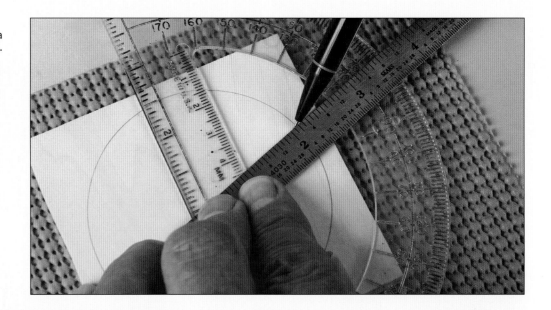

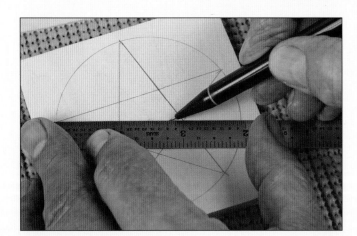

4 **Connect the points.** Use a straightedge and a thin lead pencil to draw lines connecting every other point of the star. I use a 0.5 mm lead pencil so the lines are thin and crisp.

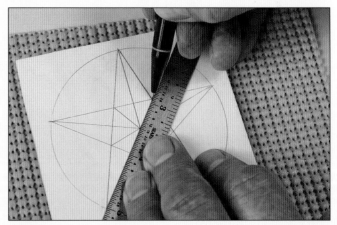

5 **Draw centerlines.** When you have the star established, draw a straight line from the tip of one wing through its center to the intersection of the legs across from the tip. Do this for each leg of the star.

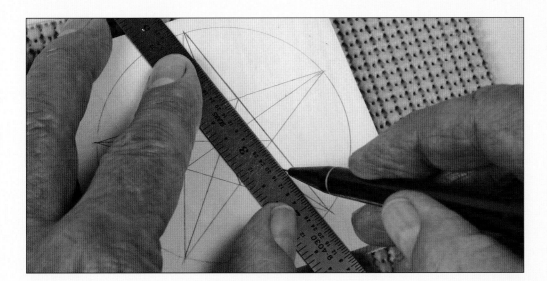

6 **Draw a line ⅛" inside**, and parallel to, each leg of the star.

It's All in the Grip

Here's a quick refresher on how to hold your chip carving knives.

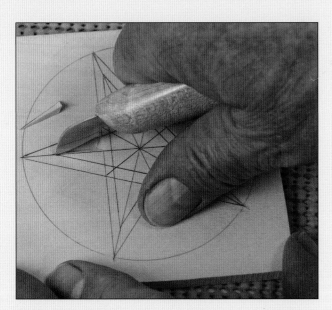

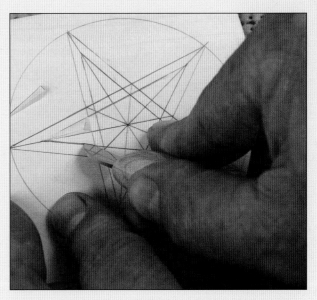

Position 1: Hold the chip carving knife as shown, with your fingers wrapped around the handle and your thumb resting on the wood. Place the tip of the blade at the top of the cut. Tilt the blade to a 65-degree angle and, as you pull the blade, sink it deeper into the wood. Your objective is to make three similar cuts to remove a triangle of wood. The first and third cuts are done using this grip.

Position 2: The second cut is done using a different grip. Place your thumb on the back edge of the blade, and place the tip of the knife vertically on the centerline. It's important to start with the blade vertical to minimize the chance of breaking out wood at the center of the triangular cut. As you begin to pull the knife, tilt the top edge of the blade toward you to a 65-degree angle from the surface of the wood, and slowly sink it into the wood as you pull it toward the bottom line.

7 **Check that your completed star looks like this.** Now it is ready to carve.

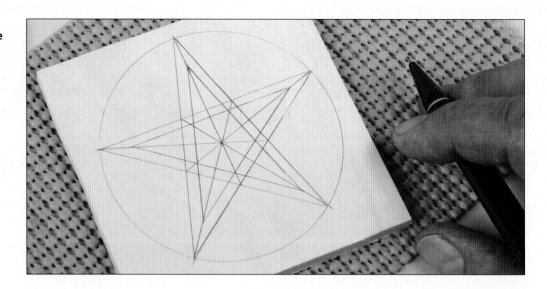

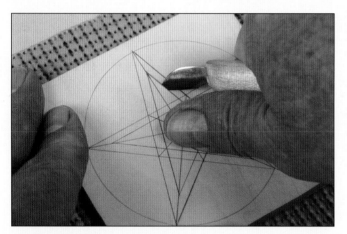

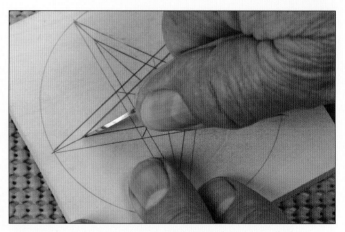

8 **Make your first cut** at the top of one of the inside legs using a standard chip carving knife (see It's All in the Grip on page 253 for a reminder on how to hold the knife). The deepest spot of the cut should be about ⅛6" deep. When you reach the bottom line, back the knife out of the wood.

9 **Turn the wood and start your second cut** along the centerline of the star's point. Keep the knife vertical as you initially start the cut to avoid breaking the star's leg, and then tilt the blade to the 65-degree angle.

10 **Continue pulling the blade** to the bottom line as you slowly sink the blade into the wood, maintaining the 65-degree angle of the blade. The tip of the blade should meet the bottom of the cut you made using Position 1. You may find it helpful to press on the back of the blade with the pointer finger of the hand that is not on the handle.

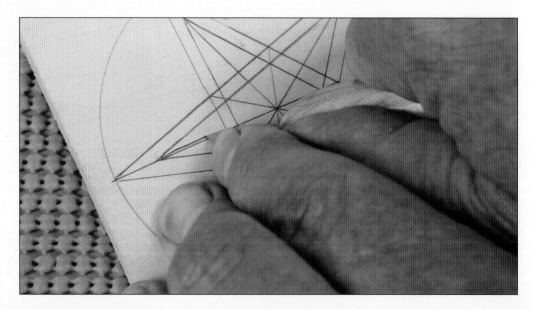

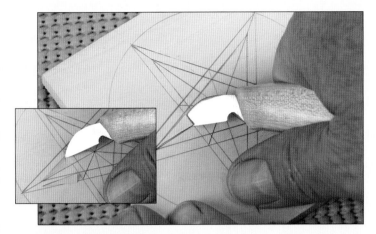

11 **Remove the chip.** When your blade touches the bottom line, back the blade out of the wood and, using Position 1, cut across the bottom of the piece you've just cut from both sides. The chip should pop out.

12 **Go to the other side of the star and repeat the sequence.** I find it helpful to use a lighted magnifying lamp when doing detailed work like this. It will give you focused light on the object you're carving and a magnified image so you can see the lines more vividly.

13 **Clean out the chips.** When you have all the legs of the star carved, a toothbrush is helpful to clean out the chips.

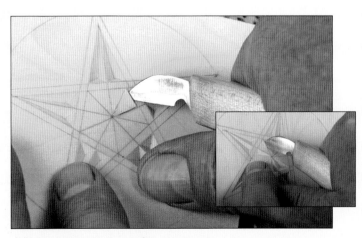

14 **Go to the center of the star and remove the chips** from each of the segments, using the same technique you did on each of the legs of the star. Continue this process for each of the segments.

15 Draw parallel lines around the outside of each of the star's legs and about 1⁄16" from the outside of the star.

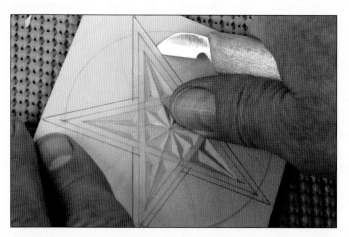

16 Tilt your knife and cut deep enough so the tip of the knife is in the wood to the center of the two lines around the star.

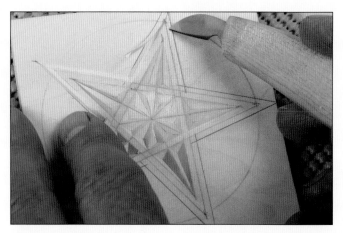

17 Cut the inside line. When you've cut all around the star on the outside line, turn the star around and cut the inside line. The piece should fall out like this.

18 Check your progress. The carving should now look like this.

19 Adjust your compass so it is 1⁄8" wider than it was when you made the initial circle, and make another circle around the previous one.

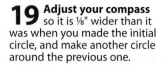

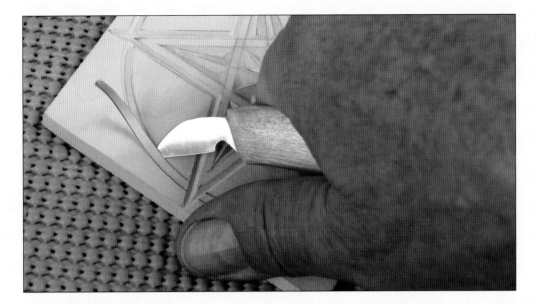

20 **Cut the circle.** Use Position 1 and sink your knife into the wood so the blade's tip is in the center of the two circle lines. Cut one side of the circle between each of the legs. When you've cut all around from one direction, tilt the handle and cut from the other direction. The piece should curl out like this. Then, continue removing the wood from each of the segments until your carving is completed (refer to Four-Quadrant Carving on page 161).

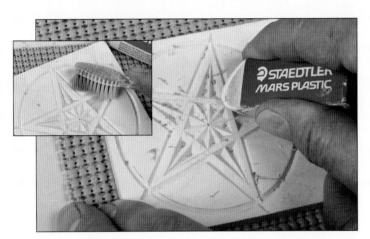

21 **Clean the carving.** To remove any pencil lines, use a white eraser. Don't use a colored eraser because it may leave color on your carving. Clean off any eraser rubber with a toothbrush.

22 **Hang the carving.** Your finished carving should look like this. If you want to hang the carving, insert an eye screw at the top of one of the legs.

23 **Make your own designs.** You can create a variety of different chip carving designs using the same basic pattern we used for this carving. It can be used to make Christmas ornaments, decorative enhancements carved in a jewelry box or napkin holder, or wherever your imagination leads you.

PIERCED RELIEF HORSE HEADS

This pierced relief is carved in a ¾"-thick walnut board. Butternut, catalpa, or cherry would also make excellent wood choices. You can really use any type of wood to carve the horse heads, but it is best if you can carve them from one board without glue joints. Unless you have an almost perfect match, the glue joint will detract from the carving. **Note:** The pattern will work at much larger or much smaller sizes.

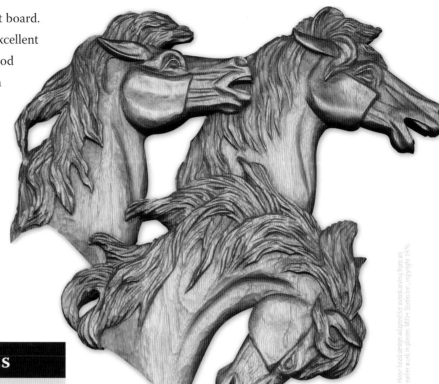

Horse head design adapted for woodcarving from an earlier work in plaster, *Miller Studio Inc.*, copyright 1976.

MATERIALS AND TOOLS

Materials
- Walnut, butternut, catalpa, or cherry (11" x 11" x ¾")
- Copy of pattern

Tools
- Band saw, scroll saw, or coping saw
- V-tool
- ⅜" (10 mm) #9 gouge
- ½" (13 mm) #5 gouge
- ³⁄₁₆" (5 mm) veiner
- Small flat skew
- Carving knife
- Drill
- ¼" drill bit
- Carbon or graphite tracing paper
- Pencil

Finishing Supplies
- Satin-finish varnish, boiled linseed oil, or tung oil
- Brush
- Brush and cloth
- Fine tip felt-tip marker or soft lead pencil

Project objectives:
- Lay out a project
- Use a band saw, scroll saw, or coping saw to cut out a project. (A coping saw will take you a period of time to cut out a carving this large.)
- Remove wood from a carving to achieve the pierced effect
- Work with various levels in a carving to give it depth
- Being aware of the anatomical structure of the object you're carving to create a realistic reproduction of the object
- Carve realistic-looking hair

Pattern appears at 50% of actual size.

1 **Make a copy from the pattern.** Transfer the pattern to the board using carbon paper or graphite paper. Then, use a band saw or a scroll saw to cut the blank. Drill holes in the pierced areas and remove the wood using a scroll saw or a coping saw.

2 **Transfer the detailed pattern to the surface of the wood** when you initially lay out the carving, or use the pattern to hand draw the detailed pattern.

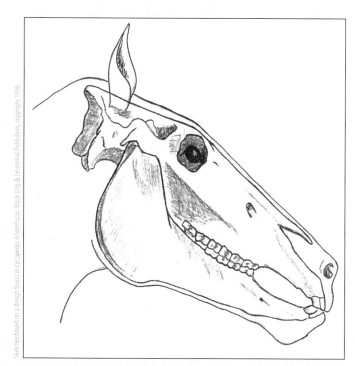

3 **Study the horse skull drawing** to visualize how the skull is situated under the skin, muscles, cartilage, and fatty tissue. Pay attention to the eye's location and the contour of the jaw. Figure out how the jaw hinges behind the eye, how the lips lie over the teeth, and where the ear is located. Any time you do a carving of a living subject, it is helpful to visualize what is under the skin. Study anatomical drawings or pictures of the skeletal and muscle structure.

4 **Establish the various levels of the carving** and use your V-tool to outline the hair masses. If you need help visualizing the levels, study the picture of the finished carving. Take your time and know what you want to achieve before you make any cut. Do not detail until you have the levels established.

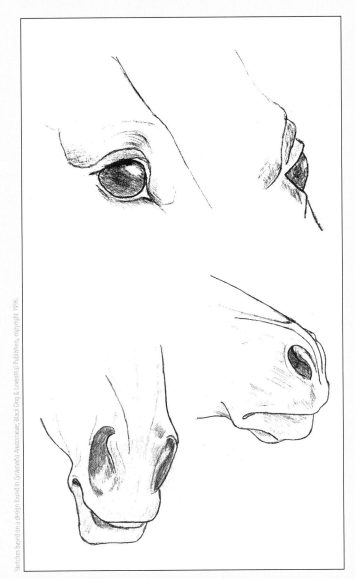

Sketches based on a design found in *Cyclopedia Anatomicae*, Black Dog & Leventhal Publishers, copyright 1996.

5 **Carve the details.** As you begin to detail, review the sketches of how the eye is shaped and how the lips and nostrils are formed.

6 **Clean up any "fuzzies", and finish your carving with varnish or one of the oils.** Sign and date the carving so 100 years from now people will know who did it and when. To facilitate hanging the finished carving, drill or rout a hole in the back of the carving.

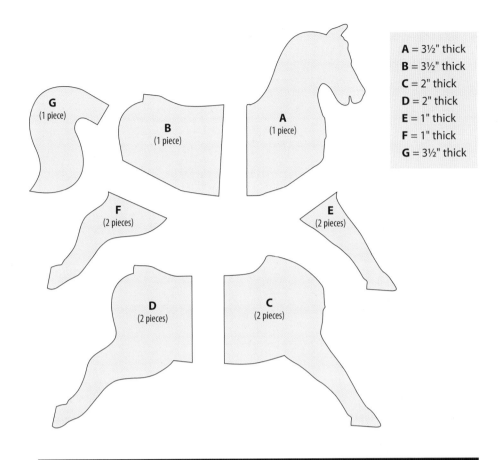

A = 3½" thick
B = 3½" thick
C = 2" thick
D = 2" thick
E = 1" thick
F = 1" thick
G = 3½" thick

ASSEMBLY DIAGRAM

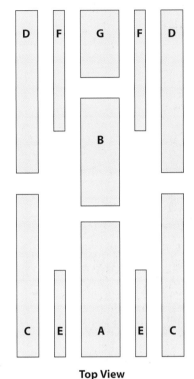

Top View

Front View

ROCKING HORSE PROJECT NOTES

- These patterns should be proportionally accurate to one another.

- The outline of each piece was cut, and then glued together. *A* was glued to *B*, using a couple of dowels to give it added strength. (It's important that each of the surfaces which join together are straight so they join showing very little seam.)

- *A* and *B* were allowed to dry, and any excess glue was removed from the sides where other pieces were joined.

- *C* and *D* were glued on both sides of *A* and *B* and allowed to dry. You will notice that joint *A* and *B* and joint *C* and *D* are not aligned with one another. They are staggered to give added strength to this area.

- *E* was glued to the inside of both of the front legs *C*.

- *F* was glued to the inside of both of the hind legs *D*.

- When all parts were assembled, except the tail, I then carved the horse.

- The tail *G* was carved, then joined to *B* by drilling a hole in both parts. Before gluing the tail in place, a dowel was inserted between the tail and the leg it rested against. When all parts fit together snugly, they were then glued.

- The rocker can be made to scale to the rest of the horse.

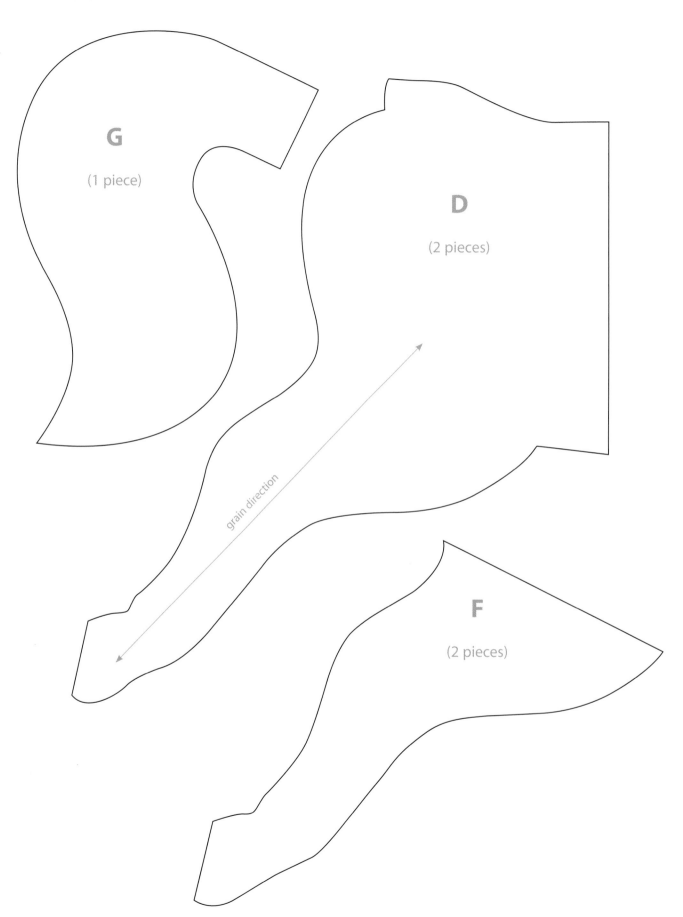

G

(1 piece)

D

(2 pieces)

grain direction

F

(2 pieces)

Pattern appears at 50% of actual size.

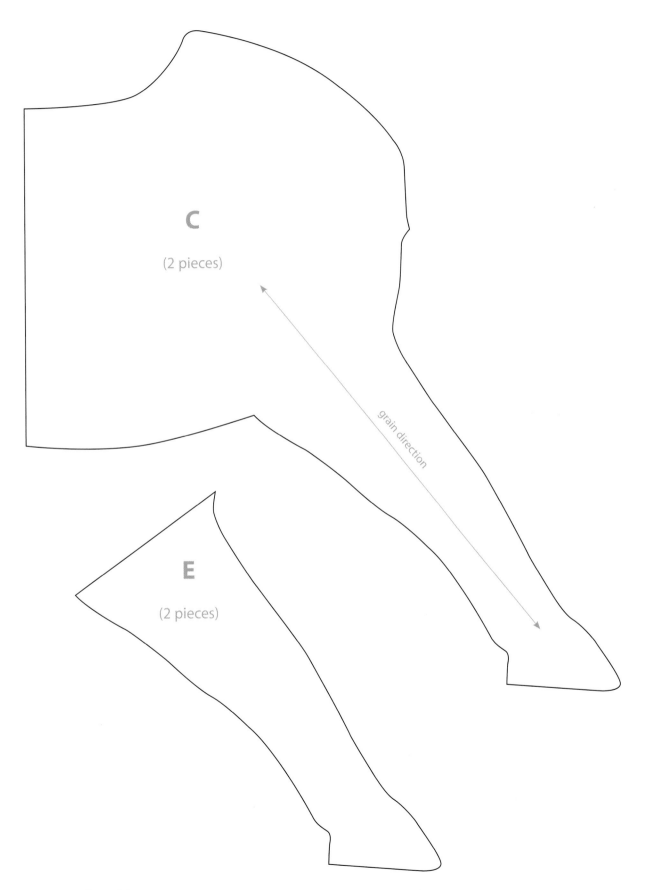

C

(2 pieces)

grain direction

E

(2 pieces)

Pattern appears at 50% of actual size.

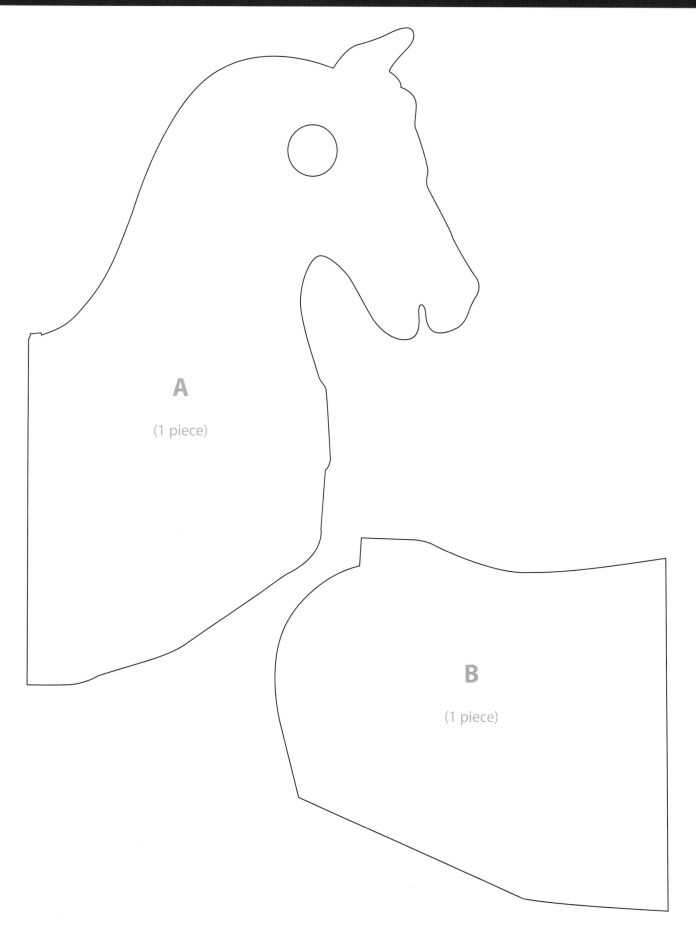

A

(1 piece)

B

(1 piece)

Pattern appears at 50% of actual size.

Wood Sources

The best way to find good sources for carving wood doesn't have to be expensive. Use common sense, network with other carvers, and you'll soon find a number of recommended sources for a variety of woods. Here are some tips:

- Talk with other carvers to find out where they get their carving wood. If you don't know any carvers in your area, try to find a carving club at *www.woodburning.com*. Open the carving club section by clicking on "carving clubs."
- Some catalogs that sell carving supplies also sell carving wood.
- Do a search on the Internet for "carving wood sources."
- Attend woodcarving shows. Many carving shows have a booth where someone sells wood.
- A good source to find carving show locations and dates is to look in *Woodcarving Illustrated* magazine, search "woodcarving show calendar" on the Internet, or look in *Chip Chats* magazine.
- When traveling, leave some extra space in your trunk for found wood. You never know what you may find.

If you have the space and time to cure wood yourself, try one or more of the following:

- Let your friends and neighbors know what you are looking for. You may be surprised what you'll find on your lawn or driveway when you least expect it.
- Contact tree removal services in your area and let them know what kind of wood you're looking for. They remove many species of trees and will normally, for a small fee, cut you some sections from the species you want.

Resources

Chipping Away, Inc.
General inquiries: 519-743-9008
Order line: 888-682-9801
www.chippingaway.com
(Carving tools, wood, roughouts)

The Woodcraft Shop
2724 State Street
Bettendorf, IA 52722
800-397-2278
www.thewoodcraftshop.com
(Everything for the woodcarver)

Moore Roughouts
P.O. Box 193
Kindred, ND 58051
800-825-2657
www.roughouts.com
(More than 500 roughouts available)

Wood Carvers Supply, Inc.
P.O. Box 7500
Englewood, FL 34295
800-284-6229
www.woodcarverssupply.com
(Woodcarving supplies—over 4000 products)

Woodcraft Supply, Inc.
210 Wood County Industrial Park
P.O. Box 1686
Parkersburg, WV 26102
800-225-1153
www.woodcraft.com
(Quality woodcarving tools and supplies)

A

Acanthus carving – A type of architectural and relief carving that utilizes stylized designs based on the acanthus plant.

Across the grain – Cutting perpendicular to the wood vessels.

Acrylics – Opaque water-based paints made from pigment mixed with acrylic resin and an emulsion.

Against the grain – Cutting at an angle to the wood vessels.

Air-drying – Drying wood by exposing it to air, allowing natural evaporation of water until the internal water reaches equilibrium with the outdoor environmental humidity.

Air filtration system – A dust collection system that removes microscopic airborne dust particles from the air in a room.

Angiosperm – Any of a variety of flowering plants that produce fruit with seeds inside, such as acorns or berries; range from small plants to tall trees.

Aniline dye – A stain made of dry pigments dissolved in either hot water or alcohol; available in a vast array of colors.

Animal carving – A style of realistic carving featuring extremely detailed animals.

Annual rings – Concentric growth rings visible in the cross section of a cut tree. Each ring represents a period of growth, normally one year.

Architectural carving – A type of carving used to accent furniture and architectural elements.

Arkansas stone – A type of whetting stone made of a soft quartz, called novaculite, mined primarily in Arkansas.

Armature – A skeleton made of wire, wood, or any other material that will support a clay model.

Artist oil paint – A combination of finely ground pigment and binders, which give the paint its consistency and working properties.

B

Back bent – A type of tool used to make cuts on the outside of curved areas; usually, only gouges are back bent. Also known as reverse bent.

Band saw – A large power tool with a continuous blade that is useful for cutting blanks.

Bar clamp – A type of clamp mounted on a bar; the heads are moveable; useful for longer spans.

Bark – The external protective covering of a tree.

Bark carving – A wood carving created in a piece of bark; usually, only one side of the bark is carved. Popular subjects include wood spirits and fantasy buildings.

Bas-relief – See low relief.

Basswood – A wood that carves easily and has a subtle grain pattern.

Bench hook table – Another name for a carving table; a portable working surface for carving.

Birch – A tight-grained wood with a uniform texture that is easily carved.

Bird carving – A style of realistic carving that features extremely detailed birds.

Bird's eye – This atypical swirling grain pattern is pockmarked with eyes that look like miniature knots; most common in maple.

Black – A color made by mixing equal amounts of the three primary colors. Adding black to any color will make it a darker shade.

Black Arkansas stone – The Arkansas-class sharpening stone with the finest hone; nicknamed the "surgical black Arkansas" due to its ability to put on the ultimate edge.

Blade – The body of the tool.

Bole – The main stem of a tree. Also known as the trunk of the tree.

Bolster – See shoulder.

Bound water – Water that saturates the walls of the wood vessels.

Branch – The part of a tree which is connected to the trunk; branches support the twigs, which in turn support the leaves.

Brown – A shade made by mixing a color with its complementary color.

Brush – Useful for cleaning chips from a carving, as well as for painting.

Burr – A wire edge formed along the cutting edge when you sharpen a tool. Also, a small cutter used in rotary tools to remove wood.

Butternut – A highly favored wood that is easy to carve and has a beautiful grain.

C

Calipers – A measuring tool with legs that can be used to measure either inside or outside dimensions of an object.

Cambium layer – The thin layer of cells between the wood and bark of a tree where cell division takes place to create new wood and bark.

CAMI – Coated Abrasive Manufacturers Institute; a grading system used to designate the grit size of sandpaper. If there is no alpha designation before the numeric value on the back of the sandpaper, it is a CAMI measurement.

Capacitance moisture meter – A device that measures moisture content in wood by generating a radio frequency field which measures the capacitance of the wood. The data is calculated by the device and displayed in percent moisture content (% MC).

Carbide cutter – A type of bit for rotary tools; used for fast wood removal.

Caricature carving – A popular type of carving that exaggerates a subject's distinctive features or peculiarities.

Carving glove – Ambidextrous protective glove worn on the hand holding the carving; made of Kevlar or stainless-steel wire.

Carving in the round – Any three-dimensional carving where wood is removed all around the subject, giving the work height, width, and depth.

Carving mallet – A helpful tool for carving hard woods, working with large carving tools, or working with a piece being held in a vise. In these cases, a carving mallet provides the extra forward motion to cut through the wood. Mallets are available with wood, brass, or urethane heads.

Catalpa – A type of wood with a similar texture to butternut, but with a more distinctive grain pattern.

C-clamp – An affordable type of clamp used to hold wood for gluing or to a surface when only a small clamping span is needed.

Central vacuum system – A dust collection system connected to the major dust-producing tools in a workshop.

Ceramic cutter – A type of bit for rotary tools; used for texturing, feathering, and fine finishing. Known for superior performance and long life.

Ceramic stone – A type of man-made sharpening stone resistant to heat and designed to combine fast cutting action with low maintenance.

Check – A split in the end grain where vessels separate from one another.

Chemical-drying – A process in which wood is stabilized artificially by using chemicals.

Cherry – A beautiful wood which will develop a beautiful patina over time from ultraviolet rays.

Chip carving – Removing chips of wood to create patterns, often in geometric shapes.

Chisel – A tool which is flat and does not have any sweep. Chisels are available as flat, flat skew, and flat skew fishtail.

Coarse grain – When the annual rings in the wood are far apart, giving it an uneven appearance. Coarse grain typically has large pores.

Color board – A reference board with squares of different tints of paint colors.

Color rendering index (CRI) – An index used to measure how much a light source shifts color as compared to another light source of the same color temperature. Sunlight has a CRI of 100, the highest level attainable.

Color temperature – A measure used to define the whiteness—or the warmth or coolness—of a light source. Color temperature is measured according to the Kelvin scale.

Compass – A type of measuring device similar to a divider that has a sharp point on one leg and a writing instrument at the end of the other.

Coniferous – Mostly needle-leaved or scale-leaved, chiefly evergreen, cone-bearing trees or shrubs such as pines, spruces, and firs.

Controlled split – A cut that helps remove wood quickly or select a piece of wood that gives strength to a long carving.

Coping saw – A handsaw with a tight cutting radius useful for cutting out blanks and other detailed work.

Crack – Separation in wood that creates visible gaps; usually runs lengthwise through the piece of wood.

Crown – The branches, twigs, and leaves that make up the foliage portion of a tree.

Cupping – Where wood has warped causing the center of the board to be lower than the edges.

Cured wood – See dried wood.

Cyanoacrylate glue – A fast-bonding glue with an acrylate base; some brands are made specifically for wood and leather bonding.

Cypress knees – Soft and unique projections that grow up from the roots of the bald cypress tree.

D

Danish oil – A surface finish made by blending a small amount of varnish with tung or linseed oil, and then thinning with mineral spirits; easy to apply.

Deciduous – Trees or shrubs that shed leaves at the end of a growing season and regrow them at the beginning of the next growing season. Basswood, butternut, cherry, and walnut are deciduous.

Dental tools – Very detailed tools, available in a variety of shapes and sizes, which can get into the most detailed areas of a carving. Can be used to clean out areas or, when sharpened, as detail knives.

Detail knife – A specialty carving knife with a sharp point for getting into tight areas.

Diamond cutter – A type of bit for rotary tools. A fast-cutting, clog-resistant bit used for stoning and texturing.

Diamond stone – A sharpening tool made of diamonds plated to a metal surface.

Differential drying – When moisture migrates from the higher moisture content in cell walls to the lower moisture content in the cell cavity.

Dishing – The concave portion of a warped board.

Dividers – A type of measuring tool with two hinged legs with sharp points at the ends; used to transfer dimensions from a model to a carving.

Dogleg – A tool used for leveling the background in a relief carving and cleaning out undercut areas.

Dogs – A type of clamp made of wooden pegs inserted into holes drilled in a bench top.

Dried wood – Wood that has had the majority of the internal water removed. Also called cured wood or seasoned wood.

Driftwood – Wood washed onto a shore of a sea or river; usually bleached.

Drill press – A large, stationary power tool used to create holes through wood.

Drills – A family of wood removal power tools used to create holes through a piece of wood, such as selected areas of a pierced relief carving.

Dust mask – A necessary piece of protective equipment that will decrease the amount of dust breathed into the lungs when carving.

Dye stain – A stain that penetrates everywhere on the wood and will cover all of the wood; may mask the grain.

E

Early wood – The part of a growth ring produced at the beginning of the growth season. Made of large cells with thin walls.

Earmuffs – An essential protective device that decreases noise damage from loud equipment in the shop.

End grain – The pattern you see in the cross section of a piece of wood.

Equilibrium moisture content – When wood has reached the moisture content of the surrounding environment.

F

FEPA – Federation of European Producers of Abrasives; a grading standard used to designate grit size of abrasive materials.

Ferrule – A metal ring that strengthens and prevents the handle of a tool from splitting.

Fiber saturation point (FSP) – The point at which vessel walls are fully saturated.

Fiddleback – A type of grain that has curls and waves. Also called curly grain.

Figure – Pattern on the wood surface created by the wood growth layers, rays, and knots.

Fine grain – When the annual rings are small and close together, creating an even texture. Has small, closely spaced pores.

Fish carving – A style of realistic carving featuring extremely detailed fish. Special tools exist to carve scales.

Fixed router – A router where the depth of cut is set prior to the tool being turned on.

Flame – A type of wavy-grained figure similar to fiddleback, but with wider bands of color.

Flat chisel – A tool that is flat across the cutting surface.

Flat-plane carving – A type of carving native to the Scandinavian countries. It features simple, controlled knife cuts that leave flat surfaces on the finished carving.

Flatsawn – See plainsawn.

Flat skew chisel – A flat tool angled across the cutting edge.

Flat skew fishtail chisel – A flat chisel where the blade contours back from the cutting edge like a fishtail.

Fluorescent lighting – An excellent source to provide general illumination in a large area. Fluorescent light creates minimal shadows, so should not be used alone when carving.

Fluteroni – Similar to a macaroni tool, the fluteroni has three working edges: a small gouge on each side and a flat chisel on the bottom.

Found wood – Any wood in its natural, unaltered state, such as bark from dead or dying trees, cypress knees, knots, weathered wood, or driftwood.

Free water – Water that fills the inside of the vessels.

Full-spectrum lighting – Artificial light that mimics sunlight by containing all colors of the rainbow in equal amounts; good lighting for coloring a carving. Full-spectrum lights are measured by the color rendering index and color temperature.

G

Gel stain – A stain that incorporates a dye into a thick carrier the consistency of mayonnaise.

Gesso – A primer base coating that gives gripping action, called tooth, so paint will stick better.

Glazing – Occurs when metal particles clog the pores of a sharpening stone.

Goggles – An essential protective device that prevents objects from flying into the eyes.

Gouge – A tool that has curvature on the cutting edge of the blade.

Grain – The pattern or figure formed by the distinction between the spring wood and summer wood. Wood grain has a variety of meanings. May be called coarse, fine, straight, cross, spiral, curly, wavy, irregular, interlocking, etc.

Green wood – See wet wood.

Grip stick – A handmade tool, made of a screw glued into a dowel. Usually inserted into the bottom of a small carving piece to make a larger gripping area.

Gymnosperm – Any seed-bearing plant with ovules exposed on the surface of leaves or leaflike structures that bear spores. Conifers are gymnosperms.

H

Handle – An important part of any carving tool; handles come in many shapes and sizes, including long handled or palm handled.

Handsaw – A wood removal tool that can remove a lot of excess wood in little time. A large handsaw with fine teeth will help when preparing a carving blank.

Hard Arkansas stone – A sharpening stone which will produce a keen edge on tools.

Hard translucent Arkansas stone – Finest grain and most dense of the natural sharpening stones.

Hardwoods – See deciduous and angiosperm.

Heartwood – The central core of a tree. No longer required to conduct water, it is composed of dead cells filled with extractives and tannins. Heartwood is normally darker in color than sapwood.

Heel – The back portion of the cutting surface.

High relief – A type of relief carving where at least half of the object's circumference projects off the wood.

Honing compound – A fine abrasive material which is rubbed into a strop to polish a tool's surface and shape the razor-sharp cutting edge.

Honing oil – A lightweight oil used to dress some sharpening stones; it keeps metal shavings from sharpened tools in suspension.

Hue – The property of a color that distinguishes it from other colors.

Human figure carving – A style of realistic carving featuring extremely detailed human figures, often concentrating on facial expressions and body language.

I

Incandescent lighting – Standard bulb lighting; particularly useful for relief carving, as shining it at a 45-degree angle to a working surface creates shadows to gauge depth.

Incised carving – Only the outline of an object is carved. Used on furniture, wood block printing, and carving letters.

India taper triangle – A type of slip stone that has a 60-degree angle used to remove burrs from the insides of V-tools.

In-lap dust collector – A dust-collecting system that can be rested in the lap during the power carving process.

Inside bevel – A small secondary angle on the inside of the cutting edge used to add strength to the cutting edge. Also called a microbevel.

Intaglio – Negative relief carving: a recess is carved, and then a subject is carved into the recess. Used mostly for molds (butter and candy) and furniture.

Into the grain – Cutting between the vessels.

Irregular grain – When the wood fibers wrap around knots or other irregularities in the wood.

J

Jigsaw – See saber saw.

JIS – Japanese Industrial Standard; a grading system used to designate the grit size of sandpaper.

Juvenile wood – The pith, together with a tree's first few annual rings.

K

Kiln-drying – Removing moisture from wood by using a thermally insulated chamber in which airflow, humidity, and temperature can be controlled.

Kiln schedule – A controlled sequence of adjusting the humidity and temperature when kiln-drying wood. The schedule is based on the wood reaching specific steps in moisture content.

Knot – The base of a limb enclosed in the bole of the tree. Dead ponderosa pines yield the best and largest knots.

Krylon matte finish – An excellent permanent non-glare spray coating to seal a carving after painting.

Kutzall cutter – A type of bit for rotary tools. Very aggressive and available in many shapes; best for fast wood removal.

L

Lacquer – A type of surface finish that is made from nitrocellulose; usually applied as a spray. Dries quickly. Available in gloss and semigloss finishes.

Late wood – The part of a growth ring produced later in a growing season. The cells are smaller and have thicker cell walls than early wood.

Leaves – The flat green structures that produce nutrients for a tree or plant through the process of photosynthesis.

Limb – The part of a tree that grows out from the trunk. Branches connect to the limbs, twigs to the branches, and leaves to twigs.

Linseed oil – A penetrating finish derived from flaxseed and available as raw, boiled, or stand oil.

Loading the strop – Rubbing a fine abrasive compound into the strop.

Long-bent tool – A tool that has a gently curved blade to allow for cutting into recessed areas without the handle interfering with the surface wood; useful for relief carving.

Low relief – A type of relief carving with the least amount of wood removed. Usually, low relief doesn't have any undercutting. Also known as bas-relief.

M

Macaroni – A multipurpose tool with three working edges: a flat chisel on the bottom and a V-tool on each side.

Mahogany – A wood favored for deep relief carvings; easy to work.

Maple – A beautiful, but difficult to carve, wood. Its density requires a mallet and sharp tools to carve.

Medullary rays – Vessels that transport food horizontally across the tree and act as food storage areas.

Microbevel – See inside bevel.

Micro tools – Small tools used for fine detail work.

Moisture content (MC) – The weight of the water in the cell walls and cavities of a piece of wood, compared to its dry weight.

N

Nagura stone – A fine-grained chalk stone used in combination with water stones to create a polishing solution that polishes the tool as it is being sharpened.

Negative transition point – A transition point that requires cutting toward it to get clean cuts.

O

Oil pencils – Similar to colored pencils, but the lead is softer and is an oil base. Most oil pencils are semi-opaque, so the wood grain will show through somewhat.

Oilstone – A type of sharpening stone; though it is the slowest, it produces the finest edge.

Opaque – Blocks the passage of light and radiant energy. Obscures the natural color of the object upon which it is applied.

Ouachita stone – A second grade of Arkansas sharpening stone; softer and coarser than most Arkansas stones.

Outside bevel – The angle ground on the front of the tool that forms the cutting edge.

Oven-drying – Removing the water from a piece of wood by drying it in an oven at a temperature of about 220 degrees Fahrenheit.

P

Palette – The surface upon which you place and mix paints before applying them.

Palette knife – A tool used to mix paints together on a palette.

Paring cut – See pull cut.

Paste wax – Inexpensive and easy to apply surface finish.

PEG 1000 – Polyethylene glycol 1000; stabilizes wood by replacing water molecules with wax-like glycol molecules.

Penetrating finishes – A family of finishes easier to apply than surface finishes; penetrating finishes are absorbed into the wood and become part of the wood rather than building on the surface.

Pentacryl – A liquid composite of siliconized polymers used to treat wet wood.

Phloem – A thin layer of cells between the bark and cambium layer, which is a food supply line to carry sap from the leaves to the rest of the tree.

Pierced relief – A type of relief carving with areas of the carving completely removed.

Pigment stain – A stain made from finely ground pigment. Collects in the pores and scratches in the wood and highlights the wood grain.

Pith – The soft center part of the trunk, branches, and twigs. Normally softer and darker than the rest of the wood.

Plainsawn – Boards created by making a series of parallel cuts in the log. The curved parts of the annual rings are visible on the ends. Also called flatsawn.

Plunge router – A type of router that has a bit that lowers itself to the correct depth as it spins.

Positive transition point – A transition point that requires cutting away from it to get clean cuts.

Prestain wood conditioner – Used under stains to promote even absorption of the stain.

Pull cut – One of two basic carving cuts. Performed by pulling the knife through the wood, as if peeling an apple. Also called paring cut.

Push cut – One of the two basic kinds of knife cuts.

Q

Quartersawn – Made by first cutting a log into quarters, then creating a series of parallel cuts perpendicular to the tree's annual rings. The boards have straight grain lines on the face and end.

Quick-grip clamp – Also known as a speed clamp. Can be operated with one hand; best for low-impact tasks.

R

Rasp – A tool with many individual teeth that can cut wood or metal. Rasps are curved on one side and flat on the other.

Reaction Wood – Abnormal wood formed in leaning trees and branches. More prone to cracking than normal wood. In hardwood trees, reaction wood is known as tension wood.

Realistic carving – A piece intended to present its subject as true to life as possible. Includes bird, animal, fish, and human figure carvings.

Relief carving – A type of carving where wood is carved away from around an object to make it look as if it is standing off the surface. Includes low, high, and pierced relief carving styles.

Resistance moisture meter – A device that determines moisture content in wood by measuring the resistance between pins which are driven into the wood. The meter then converts the measured resistance to percent moisture content (% MC).

Reverse bent – See back bent.

Riffler – A small file curved and angled to work in hard-to-reach places, such as undercut areas; rifflers feature a different head on each end.

Riftsawn – Each board is sawn in the same relation to the center of the log, giving it a slightly wavy grain pattern. Because of the way it is sawn from the log, it provides very poor yield.

Rockwell scale – A standard that determines hardness. Used to grade the hardness of tools; the lower the Rockwell number, the softer the steel used in the tool. Steel used for carving knives should be between R58c and R63c.

Roots – Grow into the ground and anchor a tree, keeping it erect. Also absorb water and minerals from the ground.

Rotary tool – A handheld power tool used to perform a variety of carving tasks, from roughing out to detailing to sanding. A variety of bits are available for the tool, including ruby, diamond, ceramic, carbide, Vanadium steel burr, Kutzall, stump cutters, and texturing stones.

Router – A type of handheld power tool with various shaped cutters that creates a groove in the wood as it moves across the piece.

Ruby cutter – A type of fast-cutting bit for rotary tools. Used for feather contouring and detail work. Leaves a smooth surface.

S

Saber saw – A handheld power saw that works well for cutting curves as well as straight lines; capable of cutting material up to an inch thick. Also known as a jigsaw.

Sandpaper – A reasonably quick and cost-effective sharpening medium. Also used in wood finishing.

Sap – Water in a tree which includes the nutrients for the tree's growth and sustenance.

Sapwood – The outer living layers of wood in a tree between the bark and heartwood, in which water and sap reside.

Scroll saw – A power tool that uses a narrow blade that can be fed through a hole in a piece of wood and used to remove internal pieces from a board, such as in a pierced relief carving.

Seasoned wood – See dried wood.

Shade – A darkened version of a color created by adding black or a small amount of the color's complement.

Shading down – Adding black to give a color a lower value.

Shellac – A type of surface finish derived from the natural resin of the lac bug. It's easy to apply and fast drying, though it has a short shelf life when mixed.

Shoe polish – A stain in a wax base that can be used to tint the surface fibers in wood.

Shop vacuum – An affordable dust collection system that can be wheeled to the source of the dust.

Short-bent tool – A tool that has a gently curved blade to allow for cutting into recessed areas without the handle interfering with the surface wood; useful for relief carving.

Shoulder – The flared section of the blade at the bottom of the tang; prevents the blade from being forced into the handle. Also called the bolster.

Slip stones – Small contoured stones made to remove metal from the inside contour of tools.

Slurry – A watery mixture of insoluble material. When sharpening, it consists of water, the metal being removed from the tool being sharpened, and abrasive particles being abraded from the top of the sharpening stone.

Soft Arkansas stone – The coarsest grained and least dense of the natural Arkansas sharpening stones; extrafine, 350 grit.

Softwoods – See coniferous and gymnosperm.

Spalted – A type of figure with irregular black lines and spots caused by fungal rot.

Spiral grain – When the grain of the wood follows a spiral course. Occurs when a tree grows twisted.

Splitting with the grain – Tearing of the wood, which normally occurs when you cut between the vessels.

Square – A measuring tool that has two straight legs that intersect at a right angle.

Stab knife – A chip carving knife used to make decorative stab cuts.

Stain – A finish that colors wood. Two basic types of colorant are used to make stain: pigment and dye.

Stamp – A type of tool used to press patterns into wood. Often used on backgrounds in relief carvings. Can be bought or made from nails, bolts, or metal rods.

Standard carving knife – The most commonly used carving knife; comes equipped with either straight or curved blades.

Standard chip carving knife – The most commonly used chip carving knife; has a 20-degree angled blade.

Stop cut – A kind of cut that marks the end of where you want to carve. It runs perpendicular to the carving you want to make; when the carving tool hits the stop cut, the waste wood falls out and you do not cut farther than you meant to.

Straight grain – The grain of the wood that runs approximately parallel with the vertical axis of the tree.

Strop – A tool that acts as a binder to hold honing compound. The strop, along with honing compound, is used to put the final edge on a tool and polish the cutting surface of the blade.

Stump cutter – A type of bit for rotary tools; features serrated edges and removes wood with light pressure.

Stylized carving – A work that emphasizes form over detail. Stylized carvings feature smooth, flowing lines and are often left unpainted.

Surface finishes – A family of finishes that offer protection from wear and tear without masking the wood grain. Slight wood penetration.

Surform file – A type of rasp similar to a cheese grater; a hole in front of each tooth allows the wood chips being removed to flow through the rasp.

T

Tabletop dust collector – A dust collection system that can be positioned on a table and pulls dust away from a carving. A good system for use in a workshop where carvings are created in one general area.

Tang – Connects the tool to the handle.

Texturing stone cutter – A type of bit for rotary tools. Primarily used for texturing.

Thumb guard – A protective item worn on the hand that holds the knife.

Tinting up – Adding white to give a color a higher value.

Tints – Lighter shades of a color that are created by adding white.

Toe – The front of the cutting surface.

Tones – Created when one color is added to another. A tone is any step as the color passes from a light shade to a dark shade, or vice versa.

Transition point – A point while carving where you need to change the direction of the cutting so the carving tool does not go between vessels.

Translucent – Some light can travel through. This is like looking through a frosted glass where you see the outline of an object but not any detail.

Transparent – Light can travel through. Colored cellophane is a good example, where you can vividly see an object behind it even if you're looking through the color.

Trunk – See bole.

Tung oil – A penetrating finish extracted from the nut of the tung tree; yields a tough, flexible, and highly water-resistant coating. It is the most durable of all natural oils.

Tupelo – A popular wood with power carvers because it does not fuzz; however, it is difficult to carve by hand.

Twigs – The small parts of a tree to which the leaves are attached.

Two-dimensional carving – Refers to carving done only on the surface of a flat piece of wood. Includes chip and relief carving.

U

Undercutting – A process where wood is removed from under an object to make it look as though it's standing off the surface.

Utilitarian carving – A style of carving that yields items intended to be useful and practical, such as spoons, bowls, and drawer pulls.

V

Value – Distinguishes a light color from a dark color.

Vanadium steel cutter – A type of bit for rotary tools. Used for very aggressive wood removal.

Varnish – A transparent finish applied to protect wood surfaces. It is available in gloss, semigloss, and satin finishes.

Veiner – A tool that makes a U-shaped cut.

Vernier calipers – A measuring tool with legs that can be used to measure inside and outside dimensions of an object.

Vessels – Strawlike tubes that transport water and minerals from the roots to the leaves.

Vetrap – A cloth bandage impregnated with latex; will stick only to itself. Makes a good thumb guard.

Vise – A mounted adjustable tool used to hold an object steady.

V-tool – Also called a parting tool. Available with angles of 30, 35, 55, 60, 75, 90, 100, and 120 degrees.

W

Walnut – A hard, but beautiful, wood to carve.

Water-based varnish – A clear, fast-drying surface finish made of microscopic beads of acrylic and polyurethane resins dispersed in water.

Water stone – A sharpening medium which requires water as the lubricant medium. Water, along with abrasive that is removed from the stone while sharpening, creates a slurry which helps to polish the blade of the tool being sharpened.

Weathered wood – Similar to driftwood. Found wood that has been exposed to the elements without decaying.

Wet wood – Wood that has not had the internal water removed or reached equilibrium with the atmospheric humidity around it. Also called green wood.

Whimsies – Nonfunctional, primarily entertaining types of carvings. Usually, feature interlocking parts carved from one piece of wood.

White – The absence of all color. Can be added to any color to make a lighter tint.

Wings – The outside edges of the blade. The distance between wings is the tool width.

With the grain – Cutting parallel to the wood vessels.

Wood clamp – A type of clamp made of wood. A clamping device made for clamping wood.

More Great Books from Fox Chapel Publishing

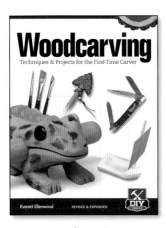

**Woodcarving,
Revised and Expanded**
ISBN 978-1-56523-800-8 **$14.99**

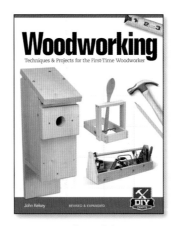

**Woodworking,
Revised and Expanded**
ISBN 978-1-56523-801-5 **$14.99**

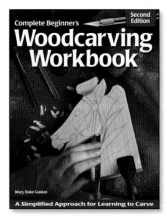

**Complete Beginner's
Woodcarving Workbook**
ISBN 978-1-56523-745-2 **$12.99**

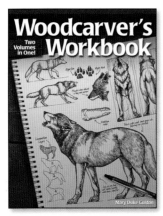

Woodcarver's Workbook
ISBN 978-1-56523-746-9 **$22.99**

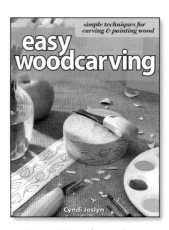

Easy Woodcarving
ISBN 978-1-56523-288-4 **$14.95**

Handcarved Christmas
ISBN 978-1-56523-605-9 **$19.95**

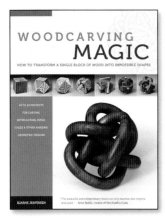

Woodcarving Magic
ISBN 978-1-56523-523-6 **$19.95**

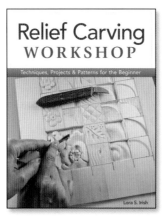

Relief Carving Workshop
ISBN 978-1-56523-736-0 **$19.99**

Chip Carving
ISBN 978-1-56523-776-6 **$16.99**

Big Book of Whittle Fun
ISBN 978-1-56523-520-5 **$12.95**

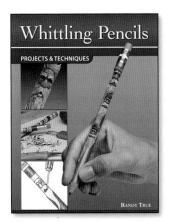

Whittling Pencils
ISBN 978-1-56523-751-3 **$12.99**

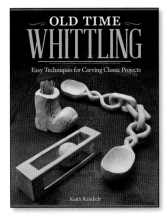

Old Time Whittling
ISBN 978-1-56523-774-2 **$9.99**

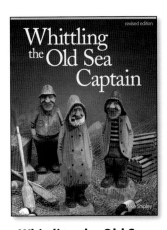

**Whittling the Old Sea
Captain, Revised Edition**
ISBN 978-1-56523-815-2 **$12.99**

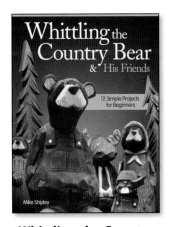

**Whittling the Country
Bear & His Friends**
ISBN 978-1-56523-808-4 **$14.99**

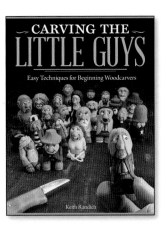

Carving the Little Guys
ISBN 978-1-56523-775-9 **$9.99**

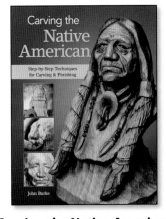

Carving the Native American
ISBN 978-1-56523-787-2 **$19.99**

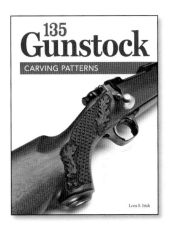

135 Gunstock Carving Patterns
ISBN 978-1-56523-795-7 **$16.99**

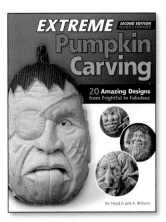

**Extreme Pumpkin Carving,
Second Edition
Revised and Expanded**
ISBN 978-1-56523-806-0 **$14.99**

More Great Books from Fox Chapel Publishing

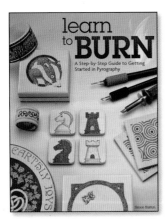

Learn to Burn
ISBN 978-1-56523-728-5 **$16.99**

**Relief Carving Wood
Spirits, Revised Edition**
ISBN 978-1-56523-802-2 **$19.99**

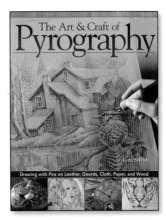

The Art & Craft of Pyrography
ISBN 978-1-56523-478-9 **$19.95**

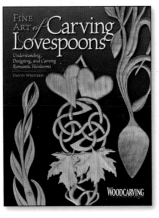

Fine Art of Carving Lovespoons
ISBN 978-1-56523-374-4 **$24.95**

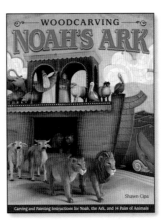

Woodcarving Noah's Ark
ISBN 978-1-56523-477-2 **$22.95**

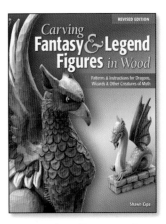

**Carving Fantasy &
Legend Figures in Wood,
Revised Edition**
ISBN 978-1-56523-807-7 **$19.99**

WOODCARVING ILLUSTRATED SCROLL SAW woodworking & CRAFTS

In addition to being a leading source of woodworking books and
DVDs, Fox Chapel also publishes two premiere magazines. Released
quarterly, each delivers premium projects, expert tips and techniques
from today's finest woodworking artists, and in-depth information
about the latest tools, equipment, and materials.

Subscribe Today!
Woodcarving Illustrated: **888-506-6630**
Scroll Saw Woodworking & Crafts: **888-840-8590**
www.FoxChapelPublishing.com